IN MY FLESH
I SEE GOD

IN MY FLESH
I SEE GOD

A Treasury of
Rabbinic Insights
about the Human Anatomy

Avraham Yaakov Finkel

JASON ARONSON INC.
Northvale, New Jersey
London

This book was set in 11 pt. Bookman.

Library of Congress Cataloging-in-Publication Data

In my flesh I see God : a treasury of rabbinic insights about the
    human anatomy : [compiled and translated] by Avraham Yaakov Finkel.
        p.   cm.
    Includes bibliographical references and indexes.
    ISBN 1-56821-425-1
    1. Rabbinical literature—Translations into English. 2. Body,
Human, in rabbinical literature. 3. Life cycle, Human—Religious
aspects—Judaism. I. Finkel, Avraham Yaakov.
BM495.I5   1995
296.3'2—dc20   94-47349

Manufactured in the United States of America. Jason Aronson Inc. offers books and cassettes. For information and catalog write to Jason Aronson Inc., 230 Livingston Street, Northvale, New Jersey 07647.

To my dear children,
Moshe and Brenda Finkel
Berish and Elisheva Weinberg
Moshe and Judy Klein
Rabbi Chaim and Naomi Finkel

To my dear grandchildren
and to my first great-grandson,
little Hillel Rochwarger

They all are a source of much *nachas*.

Ure'ei vanim levanecha shalom al Yisrael.
May you see children born to your children,
peace upon Israel.

Psalm 128:6

Contents

Acknowledgments

Odeh Hashem bechol leivav.
I thank *Hashem* with all my heart.
                              Psalm 111:1

It is with deep gratitude to *Hashem* that I present this book in the hope that its pages will inform and inspire. When my friend Mr. Arthur Kurzweil, the talented vice president of Jason Aronson Inc., suggested that I write a book on the theme "In my flesh I see God," I was hesitant at first. Was this not too esoteric a subject? But his infectious enthusiasm soon won me over, and the more I delved into the subject, the more amazed I was at the wealth of eye-opening, down-to-earth comments by the sages, who see the human body and its organs as a reflection of the higher worlds. Surprisingly, through simple analogies and metaphors they make abstract ideas intelligible to everyone. I am grateful indeed to Arthur Kurzweil for affording me the opportunity to share with the reading public the rabbis' perceptive insights and their practical advice for everyday living.

Special thanks to my son, Rabbi Chaim Finkel, a *maggid shiur* (lecturer) at Yeshivah Ner Yisrael of Toronto, who related to me a number of utterly fascinating and original commentaries that are included in this book.

I am indebted to Muriel Jorgensen and to Janet Warner, production editor on this project, for proficiently piloting this book through its various stages from manuscript to finished product.

Many thanks also to Judith M. Tulli for creating the distinctive cover design and to the entire dedicated staff of Jason Aronson Inc. for their unfailing courtesy and cooperation whenever called upon.

I am grateful to my children and grandchildren for their encouragement and for taking a lively interest in my work. They are a source of genuine *nachas* and limitless *simchah*.

Most of all, I am thankful to my wife, Suri, for patiently and cheerfully allowing me to pursue my work until the late hours of the night, for being both sounding board and reviewer, and for offering her constructive criticism and helpful suggestions.

Introduction

Modern man finds himself running on a treadmill of futility. Driven by a voracious appetite for material possessions and the comforts of life, he chases the elusive rainbow of happiness. Goaded by the media and the trends of the times, he is caught in the vicious cycle of "working in order to live, and living in order to work."

Being part of Western society, the Jew, too, is swept along in the raging maelstrom, seeking fulfillment of the insatiable desires of the body. Adrift among the surging swells of fads and fashion, he fights to keep his head above water. Still, in everyone's life there are times of tranquility, hours snatched for quiet contemplation, when a person's thoughts wander from the utilitarian, and he muses about his inner self. It is during serene moments like these that one's mind is swirling with questions about God, the world, and the meaning of life.

Such questions have occupied the minds of the great Jewish thinkers of all ages. The prophets of the Bible, the teachers of Talmud and *Midrash*, the foremost philosophers and kabbalists, as well as the chasidic masters and the teachers of the *Mussar* movement of the more recent past, all have grappled with the mystery of man and his relationship with God and the world. Although the books these thinkers wrote could fill a library, their thoughts can be condensed into two sublime Scriptural verses that jointly hold the solution to this baffling enigma.

The first passage reads, "God created man with His image. In the image of God, He created him" (Genesis 1:27). Concealed in these seemingly simple words is the profound truth that man is a reflection of God's image. The implication is that man, who is less than a speck of dust in comparison to the Infinite, is a small-scale replica of all the forces of Creation. Everything God created in the world, He created in man.

As a corollary, the other key phrase states, "In my flesh I see God" (Job 19:26). Since man is a miniature model of the universe, whatever you see in your physical body has a parallel above. By analyzing your inner self and contemplating the marvels of your body, you come to recognize the Creator and attach yourself to Him.

The logical outcome of this premise is that there exists an interaction between man and his Maker, as each part of the human body has a direct link to a corresponding entity in the higher world. Thus, every act you perform makes an impact on the higher world. The kabbalists compare this relationship to a long rope; when you shake your end of the rope, the other end will move concurrently.[1] By doing a *mitzvah* you create harmony in the spheres above and unclog the channels through which divine abundance flows to our world. Conversely, a transgression causes disruption in this flow of plenty. It is clear that man plays a role of supreme importance in Creation. In fact, speaking of man, the psalmist exclaims, "You have made him little less than divine" (Psalm 8:6). The *Zohar* goes so far as to say that "by doing righteous deeds, a Jew imparts strength and power to God, as it says, 'Give might to God' (Psalm 68:35). How can you do that? Through good deeds and mitzvot" (*Zohar*, beginning of *parashat Bo*).

The Talmud tells us that the 248 limbs of the body are linked to the 248 positive *mitzvot* of the Torah (things you must do). These are the cables that lift you from the constraints of your mundane existence, the conduits that connect you to the divine throne. The *Tanach* (Bible), Talmud, Midrash, Kabbalah, and the writings of the later sages abound with a profusion of profound insights, eye-opening commentaries, poignant anecdotes, and mind-boggling letter/number permutations about the significance and the functions of the limbs and organs of the human body and their counterparts in the spiritual world.

The chapters that follow present selections of such colorful and inspiring nuggets of wisdom and their philosophical underpinnings. The reader, whether he is steeped in Torah learning or has only a nodding aquaintance with Jewish tradition, will find in the words of the rabbis a comprehensive system of thought that makes sense, removes doubt, and resolves dilemmas. The jumbled pieces of the puzzle of life fall into place, and a unified picture of Judaism appears.

By offering easy-to-understand translations of the original Hebrew texts, most of which have never been translated before, I aim to make the words of the sages accessible to a wide circle of readers. It is my hope that the reader will be moved and inspired by the sublime greatness of our *chachamim* (sages), whose nobility of character and vast scholarship are evident on every page. Since the chapters of this book encompass a broad spectrum of the manifold facets of Jewish life, a comprehensive picture emerges of the Torah perspective on the human body and its organs. The subjects discussed range from the human anatomy to hygiene, marriage, pregnancy, circumcision, dream interpretation, and a host of related topics. Amazingly, the timeless advice of the ancient rabbis regarding our physical and mental health provides solutions to many of our present-day woes and afflictions. As we read their comments, new vistas come into view that give hope to the despondent and guidance to the perplexed. We see man and the world from a new perspective. We learn that our body is much more than a physical form of flesh, blood, and bones covered by a layer of skin. We come to recognize ourselves as the handiwork of the Creator, our limbs as tools for attaining perfection, and our bodies as receptacles of God's boundless kindness.

I

MAN IS
A SMALL WORLD

Part I sets the stage and provides the philosophical foundation for the central idea of this book.

In the view of the sages, man is an *olam katan,* a "miniature world," a microcosm. They describe the human body as a small-scale replica of the macrocosm, encompassing in its limited confines the vast universe in its infinite variety. This fundamental thought is a recurring theme in the writings of the early and later great thinkers. It comes to full bloom in kabbalistic literature, which deals at great length and in profound depth with the creation of the world and of man. Kabbalah addresses the mystery of how God, who is a purely spiritual and unfathomable Being, brought into existence a world that is physical and tangible in nature.

The selections in Part I offer a sampling of the thoughts of the great philosophers, including the Rambam, the Chovot Halevavot, the Kuzari, and the Maharal. The kabbalistic perspective of man and the world, as well some of the basic teachings relating to the Ten *Sefirot,* are discussed in general terms. The selections of the writings by the exponents of Kabbalah, including the Maggid of Mezritch and the Maor Vashemesh, as well as the writings of Rabbi Eliyahu E. Dessler, will help to shed some light on this difficult subject.

1

A Replica
of the Universe

One of the earliest sources where the original idea of man being an *olam katan*, "a small world," is ingeniously illustrated is *Avot deRabbi Natan* 31:3,[1] where we read:

"God created in man everything He created in the world. The forests correspond to the hair, wild [meat-eating] animals to his intestines. Caves resemble his ears, aroma corresponds to his nose, the sun to his vision, foul-smelling water to nasal mucus, and the salt water of the sea reflects tears. Flowing rivers parallel the urinary flow, gates correspond to lips, doors to teeth, sweet water to saliva, the stars to cheeks[2] . . . water from a spring is mirrored in blood, a tree in man's bones, and the head is the king of all of man's limbs. So you see that whatever God created in the universe, He fashioned [on a small scale] in man."

✤

MAN'S ACTIONS AFFECT THE ORDER OF THINGS

Commenting on the above-mentioned paragraph, Rabbi Yehoshua Falk[3] says:

"The notion that man is a miniature replica of the universe implies that he is the ultimate purpose of Creation, and everything was created for his sake.

"As a result, if he misuses any of the limbs of his body [by transgressing the commandment with which it is associated],[4] he causes a defect in the corresponding part in the grand universe. If he violates all the commandments, he mars all the limbs of his body and thereby disrupts the balance of the entire cosmos. This is, in fact, what happened at the time of the Flood.[5] By the same token, each good act repairs the whole universe[6] and raises the world to a higher level."

The above commentary by Rabbi Yehoshua Falk is based on the talmudic saying according to which the 248 positive *mitzvot* of the Torah (things you are required to do) correspond to the 248 limbs in the human body (*Makkot* 23b). Although, compared to the infinite universe, man is smaller than a speck of dust, his actions have far-reaching significance. In fact, they affect the harmonious order of the entire cosmos. When performing a *mitzvah*, he restores and elevates both the physical world and the higher realms. Conversely, a transgression causes a disruption in the flow of divine abundance.

✦

MAN'S DEEDS ARE OF
IMMEASURABLE SIGNIFICANCE

Maharal:[7] Although the *mitzvot* may appear to be insignificant rituals, each *mitzvah* comprises dimensions that reach the loftiest heights of the world to come. In that respect, the *mitzvot* form a perfect analogy to man and his soul. Just as a man, standing in the mundane world, harbors a soul that reaches to the world to come, so too do Torah and *mitzvot* delineate actions in the physical world that are moored in the exalted heights of the spiritual world.[8]

THE *ZOHAR*'S VIEW

The *Zohar* puts it this way: The 613 limbs in the human body correspond to the creation of the world. That is the reason why man is characterized as a small world. Therefore, if you make God King over each of your limbs, it is the same as if you made Him King over the entire world.

Tikkunei Zohar 70, p. 175a

GOD IS YOUR SHADOW

The correlation between God and man is aptly expressed in the following comment by the Ba'al Shem Tov:

"Whatever action you do down here in this world, evokes a similar action by God, for it says, 'God is your shadow' (Psalm 121:5). Your shadow mimics everything you do. If you jump, your shadow jumps; if you wave your hand, your shadow does the same. Now man was created in the image of God, and just like a shadow, God imitates every motion you make. If you open your hand to the poor, God opens a wellspring of goodness to flow down to you. If you are humble, God, as it were, humbles Himself before you and fulfills your wishes."

Sefer Ba'al Shem Tov, Kedoshim, 23

A SMALL TOWN

The idea that man is a reflection of the entire universe is prevalent throughout the writings of the sages. The Talmud finds an allusion to it in the biblical verse that states, "There was a small town, with only a few inhabitants. A mighty king came upon it and surrounded it, and built great siege works over it. Present in the city was a poor wise man who by his wisdom saved the town. Yet no one remembered that poor man" (Ecclesiastes 9:14, 15).

The *Gemara* (*Nedarim* 31b) interprets this story allegorically. The small town refers to the human form; the few inhabitants are the limbs. The mighty king who surrounded the town symbolizes the evil inclination. Why is it called "mighty"? Because it is thirteen years older than the good inclination. For the first thirteen years of his life, man is dominated by the *yetzer hara*, his evil inclination. He is born a self-centered, greedy, and self-indulging creature that only takes and does not give. The *yetzer tov*, the good inclination, enters man only when he reaches the age of thirteen.[9] Only then is he mature enough to subdue his selfish instinct and learn to give to others.

The siege works built by the great king represent the misdeeds a person commits at the instigation of the evil inclination.

The poor wise man who saved the town stands for the good inclination. Why is he called poor? Because most people ignore him. By his wisdom the wise man saved the town, for whoever follows the advice of the good inclination is saved. Yet no one remembers that poor man, because when the evil inclination gains the upper hand, no one remembers the good inclination.

✤

THE RAMBAM'S (MAIMONIDES') VIEW

The Rambam[10] in his *Guide for the Perplexed*[11] devotes an entire chapter (1:72) to the parallel between the universe and man. Here are a few excerpts from that chapter:

Note well that the entire universe is nothing but one individual being; that is to say, the outermost heavenly sphere and all that is in it are unquestionably one single being, a person like Reuven and Shimon. . . . Just as, for example, Reuven is one individual composed of various parts, such as flesh, bones, and tendons, various bodily fluids, and spiritual elements, so is the entire universe composed of heavenly spheres, the four elements,[12] and their combinations. . . .

The human body contains primary organs, like the heart, the liver, and the brain. It also comprises secondary parts, like the stomach and the intestines. The secondary organs depend on the primary ones and cannot exist without the control of those organs. In the same way, the universe consists of principal parts, namely, the quintessence[13] that encompasses the four elements, and other parts that are secondary and require a leader, namely, the four elements and the things composed of them. . . .

In the universe, too, there exists a certain force that is in control. It sets the main parts into motion and gives them the driving force to govern the rest. Without that force, the existence of this sphere with its principal and secondary parts would be unthinkable. It is the source of the existence of the universe in all its parts. This force is God, blessed be His name. It is because [he is a reflection] of this force that man is called *olam katan*, "miniature world" or microcosm, for he, too, possesses a certain capacity that regulates all the forces of his body. And it is for this reason that God is called the Life of the Universe, as in the passage, "and he swore by the Life of the Universe" (Daniel 12:7).

❧

IN MY FLESH I SEE GOD

A detailed discussion of the notion that man is a small-scale representation of the universe is found in *Chovot Halevavot*, "The Duties of the Heart," written by Rabbi Bachya ibn Pakudah.[14] This work has been described as perhaps the noblest work of posttalmudic literature on Jewish ethics.[15] *Chovot Halevavot* teaches that by studying his body and its functions man will recognize the infinite wisdom, goodness, and power of the Creator.

In *Shaar Habechinah*, the "Chapter on the Evidence of the Divine Wisdom," chapter 5, Rabbi Bachya writes:

Philosophy is man's knowledge of himself, so that through the evidence of the divine wisdom that is manifest within himself he will come to recognize the Creator; as Job said, "In my flesh I see God" (Job 19:26). . . .

At the outset I want to call your attention to the origin and earliest development of a human being. You will then recognize the divine kindness that has brought man into existence out of nothingness. How he passes from the mineral into the vegetable state that in turn becomes food and changes into seed and blood.[16] This is transformed into animal life, which finally takes on the form and nature of a living, thinking, and mortal[17] human being. . . . To this human body God has joined a spiritual element: the soul. . . .

At the beginning of a human being's existence, the Creator appointed the mother's body to serve as a couch for the fetus, so that it stays in a safe and well-protected place, where no hand can touch it, where it is shielded from heat or cold, and where its food is ready for it. . . .

Then it emerges from the womb through a narrow passage without any skill or help on its part, but only by the power of the wise, merciful, and gracious One who shows compassion to His creatures, as He said to Job, "Do you know the season when the mountain goats give birth? Can you mark the time when the hinds calve? Can you count the months they must complete? Do you know the season they give birth?" (Job 39:1,2). . . .

When the infant has emerged into the world, the Creator provides for it food from its mother's breast. The blood that has been its nourishment in the womb, is now converted into milk in the mother's breast, pleasant and sweet, flowing like a gushing spring whenever needed. The milk is not so abundant that it might be too heavy for the mother and flow without suction. Neither is it so scanty as to tire the child when it is suckling. God's grace is also evident in the fact that He made the opening of the nipple like the eye of a needle, not so wide that the milk would run without suction, in which case the child might choke, and not so narrow that the baby would have to exert itself while nursing. . . .

If you think about it, you will take notice of the natural processes by which the food is distributed to every part of the body. The wisdom you observe will inspire you to thank the Creator and praise Him, as David said, "All my bones shall say, 'Lord, who is like You?'"(Psalm 35:10). You will observe that the food passes into the stomach through a tube, called esophagus, that is absolutely straight, without any bend or twist. The stomach grinds the food more thoroughly than the teeth have done before. Then the food is carried into the liver through thin connecting veins that act as a strainer, preventing anything coarse from passing through to the liver. The liver converts the food it receives into blood, which it distributes all over the body through tubes that look like water pipes and were formed specifically for this purpose. . . . The waste substances that are left are eliminated through channels suited for this purpose. . . . The refuse of the blood passes into the bladder.

Now, dear brother, consider the wisdom of the Creator manifested in the composition of your body; how he set the organs in the right places, to receive the waste substances, so that they should not spread in the body and make you sick. . . .

Then think about the formation of the organs of the voice and the instruments of speech. The trachea (windpipe), hollow for the production of sound; the tongue, the lips, and the teeth designed for the clear articulation of consonants and vowels. These organs have other uses too. The air enters the lungs through the windpipe; the tongue is the organ that enables you to taste savory dishes, and it helps you swallow food and drink. The teeth serve to chew solid food. The lips serve to keep liquids in the mouth and to swallow the desired quantity. Regarding the other organs, the purpose of some is known; of others, unknown. . . .

Next consider the powers of the soul. . . . Take memory, for instance. How much loss would a person incur if he were unable to remember what he owned and what he owed; what he had taken and what he had given; what he had seen or heard. . . . Forgetting also has its uses. For if not for the ability to forget, a person would never be free from depression. No happy occasion would dispel his sadness. . . .

The great goodness of God is manifested in the ability to think and perceive that He has bestowed on us. It is through these capabilities that we are different from other living creatures. . . . Through our intellect we know that we have a Creator who is wise, everlasting, a Oneness, who has existed from all eternity, infinite in power, unlimited in time and space, exalted above the qualities of his creatures and beyond the comprehension of all existing beings. . . .

Think about the benefits God has granted man by the gift of speech and the orderly arrangement of words. Man thereby gives expression to what is on his mind and soul, and understands the concerns of others. The tongue is the heart's pen and the mind's messenger. Without speech, there would be no social contact between one person and another; human beings would be like cattle. Man, so the proverb goes, is heart and tongue . . . and by speech he is different from the animals. . . .

Then consider the advantages inherent in written characters and the art of writing. By means of the written word, the deeds of those who have passed away and those who are still alive are recorded for the benefit of those who will come after them. . . .

One of the greatest benefits bestowed on man is that he has been provided with hands and fingers with which he can draw, write, embroider, kindle fire, and do other things and perform precision work. . . . I can safely say that there is not one of the organs that I have mentioned that does not exhibit to a thinking person the marks of divine wisdom in its structure, form, and combination with other organs.

FROM LARGE TO SMALL

Rabbi Avraham ibn Ezra,[18] the classic Torah commentator, touches on the theme of man being a microcosm. He sees both man and the Sanctuary and its furnishings as a reflection of a higher world.

In his commentary on Exodus 25:40 he says the following: "[God said to Moses,] 'Note well, and follow the pattern that you will be shown on the mountain and make [the menorah] in that manner' (Exodus 25:40)."

Ibn Ezra goes on to say:

We know that the energy of the soul radiates throughout the entire human body. Some organs in the body, like the eyes and the ears, are suffused with nerves and are therefore more sensitive than, for example, the liver or the bones, which have fewer nerves. Now, the heart receives more energy from the psyche[19] than any other part of the body does. That is why the heart is served by many other organs.

We can draw an analogy from this to God. We know that His glory fills the whole world. However, in some places His power is more evident than in others. . . . The *Bet Hamikdash* (the Holy Temple) is the location chosen [for the greatest concentration of holiness].

If God grants you wisdom, you will understand the mystery of the Holy Ark, its cover, and the two cherubim whose wings were spread out. [These holy furnishings were situated in the Holy of Holies.]

You will also understand [the mystery of] the menorah, the incense altar, and the table, which were outside the partition [of the Holy of Holies], as well as the sacrificial altar and its utensils, the washstand and its base, which were situated outside the Tabernacle's entrance. Because these things express the glory of God. . . .

If you know the secret of your soul and the makeup of your body you can grasp the nature of the Higher World, *because man is a miniature cosmos.* He was last to be created during the six days of Creation. You can find an allusion [to the idea of man being a microcosmos] in the verse, "He began with the largest and ended with the smallest" (Genesis 44:12).[20]

ANGELS IN HUMAN FORM

Rabbi Yehudah Halevi,[21] in his seminal work the *Kuzari,*[22] expounds on the concept of man being a small world:

Philosophers have compared the world to man, and man to a small world. Accordingly, God being the spirit, soul, mind, and "life" of the world, it is reasonable to compare Him to man. If this comparison is plausible on an intellectual level, then it certainly is valid in the eyes of the prophets, whose vision is far more accurate than theoretical speculation. The prophets' vision penetrated the heavens, and they saw the heavenly hosts "eye to eye." They saw those who dwell on high, both the angels closest to God and those who are more distant; all appeared in human form. It is to the form of these angels that the Torah alludes in the verse, "Let Us make man in Our image, after Our likeness" (Genesis 1:26).

The reason why angels appear in human form is this: We have previously indicated that the world was created in the following sequence—first the basic elements (light, earth, water, and air), then the minerals, then the water animals as well as those that live in the air, and finally man with his fully developed senses and brilliant natural instincts. There is only one higher level of creation—that of the celestial and the divine, the angels. God created man in the form of the ministering angels that are near Him in rank, not in place (as we cannot speak of place in connection with God).

Kuzari, chap. 2

ISRAEL, HEART OF THE NATIONS

One of the best-known passages in the *Kuzari* reads: Israel among the nations is like the heart among the organs of the body. It is at once the sickest and the healthiest of all organs. . . . The heart is always threatened by ailments of all sorts. The continuous changes of emotions, alternating between too much and too little, harmful food, excessive work, sleep and wakefulness, all impair the heart, while all the other organs remain unaffected.

In what sense is the heart the healthiest of all organs?

It is impossible for the heart to be afflicted by cancer, a wound, or paralysis, for any of these would cause death. The heart reacts with such sensitivity to the remotest threat to its health that it combats the danger as long as it has the power to do so. Other organs lack this fine sense, and diseases can, therefore, freely develop in them.

Kuzari 2:36 and 2:44

The commentary *Otzar Nechmad* explains that the heart is the most sensitive organ in the body. A disease in any other organ—whether in the liver or the stomach—immediately affects the heart. The same way, by assimilating to the surrounding society, the Jewish people are stricken by the corrupting diseases from which that society is suffering, as it says, "They mingled with the nations and learned their ways" (Psalm 106:35).

THE TABERNACLE, THE UNIVERSE, AND MAN

Rabbeinu Bachya[23] draws a striking parallel between the Tabernacle, the universe, and man. In his commentary on Exodus 25:9 he makes the following observation: "[God says to Moses,] 'You must make the Tabernacle and all its furnishings following the plan that I am showing you'" (Exodus 25:9).

Rabbeinu Bachya: The Tabernacle and its furnishings are tangible objects that are designed to help you understand the higher spiritual concepts they represent.

Take for example the Tabernacle. It is made up of three sections: (1) the space behind the cloth partition, [which is the Holy of Holies], (2) the chamber outside the partition, which is the *Ohel Mo'eid*, the Communion Tent, and (3) the *Chatzeir*, the Outer Enclosure.

These three sections correspond to the totality of physical existence. Existence, too, is composed of three elements: (1) the spiritual world of angels and celestial beings, (2) the physical universe with its galaxies, stars, and planets, and (3) the lowly earth.

In the same way, man, the crown of Creation, is a replica of the totality of existence. In fact, he is called *olam katan*, "a miniature world," or microcosm. He, too, can be divided into three main segments: (1) the element of thought and speech, (2) his life force, and (3) his natural functions [such as his digestive system].

The primary section of the Tabernacle, the Holy of Holies, is the repository of the two Tablets of the Covenant, which were placed in the Ark with the two cherubim on its cover. These are esoteric, hidden things, as it says, "[W]ith the Presence of the God of Israel above them" (Ezekiel 10:19).

The Holy of Holies parallels the world of angels and celestial beings. Its counterpart in man is the head, the seat of his intellect and the power of speech. Just as the *Shechinah* (Divine Presence) rests on the cherubim, so does it rest on man when he puts on his *tefillin*; his head *tefillin* opposite his brain and his arm *tefillin* opposite his heart. For the *tefillin* correspond to the cherubim. This gives you an inkling of the importance of the *mitzvah* of putting on *tefillin*.

The outer chamber of the Tabernacle houses the holy vessels, the table, the menorah, and the incense altar. It is indicative of the universe, filled with countless orbiting heavenly bodies that declare the glory of God. In man, it conforms to the life force that is concentrated in the heart, the central organ that radiates vitality to all parts of the body.

The third part of the Tabernacle is the Outer Enclosure, the site of the Copper Altar on which the sacrifices are offered and animal life comes to an end. It is symbolic of our lowly world, which is marked by the recurring cycle of birth and death. It parallels the natural functions of man which are seated in the lower part of his body, that is to say below his navel, meaning his digestive system, the carnal element of his existence.

Thus, the spiritual realm, the universe, and man are all reflected in the Tabernacle.

THE HOLY OF HOLIES

Rabbi Levi Yitzchak of Berditchev[24] said: In whatever you do, you should consider your body as the Holy of Holies. Think of it as a *chelek Elokah mima'al*, a part of the manifestation of the Almighty on High. If you do, you will keep the Evil Impulse at bay.

The brain of man can be compared to the Ark and the Two Tablets of the Covenant. It is the noblest part of man. Therefore, whoever thinks unholy thoughts is placing an idol in the Holy of Holies. Whenever you lift your hands to do an action, consider your hands the messengers of God.[25]

LET US MAKE MAN WITH OUR IMAGE

God said, "Let us make man with our image and likeness. Let him dominate the fish of the sea, the birds of the sky, the livestock animals, and all the earth—every land animal that walks the earth" (Genesis 1:26).

Malbim:[26] Let us make man in our image and likeness. To whom did God say, "Let us make man"?

Everyone agrees[27] that God was speaking to all the forces of Creation that He had brought into being. God said, "Let us make a man who is a microcosm. Let us fashion a man who contains precisely everything there is in the great universe, the macrocosm. Thus man will be 'in our image,' meaning, he will be a small-scale model of the great world, possessing also the divine part that gives life to the great world. . . ."

In all creation, only man resembles God in that he has a free will. He thereby is the ruler of his small world. Everything else created by God must follow the dictates of nature. Angels have no freedom; they can only act according to the will of God. And surely the actions of all the creatures of the physical world are determined by the laws of nature. Man is the only exception. He is the master over his actions, to do or not to do, as he chooses.

If we search the macrocosm for the being in whose mold man is cast, we find that the only One who has the power to change the laws of nature at His discretion is God who dwells in all the worlds and infuses them with life. He has the capacity to subdue the forces of nature and perform miracles. Similarly, man has the ability to subdue the natural instincts of his microcosm—his "small inner world"—by means of his free will. Thus, man truly is made in the likeness of God.

2

The Kabbalistic View

WHAT QUESTIONS DOES KABBALAH ADDRESS?

Kabbalists strive to comprehend God and His relationship to man and the world. Specifically, they seek to understand the paradox that God, who is One, an inseparable, nonphysical, infinite Being, created the universe that is physical, multifaceted, and finite. They are puzzled by the incongruity that kindness and strictness, infinite mercy and unmitigated justice, all come forth from one indivisible, beneficent, and compassionate God.

Of course, knowledge of God is unattainable. Not even Moses, the greatest human being who ever lived, was capable of apprehending the Divine Essence. He desired to know the true nature of God when he asked, "Show me Your glory" (Exodus 33:18). God replied that this was impossible. He told Moses, "You cannot see My face, for no man can see Me and live" (Exodus 33:20).

To a certain extent, however, Kabbalah lifts the veil that shrouds these mysteries and reveals some of the secrets of the higher worlds. This esoteric body of knowledge is accessible to *yod'ei chein*, "those who understand *chein* [an abbreviation of *chochmat nistar*], the wisdom of mysticism."

These are the great and holy kabbalistic scholars who pine for closeness and attachment to God and who live a life devoted to Torah study, piety, prayer, and contemplation. For all others, including the author of this book, this wisdom remains an unfathomable secret, an inscrutable enigma that can be touched upon in only the most cursory and over-simplified terms.

CREATION AND *TZIMTZUM*

To what purpose did God create the world? How did the universe come into being?

Kabbalah finds an indication in the verse, *Olam chesed yibaneh*, "The world is built on kindness" (Psalm 89:3). God, in His infinite love, desired to bestow *chesed*, kindness, on a being who would deserve His bounty by freely choosing to worship Him. Thus He created the universe for the sake of man,[1] whom He endowed with *bechirah*, the freedom to choose between good and evil. Unlike the angels, man received the *yetzer tov* (the good impulse) and the *yetzer hara* (sensuality, the temptation to follow the attraction of the senses). By freely choosing to do good and rejecting evil in spite of its powerful allure, man earns the boundless flow of kindness God wants to bestow on him.

How does the flow of kindness make the transition from the lofty metaphysical realm down to earth? How does the intangible become tangible?

Kabbalah[2] teaches that at the beginning of Creation, God's Infinite Light filled all reality. Within this Divine Light nothing else could exist. Therefore, before bringing the universe into being, God made "room" for it by yielding space, in a process called *tzimtzum*, which means stricture, or contraction of His Infinite Light. To put it another way, God withdrew into Himself, leaving a vast primordial void in the middle of His Infinity. Into this newly created "space" flowed the *Or Ein Sof*, the Divine Infinite Light, descending through a series of ten *Sefirot*. For lack of a better term, *Sefirot* commonly are called attributes, vessels, or emanations. It should be understood that *Sefirot* are purely metaphysical in nature and not in any sense material; their essence is completely beyond human comprehension.

The *Sefirot* guide the Divine Light down to the lowly regions of our universe. They constitute the channels through which the divine flow of plenty surges from the lofty heights of the spiritual realm to our coarse material world. It is a stream of divine beneficence through which God continually brings His world into being and sustains it, as we say in *Tefillat Shacharit*, the Morning Prayer, "He renews daily, perpetually, the work of creation."

Simply put, the *Sefirot* are the divine attributes through which God reveals Himself to a limited degree. As the Infinite Light flows from the higher to the lower *Sefirot*, its intensity progressively wanes; its splendor is concealed more and more.

WHERE IS THE PRIMEVAL LIGHT HIDDEN?

The biblical account of Creation gives rise to a thorny question. On the *first* day of Creation, "God said, 'Let there be light,' and there was light" (Genesis 1:3). This seems to contradict the account of the creation of light in Genesis 1:17–19, where we are told that "God placed [the sun, the moon, and the stars] in the heavenly sky to shine on the earth. . . . It was evening and it was morning, a *fourth* day."

If the sun was created only on the fourth day, what was the source of the light of the first day, and what happened to this mysterious light?

The Talmud explains, "The light that the Holy One, blessed be He, created on the first day, [was of such intensity] that a person could see from one end of the world to the other. But as soon as God saw the corruptness of the generation of the Flood and the generation that built the Tower of Babel, He hid it from them. And for whom did He reserve it? For the righteous ones to come" (*Chagigah* 12a).

Where did God store this glorious light of the first day of Creation? He concealed it in the Torah, which is the embodiment of the *Or Ein Sof* (the Infinite Light).[3] Its letters and words, as they appear in the Written and the Oral Torah, are the manifestation of God's will and wisdom. By studying the Torah you are in contact with God, you connect with eternity. You are seeing the brilliant light of Creation that is hidden in the Torah. This primordial light lifts you above the constraints of time and space. You are indeed capable of seeing "from one end of the world to the other."

By performing a *mitzvah* you are implementing the master plan God envisaged when He created the world. An act as simple as reciting a *berachah*, eating *matzah* at the Seder, putting on *tefillin*, or giving *tzedakah* affects countless forces in the cosmos, creates harmony, and restores order in the higher realms. By doing a *mitzvah* you are "cleansed and sanctified from above" and you "cause abundant bounty to flow in all the worlds."[4]

In the words of *Mesillat Yesharim*, "If a person is drawn to the worldly pleasures and moves away from his Creator, he causes harm to himself and brings ruin on the world. But if he controls himself, clings to his Creator, and uses the world only as a means to serving God, he is elevated and the world is elevated along with him."[5]

❧

FROM DARKNESS INTO LIGHT

Rabbi Tzadok Kakohen of Lublin,[6] one of the most profound thinkers of the chasidic movement, detects a striking correlation between Creation and events in Jewish history:

The pattern of God's Creation in which darkness preceded light is evident throughout history. You will find that light always emerges from darkness. For example, the light of the Giving of the Torah came only after the darkness of Egyptian bondage. The building of the Temple was preceded by capture of the Holy Ark by the Philistines (1 Samuel 4:11). The Sanctuary in the Desert was erected as a result of the sin of the golden calf. When Moses had gone up the mountain to receive the Tablets, the children of Israel said to Aaron, "Make us a god to lead us. We have no idea what happened to Moses" (Exodus 32:1). They wanted a visible, tangible god. As a result of their transgression, they received the holy Sanctuary, a tangible, visible structure to go before them, where they could reach closeness to God. As it says, "Whoever sought God would go to the Meeting Tent outside the camp" (Exodus 33:7).[7]

THE CLOUDY ORIGINS OF *MASHIACH*

The principle of light emerging from darkness that has been embedded in the matrix of the world since the first day of Creation can be detected at every juncture in Jewish history.

Abraham, the father of the Jewish people, the man who discovered God and taught His existence and the love of righteousness to all mankind, was the son of an idol worshiper and grew up in the depraved pagan society of Ur Kasdim.

The origins of *Mashiach*, the Redeemer who will usher in the age of God's sovereignty on earth, are shrouded in the shadows of incest. It all began when Lot's daughters, thinking that they were the only people left on earth, made their father drunk, lived with him, and gave birth to Ammon and Moab (Genesis 19:36–38). Eight centuries later, Ruth, a descendant of Moab, became the great-grandmother of David. David, in turn, is the ancestor of the future *Mashiach*.

The *Midrash* sums up this idea in a succinct comment: "Who can produce a clean thing out of an unclean one?" (Job 14:4). Abraham came from Terach, Hezekiah from Achaz, Yoshia from Amon,[8] Israel from the nations, the World to Come from this world. Who could do this? Who could decree this? No one but God the only One on earth" (*Bamidbar Rabbah* 19:1).

GIVING AND RECEIVING

Ever since God created the world out of a desire to bestow His kindness on man, the process of giving and receiving— the kabbalists call it *mashpia* and *mekabbeil*—has become the universal pattern for all existence. It is manifest in the flow of the Divine Light through the chain of the Ten *Sefirot*, whereby a *Sefirah* receives the Light and passes it on to the *Sefirah* below it. The receiving *Sefirah*, in turn, conveys the Light to the next *Sefirah*, in a continuous chain of giving and receiving.

THE GIVER AND THE TAKER

Rabbi Eliyahu E. Dessler[9] says: When the Almighty created human beings He made them capable of both giving and taking. The faculty of giving is a sublime power; it is one of the attributes of the blessed Creator of all things. He is the Giver par excellence; His mercy, His bounty, and His goodness extend to all His creatures. His giving is pure giving, for He takes nothing in return. He can take nothing for He lacks nothing, as the verse says, "If you are righteous, what do you give Him?" (Job 35:7).

Our service to Him is not for His need but for our own, since we need a means of expressing our gratitude to him.

Man has been granted this sublime power of giving, enabling him too to be merciful, to bestow happiness, to give of himself. "God created man in His own image" (Genesis 1:26). . . .

These two powers—giving and taking—form the roots of all character traits and of all actions. And note: there is no middle way. Every person is devoted, at the deepest level of his personality, to one or the other of the two sides, and in the innermost longing of the heart there are no compromises. It is a basic law that there is no middle path in human interest. In every act, in every word, in every thought (except perhaps those directed toward his innermost self without any connection with anything outside himself), one is devoted either to loving-kindness and giving or to grasping and taking.[10]

MALE AND FEMALE

The heavenly principle of *mashpia* and *mekabbeil*, giving and receiving, has its counterpart here on earth where it took on material form in Adam and Eve, or, in a broader sense, in the male and female. The marital union and the gift of man to woman are essentially a reflection of God's outpouring of goodness through the *Sefirot* with which He built the world.

Commenting on this idea, Rabbi Eliyahu E. Dessler says:

Why do we find so often that this husband-wife affection does not seem to last? The answer is simple. People are generally "takers," not "givers." When their biological instincts gain the upper hand they become "givers" and "lovers." But before very long, nature relaxes its grip and they relapse into a state of "taking" as before. This change takes place imperceptibly. Previously they were joined together in an atmosphere of love and mutual giving. From now on they are "takers" once again, and each begins to demand from the other the fulfillment of his or her obligations. When demands begin, love departs.

This is why I always say to a couple in the joyousness of their wedding day: "Filling your hearts at this moment is a wondrous desire to give pleasure and happiness to each other. Take care, my dear ones, that you strive to keep this desire always as fresh and strong as it is at the present time. You should know that the moment you find yourself beginning, instead, to make demands upon each other, your happiness is at an end."[11]

TEACHER AND STUDENT

The theme of *mashpia* and *mekabbeil* is also apparent in the relationship between teacher and student, whereby the teacher, the *mashpia*, transmits his learning to the pupil, the *mekabbeil*. The teacher, emulating the divine *tzimtzum*, must concentrate his knowledge, streamline and distill it to essentials, in order to make the student understand his teaching.

Rabbi Dov Ber,[12] the Maggid of Mezritch, offers a fitting analogy:

Many times, a teacher must act like a man who uses a funnel to pour liquid from one bottle into another. In the same way, the teacher must condense his wide-ranging knowledge into words suited for the understanding of his students. If he is unwilling to simplify his thoughts and tries to convey the full scope of his comprehension of the subject, his students will learn nothing, because his teaching will be beyond their grasp.[13]

SHABBAT

Shabbat, too, is a manifestation of the flow of plenty that runs from giver to receiver. For six days, God created a world that culminated in the formation of the first man. On the seventh day, God rested. Man, who is in the likeness of God, was placed in the Garden of Eden and given the task "to work it and watch it" (Genesis 2:15). Imitating God, he must labor for six days, and on *Shabbat*, he is to cease from working and to retreat into a world of rest, peace, and holiness.

The *Zohar* says that the spiritual wealth of *Shabbat* radiates throughout the ensuing six weekdays. *Shabbat* is the *mashpia* (giver), the six weekdays are the *mekabbeil* (receiver). The blessings of *Shabbat* sustain and vitalize us during the week of working on the material world. *Shabbat* is *mei'ein Olam Haba*, a semblance of the World to Come, and we are the beneficiaries of its bountiful blessing. *Shabbat* catapults us into the highest regions of nearness to God and enables us to create an oasis of the spirit in the middle of the desert of materialism.

A TWO-WAY STREET

The stream of plenty runs from giver-*Sefirah* to receiver-*Sefirah*, whereby the receiving *Sefirah* passes on the divine abundance to the *Sefirah* below it until it reaches the physical world in which we live. There it breathes life into all existence, as it is written, "It is You alone, God. You made the heaven, the most exalted heaven [the highest spiritual spheres] and all their legions, the earth and everything on it, the seas and everything in them, and You give them all life" (Nehemiah 9:6).

Even inanimate objects have "life," in the sense that their continued existence depends on God's will.

The *Sefirot* through which the life-giving Divine Light flows in a downward direction have a double function. They also serve as the conduit through which man can elevate himself to higher spiritual levels. By performing *mitzvot*, he can climb the spiritual ladder and reach lofty heights. In fact, Moses, the "man of God," attained such a high degree of perfection as to be able to speak with God "face to face" (Numbers 11:27).

The idea of the two-way movement between heaven and earth is metaphorically expressed in Jacob's dream in which he had a vision of "a ladder standing on the ground, and its top reached up toward heaven. God's angels were going up and down on it" (Genesis 28:12). In other words, the Divine Light flows downward and the soul climbs upward by way of the *Sefirot*.

THE TEN GARMENTS

Rabbi Klonymos Kalman Epstein of Cracow,[14] in his work *Maor Vashemesh*,[15] makes the following insightful comment on this theme:

The essence of God's Being is beyond human comprehension. However, God in His wisdom, rigorously restricted His Divinity in order that man should be capable of gaining a very minute glimmer of understanding of the splendor of His Divine Light. God restricted Himself within ten "garments"—the Ten *Sefirot*, vessels through which the Light of the Creator is emanated to man. By virtue of this *tzimtzum* (divine restriction), man can attain cognizance of God, ascending progressively to ever higher levels of understanding. He can achieve this by removing one restrictive "garment" after another until he reaches the stage of attaching himself to the Great Light of the *Ein Sof*, the Infinite.

God created the world after subjecting Himself to thousands of restrictions of His spirituality, enveloping Himself with numerous enclosures and barriers. He placed man in this physical world and rewards him for attempting to break through these barriers with all his might, striving to approach God and attach himself to Him. It is an arduous quest of searching and probing the ultimate Truth until he has erased the final obstruction and reaches the splendor of the Divine Light. Thus, the greater the *tzimtzum*, the greater is man's reward for shattering the restrictive barriers.

Indeed, this is the intent of the *Mishnah* (*Avot* 5:1), which states: "With ten utterances the world was created . . . in order to bestow goodly reward on the righteous who sustain the world that was created with ten utterances." Although God created the world under a cover of ten "garments," the *tzaddikim* endeavor with their worship to penetrate through these "garments" and reach the nearness of God. By rising above the physical aspects of the mundane world and reaching out to the spiritual world, they earn a rich reward.[16]

❧

RUN AND RETURN

The concept of the two-way current that flows between heaven and earth is rooted in the principle of *ratzoh vashov*, "run and return," that is the basis of all of Creation.

The kabbalistic masters find an allusion to this basic rule in the *Ma'aseh Merkavah* [the vision of the Divine Chariot] of Ezekiel in which he saw that "the *Chayot* [the highest category of angels] ran and returned as the appearance of a flash of lightning" (Ezekiel 1:14).

The phenomenon of "run and return" is apparent in all of existence. For example, we see a manifestation of the "run" in the Divine Light that brought Creation into being, and the "return" in God withdrawing from Creation.

To illustrate the principle of "run and return," let us think of a father who teaches his child to walk. He will begin by holding and supporting him, yet at the same time he moves away from him and encourages him to take his first hesitant steps. As the child moves closer, the father withdraws farther.

Since man is an *olam katan*, a "small-scale universe," the motif of "run and return" is evident in the function of the human anatomy. It is, in fact, the basis of all life. A prime example of this is the circulatory system, in which the heart is the central, life-giving organ. The throbbing, rhythmical pulses of the heartbeat, alternately expanding and contracting, are characteristic indications of the universal principle of *ratzo vashov*, "run and return."

The analogy with the circulatory system can be taken one step further. The current of Divine Light flowing from the higher to the lower *Sefirot* is reflected in the human heart, which receives the oxygenated blood from the lungs and pumps it into all parts of the body. The heart, which is the primary organ, receives blood that has been invigorated with oxygen—a gas of little substance, something akin to spirit—and transfers it via the blood vessels to the subordinate organs. The life force inherent in the blood activates the brain, which prompts man to act in accordance to God's will, to sing His praises and fulfill His *mitzvot*. He thereby elevates himself and all of Creation. To put it another way: The heart that receives the blood that has been enriched with "spiritual" oxygen and pumps it into all parts of the body is the materialization of the cosmic cycle of *ratzo vashov*, "run and return."

THE "RUN AND RETURN" OF LIFE

Our entire relationship with God is dominated by the fluctuations of "run and return." At times, we are overcome by a desire to run away and withdraw from the world, go into seclusion, uplift ourselves, and totally immerse ourselves in prayer, Torah study, and *mitzvot*. This feeling alternates with an equally strong urge to return to the world with its physical joys and pleasures.

When Moses announced to the people that his death was imminent, he phrased it in terms of "run and return." He said, "Today I am 120 years old and I can no longer go out and come back" (Deuteronomy 31:1). Feeling that he could only ascend to heaven but not return to the World of Action, he knew that death was approaching.

Moses asked God to appoint as his successor a man "who shall take them out and bring them in" (Numbers 27:17). He meant to say that one of the qualifications of a leader of the Jewish people is the ability to "take them out"— to inspire and elevate them to lofty spiritual heights ("run") and "to bring them in"—to bring them back to reality and deal with their mundane problems ("return").

LIKE AN EAGLE

Rabbi Dov Ber, the Maggid of Mezritch, explains the principle of "run and return" by pointing to a verse in the Torah: "Like an eagle arousing his nest, hovering over its young, He spread His wings and took them, carrying them on His pinions" (Deuteronomy 32:11).

Says the Maggid of Mezritch: In order not to crush her young and their nest, the eagle hovers over her nest when feeding her young, "touching, yet not touching."

The eagle represents God in relation to His children, the people of Israel, and to the totality of His Creation in general. If God openly revealed His Presence, the world would be consumed by the splendor of His glory. On the other hand, if He completely withdrew His continuous guidance and supervision, the world would instantly cease to exist. Therefore, God hovers over Creation, "touching, yet not touching."[17]

GOD'S GREATNESS AND HUMILITY

The principle of "run and return" is the underlying theme of the following talmudic exposition:[18]

Wherever you find mention of the might of the Holy One, Blessed be He, you will also find mention of His humility. This is written in the Torah, "For the Lord your God, He is the God of the heavenly forces [i.e., of the angels], and the Master of masters" (Deuteronomy 10:17). And immediately after this it is written, "He performs justice for the orphan and widow" (Deuteronomy 10:18).

This is repeated in the Prophets, "So says the Exalted and Uplifted One, who abides forever, and [whose name] is holy" (Isaiah 57:15). And immediately after this it is written, "But [I am] with the contrite and lowly of spirit" (at the conclusion of this verse).

This is stated a third time in the Writings, "Extol Him who rides in the highest heaven with His name—God" (Psalm 68:5). And immediately after this it is written, "Father of orphans and Judge of widows" (Psalm 68:6).

"RUN AND RETURN" IN THE HUMAN FORM

Ratzo vashov, the universal principle of reciprocation, is evident in the human body. On the one hand, God in His infinite wisdom condensed the entire universe in the human form, making man a microcosm of the higher and lower realms. In return, man, contemplating the marvels of his anatomy and the miracle of life, recognizes the greatness and all-embracing love of the Creator and proclaims, "In my flesh I see God" (Job 19:26).

THE HIDDEN LIGHT

Before Creation, God alone reigned in majestic splendor; "He and His name were alone."[19] His Infinite Light filled all reality, *leit atar panui mineih*, "there was no place devoid of Him."[20] When God wanted to create the universe, He restricted and concealed Himself in an act of ultimate kindness, in order to make "room" for the world in a process called *tzimtzum*. He then poured out His Infinite Radiance through the Ten *Sefirot*, the ten channels of light that convey the purely spiritual light to the physical universe. The *Sefirot* are, in fact, the link that connects the physical world to God. They are His instrument for guiding the universe that is sustained by the continuous flow of divine plenty. If this flow were to cease even for an instant, the entire universe would revert to nothingness.[21]

As the Divine Light, the *Or Ein Sof*, descends through the *Sefirot*, it becomes increasingly more hidden, and by the time the sublime splendor reaches our universe, it is obscured by thick layers of physicality, enveloped by an opaque cloak of naturalness. This concealment reaches a point where, here on earth, the divine is virtually invisible, and many people are unable to discern godliness through the mist of earthiness. Surrounded by the comforts of life and the marvels of modern technology, their senses are beclouded by the fiction that they, rather than God, are the masters of their destiny. Intoxicated with the joys of sensuousness, they neglect to look beneath the surface of their material existence and falsely attribute the vicissitudes in their lives to natural causes, fate, fortune, or coincidence. They are not aware that God is the source of their bountiful blessings, that He is the prime mover who controls events and guides the affairs of the world and of each individual. Encased in their bodily nature, they do not recognize His *hashgachah kelalit*, His general supervision of the laws of nature and His *hashgachah peratit*, His close supervision over each person according to his own deeds. They are not aware that "God looks down from heaven; He sees all mankind. From His dwelling place He oversees all the inhabitants of the earth" (Psalm 33:13, 14).

HIDING THE CONCEALMENT

Rabbi Yitzchak Meyer Alter of Ger,[22] the Chidushei Harym, expounds on the subject of divine concealment, citing the verse, "On that day I will utterly hide My face . . ." (Deuteronomy 31:18).

Chidushei Harym: I will utterly hide My face—the Hebrew text uses a double phraseology, *hasteir astir*, literally, "hide, I will hide." What is the significance of this redundancy?

As long as people notice that God's Presence is concealed, there is as yet no real concealment; the tragedy is not too great. An awareness of God's concealment will spark a yearning to return to Him. Such longing will breach all barriers and lead to the highest form of *teshuvah*. The trouble is when the concelment itself is hidden, when no one senses that God's face is hidden, when no one seeks God, and no one feels the need for spirituality and sanctity. Thus the meaning of *hasteir astir* is "I will hide My concealment." I will dull their senses, benumb and stupefy them so that they don't feel the lack of divine radiance and the resultant emptiness in their lives.

TORAH AND NATURE

Where can you find the hidden Infinite Light here on earth?

First, you can find it in the Torah, the repository of God's wisdom. When you study the Torah, exploring its laws, yes, even a law as mundane as that relating to an ox that has gored a cow, you are linked to the higher worlds and in tune with the absolute truth. You sense a closeness to God. The same way, when you perform a *mitzvah*, any *mitzvah*, even one as simple as putting on *tefillin* or lighting *Shabbat* candles, your action connects you to the spiritual realm. You are making a significant impact on the forces of the universe. Indeed, with every *mitzvah* you perform you are repairing and restoring the cosmic balance that has been disturbed.

Second, God's greatness is revealed in nature, in the majestic beauty of a towering mountain and the delicately fluttering wings of a gentle butterfly. It is manifest in the swirling galaxies in outer space and in the structure of the atomic nucleus surrounded by electrons. Nature, like the Torah, is God's manuscript, where each blade of grass bears the signature of its divine author. Nature is the mantle that enwraps God's majestic Light. This is alluded to in the fact that the Hebrew words for God and nature, *Elokim* and *hateva*, have the same numeric value. *Elokim* is written *alef* = 1, *lamed* = 30, *hei* = 5, *yud* = 10; *mem* = 40; 1 + 30 + 5 + 10 + 40 = 86; *hateva* is written *hei* = 5, *tet* = 9, *bet* = 2, *ayin* = 70; 5 + 9 + 2 + 70 = 86, both adding up to 86.

GOD IS APPARENT IN MAN

In addition to the Torah and nature, there is a third manifestation of God in this world: His hidden Light can be found in man. God created man in His image and endowed him with a soul that is characterized as *cheilek Elokah mima'al*, "a part of God above." Man's divine soul sets him apart from the rest of Creation. All creations, plants and animals, stars and planets, even angels, inexorably must obey the divine will as laid down in the fixed laws of nature. Only man resembles God in having moral freedom and will. By dint of this freedom, only he can rise beyond the level of his material existence to reach the nearness of God, as it is stated, "You have made him little less than divine, and adorned him with glory and majesty. You have made him master over Your handiwork, laying the world at his feet" (Psalm 8:7). To put it another way, man's freedom of will is the divine spark inherent in his soul.

THE RAMBAM'S PERSPECTIVE

The Rambam (Maimonides) explains it as follows:

Every human being was granted freedom of choice. If a person wants to follow the proper road and be a *tzaddik* (a righteous man) he has the freedom to do so, and if he wants to choose the wrong road and become an evildoer, he can do that too.

And so it is written in the Torah. "[After Adam's transgression,] God said, 'Man has now become like one of us in knowing good and evil'" (Genesis 3:22). In other words, [God is saying that] mankind has become unique in the world. Unlike any other species, man has the ability to distinguish consciously between good and evil and do whatever he wants to do without anyone deterring him from doing either good or bad.[23]

HABIT BECOMES SECOND NATURE

The Rambam (Maimonides) states: It is as impossible for one to be born with good or bad traits as it is for one to be an accomplished craftsman from birth. It is possible, however, that a person is born with a natural inclination to a particular virtue or vice, so that one type of activity will be easier for him than another.

For example, it is easier for a person whose brain matter is clear and contains only a small amount of fluid to learn, remember, and understand things than a phlegmatic man whose brain is overloaded with fluids.[24] But, if one who has these natural gifts fails to stimulate his talent, he surely will remain ignorant. On the other hand, if an inherently dull and phlegmatic person is taught and enlightened, he will gain knowledge and understanding, albeit with great difficulty. In exactly the same way, a person whose blood is warmer than normal has the potential to become a brave man. If this man is trained to be brave he will become boldly daring in short order. Someone else whose temperament is colder than normal would be naturally inclined to coward-ice and fear. If he is taught to be fearful, he will quickly become a coward. But if he is conditioned to be fearless, he will eventually learn to be valiant, although it will take a great deal of hard work. In spite of his disposition, he can achieve heroism if he receives the proper training.[25]

ADAM

God said, "Let us make man with our image and likeness."

Rabbi Samson Raphael Hirsch:[26] The name Adam, man, reflects the essential nature of the first man. The word Adam is cognate to *adom*, red, the least-broken ray of the spectrum of the pure ray of light; which is to say, man is the nearest revelation of the divine on earth.

The word Adam is related also to *domeh*, likeness.[27] Man is a being whose entire mission consists of being a "likeness of God" but who is to actualize this likeness through his own free-willed energy. He thereby becomes the representative and alter ego of the Supreme Being.

Furthermore, the name Adam can be seen as a deriva-tive of *damah*, "to be silent." Man must in no way contra-dict the likeness to God expected of him. Being similar to God, man should not tolerate anything in himself that is contradictory to God.

FOUR WORDS DENOTING MAN

Rabbi Yitzchak Eizik Chaver, a distinguished disciple of the Vilna Gaon, in his commentary *Or Torah*[28] notes that the Hebrew uses four words to signify man: *enosh, gever, ish,* and *adam.* He finds that each term represents a different stage in the spiritual development of man.

Enosh אֱנוֹשׁ, (*alef* = 1, *nun* = 50, *vav* = 6, *shin* = 300) is man at the lowest level. *Enosh* has a numeric value of 357. This is *almost* the same as the value of *nachash* נָחָשׁ, snake, (*nun* = 50; *chet* = 8; *shin* = 300), the symbol of evil, which adds up to 358. Note that the difference between *enosh* (man) and *nachash* (serpent) is only 1. Man at the level of *enosh* is under the total dominance of the *nachash,* the snake. His soul has almost been smothered completely, but not quite. There still is *one* tiny spark of *emunah* (faith) flickering in his soul. As long as this spark is still glowing, it can ignite into a blazing flame of *teshuvah.* The *enosh* will yet rise to the heights of Torah greatness.

Gever, the next stage in spiritual growth, is akin to the word *gevurah,* "power, might." Hence, *gever* denotes the man who is struggling mightily with his carnal instincts and is trying to subdue these tendencies and eventually will emerge victorious.

Ish, אִישׁ, signifies a man who has mastered his evil inclination. In the word אִישׁ *ish,* the letter *yud,* symbol of divinity, is firmly anchored between the *alef* and the *shin.* The *yud* separates these two letters, which together form *eish,* fire. In other words, harboring God in his heart, he has doused the flames of forbidden passion.

Adam cognate to *adameh le'Elyon,* "I will match the Most High" (Isaiah 14:14), represents man as he was meant to be, the perfect man who clings to God and His Torah.

❧

FROM EARTH TO HEAVEN

The Talmud teaches: The first man reached from earth to heaven, but when he sinned, the Holy One, blessed is He, laid His hand on him and diminished him (*Sanhedrin* 38b).

On this passage in the Talmud, Rabbi Chaim Shmulevitz comments:[29] This is a metaphor and should not be taken literally. The point the *Gemara* wants to make is that man's potential was unlimited. The whole world was within the reach of his intellect; nothing was beyond his grasp.

When Adam transgressed, God diminished him, curbed his mental capacity, and placed many lofty concepts beyond his reach. Still, even after being diminished, man's mental powers enable him to do things that seem physically impossible.

For example, we read that on arriving in Charan, Jacob saw a well that was covered with a huge boulder. Ordinarily, it required the combined efforts of a large number of shepherds to remove the stone and water the sheep. Yet "Jacob stepped forward and rolled the stone from the top of the well" (Genesis 29:10), "like removing a cork from a bottle" (Rashi). Such superhuman power stems from single-minded dedication. We see evidence of this in daily life when, for example, a man caught in a fire will perform heroic feats that, normally, ten people could not achieve.

There is no limit to the things you can achieve with steadfast devotion and indomitable willpower. Man still can reach from earth to heaven.

Sichot Mussar, 5731 / 1971:5

3

Man, a Reflection of the Ten *Sefirot*

THE MYSTERY OF THE TEN *SEFIROT*

One of the fundamental principles of the Jewish faith is that it is impossible to comprehend God. As the Rambam puts it: We believe that God is totally nonphysical. He is not a body or a physical force. Thus we cannot say that God moves, rests, or exists in a given place. . . . Very often, however, our holy Scriptures do speak of God in physical terms. Thus, we find such concepts as walking, standing, sitting, hearing, seeing, and speaking used in relation to God. In all these cases, though, Scripture is only speaking in a figurative sense, formulating esoteric concepts in terms the human mind can grasp. Our sages teach us, *dibrah Torah bilshon benei adam*, "The Torah speaks the ordinary language of man" (*Berachot* 31b).[1]

And so, when discussing the mystery of the *Sefirot*, we must bear in mind that all descriptions of conduits, emanations, radiations, and channels are only metaphors to express the means by which the *Ein Sof* (the Infinite One) makes His existence known. It is impossible to fathom the reality of the Ten *Sefirot*, since, in essence, they are manifestations of divine attributes that are beyond human understanding.

Rabbi Moshe Cordovero,[2] the revered kabbalist, in his work *Pardes Rimonim*[3] describes the Ten *Sefirot* in their utter complexity. In descending order, the following are the Ten *Sefirot*:[4]

1. *Keter* (Crown)
2. *Chochmah* (Wisdom)
3. *Binah* (Understanding)
4. *Chesed* (Kindness)
5. *Gevurah* (Power)
6. *Tiferet* (Beauty)
7. *Netzach* (Eternity)
8. *Hod* (Splendor)
9. *Yesod* (Foundation)
10. *Malchut* (Kingdom)

THE *SEFIROT* IN HUMAN FORM

Kabbalah sees man not only as a replica of the physical universe but also as a model of the spiritual realm. Man was created "in the image of God," thus he can be thought of as a small-scale projection of the Ten *Sefirot*. With that in mind, Rabbi Moshe Cordovero in *Pardes Rimonim*, in the chapter *Shaar Hatzinorot* (Gate of the Conduits), presents a symbolic diagram that depicts the *Sefirot* in the shape of a human figure, wherein each of the major limbs and organs matches one of the *Sefirot*.[5]

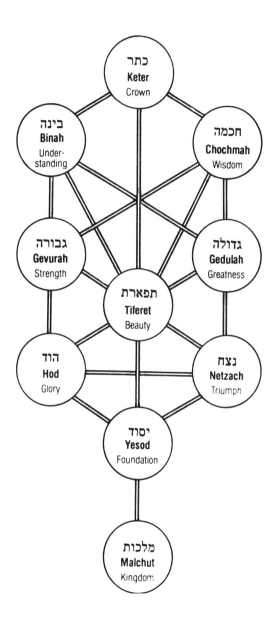

Illustration from *Pardes Rimonim*—representation of the spiritual *Sefirot*.

THE *GEMATRIA* OF GOD'S NAME

The *gematria*, numeric value, of the four-letter Divine Name Y-H-V-H amounts to 26 (*yud* = 10; *hei* = 5; *vav* = 6; *hei* = 5; 10 + 5 + 6 + 5 = 26).

It should be noted that a letter of the *alef-bet* can be written as a single letter, א, *alef*, ב *bet*, ג *gimel*, but it can also be written in its *milui* form, "in full." The four-letter Name in its *milui* form is as follows:

יוד, *yud*, spelled *yud* (10); *vav* (6); *dalet* (4). 10 + 6 + 4 = 20.
הא, *hei*, spelled *hei* (5); *alef* (1). 5 + 1 = 6.
ואו, *vav*, spelled *vav* (6); *alef* (1); *vav* (6). 6 + 1 + 6 = 13.
הא, *hei*, spelled *hei* (5); *alef* (1). 5 + 1 = 6.

Thus, the four-letter Divine Name written in its *milui* (full) form is composed of ten letters, clearly an allusion to the Ten *Sefirot* and an indication that the Ten *Sefirot* are manifestations of God.

Furthermore, the total numeric value of the Divine Name in its *milui* form adds up to 45 (20 + 6 + 13 + 6 = 45), which is exactly the value of the letters of אדם, *adam*, man (*alef* = 1; *dalet* = 4; *mem* = 40; 1 + 4 + 40 = 45).

The equation of God's name and man tells you that man is created in the likeness of God and endowed with a divine spark, the human soul. The Godlike quality of man is expressed in the following verse: "You have made him little less than divine, and adorned him with glory and majesty" (Psalm 8:6).

OLAM, SHANAH, NEFESH: WORLD, YEAR, AND SOUL

God created man with His image. In the image of God He created him (Genesis 1:27).

Rabbi Yaakov Yosef of Polnoye:[6] Since man is an *olam katan*, "a miniature universe," he exemplifies the Ten *Sefirot*. Whatever exists in the higher worlds is present in man and can be found in the three dimensions of human activity:

olam—world,
shanah—year,
nefesh—soul

To put it another way, *olam* (world) symbolizes the dimension of space, *shanah* (year) represents the dimension of time, and *nefesh* (soul) refers to the moral dimension. For in this world, man operates within the confines of time and space, and he is bound by the laws of morality. (*Ashan*, the acronym formed of the initials of *olam*, *shanah*, *nefesh*, is a recurring term in kabbalistic writings.)

THE FOUR WORLDS

The sages of kabbalah teach that the totality of existence is composed of four worlds. In descending order they are:

Atzilut (Emanation),
Beriah (Creation),
Yetzirah (Formation),
Asiah (Action)

In kabbalistic literature the four worlds, *Atzilut*, *Beriah*, *Yetzirah*, *Asiyah*, are generally referred to by the acronym *Abiyah*. These worlds can exist only because God has made "room" for them, for when the divine radiance shines in unrestricted brilliance, nothing else can exist. And so, God has withdrawn and hidden His all-pervasive Self, allowing the physical universe to come into being. Descending from the higher to the lower worlds, God's concealment gradually increases. His radiance is most evident in the World of Emanation, and it is almost completely obscured in the World of Action, which is our world. What this means is that the creatures of the higher worlds—angels like *Ofanim*, *Serafim*, and *Chayot*—are more Godlike and less separate from God. They more clearly perceive the Divine Light.

By contrast, the inhabitants of the World of Action, meaning man, are separated from God by a massive barrier of corporeality. This barrier effectively shuts out the divine radiance and leads many people to doubt or even deny the existence of a Creator. They delude themselves into thinking that they are master of the world. They take their cue from Pharaoh, the archetypical atheist, who proclaimed, "My Nile is my own; I made it myself" (Ezekiel 29:3).

Only when disaster struck in the form of the Ten Plagues did Pharaoh "see the light." At last he declared to Moses, "God is just! It is I and my people who are wrong! Pray to God" (Exodus 9:27, 28).

DISCUSSION OF THE *SEFIROT*: *KETER, CHOCHMAH, BINAH*

Of the uppermost three *Sefirot*, the highest and holiest is *Keter* (Crown). It is the one nearest to God, the manifestation of God's will, and as such, transcends all human understanding and defies all logic.

The group of the three highest *Sefirot*, consisting of *Keter* (Crown) along with *Chochmah* (Wisdom) and *Binah* (Understanding), are called *mochin*, which means the brain. They are "the *Sefirot* of the head" and represent cognition, intelligence. In human terms, *Chochmah* can be described as intuitive or direct knowledge, *Binah* as the *Sefirah* of intellectual analysis, where intuition develops into actual thought.[7]

The group of *mochin* (*Keter*, *Chochmah*, and *Binah*) is also called *imot*, mothers. This is a fitting description because these three *Sefirot* of intelligence "give birth" to the seven lower *Sefirot*.

THE THREE UNFATHOMABLE *SEFIROT*

The parallel between the *Sefirot* and man extends even further. The three highest *Sefirot*, namely, *Keter*, *Chochmah*, and *Binah*, are often referred to as *reisha delo ityada*, "the unknowable head." The "unknowable head" (the three highest *Sefirot*) compares to the lower seven *Sefirot* as man's soul compares to his body. And just as man's soul—his inner self—is hidden from others and is apparent only through one's words and actions, so is the essence of God completely concealed and is revealed only in the *midot* (divine characteristics), the seven lower *Sefirot*.

YOUR ELUSIVE SELF

Taking this thought one step further, we can say that a person's inner self, his soul, is hidden, not only from others, but even from himself. Just as God is unknowable, so it is impossible for you to perceive your innermost self. It sounds absurd, but you can easily prove it to yourself. As you read these lines and reflect on them, try to think about yourself. Try to pinpoint your "I," your conscious mind, that is doing the reading and the thinking. As you reflect about your mind and think about your "self," you discover that there are really two "selfs" within you. There is the "active

I" that is doing the thinking, and the "passive I" that is the object of your thinking. Now, if you try to analyze this "active, thinking I" with which you are examining your "self," you find that there is yet an even higher "I" that is thinking about your "thinking self." You suddenly realize that, no matter how high you reach in thinking about thinking about thinking . . . about yourself, your true, primary "thinking self," your innermost "I," can never be apprehended. It is impossible to think about your "real self" or to understand your "real self," because it is the hidden divine spark within you. Like the infinite, it is elusive, beyond your grasp. You have proved to yourself and know with absolute certainty that there is a thinking "I," but you cannot comprehend it.

And so, by looking within yourself, searching for your hidden "I," you discover your soul, which is a small particle of God. In the process, you have found God, the Life-giver of the world. As Job put it, "In my flesh I see God" (Job 19:26). By contemplating my "self" I come to recognize God.

THE "LOWER" SEVEN *SEFIROT*

The "lower" seven *Sefirot* are the channels with which the world was created. In *Sefer Yetzirah*[8] (1:5) they are called *midot*, divine attributes, characteristics through which God administers the world, like kindness, strict justice, or mercy.

The word *midot* can also be translated as *measures*. The term *measures* is equally appropriate because, in contrast to the three higher *Sefirot*, which are unlimited, the seven lower *Sefirot* are measured and restricted.

The mother-child relationship between the *Sefirot* of *mochin-imot* and *midot* is strikingly paralleled in man. Just as the *mochin* (*Sefirot* of intelligence) give birth to the *midot*

(*Sefirot* of character traits), so is man's intellect the source of his behavior, because all human qualities and emotions, such as love, fear, generosity, and pride, originate in his thinking process.[9]

The *Sefirot* can be seen as a configuration resembling an upright human figure, each of whose main limbs corresponds to one of the *Sefirot*. The head represents the highest three *Sefirot*. The next group of three *Sefirot* corresponds to the heart and the two arms. The lowest three *Sefirot* parallel the parts of the body that sustain life: the two legs and the reproductive organ.

As shown in the diagram, the *Sefirot* are set in groups of three. The two outermost *Sefirot* on the right side represent *chesed* (kindness), and those on the left represent *din* (strictness). The third *Sefirah* in the center reconciles the two opposing extremes.[10]

The *Sefirot* on one side balance those on the other. For example, *Chochmah* (Wisdom), which is intuitive knowledge, is balanced by *Binah* (Understanding), logical analysis. Similarly, *Chesed*, the *Sefirah* of limitless, unrestricted love, is kept in check by *Gevurah* (Power), the *Sefirah* of restraint, fear, and awe.

EMULATING THE DIVINE ATTRIBUTES

It is man's task in this world to improve himself and thereby the world. He does it by emulating the divine traits that are manifest in the seven "lower" *Sefirot*,[11] in particular the quality of *chesed*, kindness.

This thought is spelled out in the Talmud:

"Follow God your Lord" (Deuteronomy 13:5). Is it possible for man to follow the Divine Presence, which is described as "a consuming fire" (Deuteronomy 4:24)? But it means rather to follow the attributes of the Holy One,

Blessed be He. Just as He clothes the naked, as it says, "And God made for Adam and his wife garments of skin and clothed them" (Genesis 3:21), so you clothe the naked; just as the Holy One, Blessed be He, visited the sick, as it says, "And God appeared to him [Abraham, after his circumcision] in the plain of Mamre" (Genesis 18:1), so you visit the sick . . . (*Sotah* 14a).

CHESED (KINDNESS), THE FOURTH *SEFIRAH*

Chesed is the trait of outpouring of benevolence to others, bestowing unlimited love and kindness on them, whether they deserve kindness or not. It is the cornerstone of this world, as it says, *Olam chesed yibaneh*, "The world will be built on kindness" (Psalm 89:3). God continuously showers His kindness on the world by nourishing and sustaining all His creatures. But the greatest act of divine kindness is that He gives of Himself, implanting in each of us a part of Himself, our soul.

Man, who has a spark of the Divine Essence and exemplifies the *Sefirot*, is urged to emulate the divine attributes in the phrase *hidabeik biderachav*, "cling to His ways."[12] How can you make the *Sefirah* of *Chesed* (Kindness) a reality in your life? By loving God with all your heart and soul and by loving your fellowman, treating him with goodness and kindness. The *Sefirah* of *Chesed* is the right arm of the human body in the *Sefirah* diagram, symbolic of the helpful arm that is extended in welcome, friendship, and aid.

ABRAHAM, PILLAR OF *CHESED*

Abraham, more than anyone, exemplified the quality of *chesed* (kindness). He is called the *amud hachesed*, the pillar of kindness, and became the personification of the *Sefirah* of *Chesed*. In the *Shemoneh Esrei* (*Amidah*), *Chesed* corresponds to the first *berachah*, in which we praise God as *Magein Avraham*, "Shield of Abraham."

Abraham, the father of the Jewish people, discovered God and spread the knowledge of God among the pagan world of his time. He thereby emulated God, who showers His infinite kindness on an undeserving world. The Torah gives an illustration of Abraham's unparalleled kindness as it came to the fore when, on the third day after his circumcision, weakened and frail from the ordeal, he graciously received three Arab wayfarers and personally served them an elaborate meal.[13]

The *Gemara* tells us how Abraham's kindness inspired the unbelievers to recognize God. He established an inn where he would offer room and board to hungry and tired wayfarers. When the guests wanted to thank Abraham for his hospitality, he would explain to them that all the food he offered them came from the bounty of the One to whom the world belongs. Therefore, he told them, "Bless God of whose food you have eaten" (*Sotah* 10a).

GEVURAH (POWER), THE FIFTH *SEFIRAH*

Gevurah (Power), the opposite of *Chesed* (Kindness), is the trait of restraint, fear, and awe. It means giving in a limited, controlled way. On the human level it involves fearing God, standing in awe of Him, and shuddering at the very thought of transgressing His *mitzvot*. It means controlling yourself by making a protective "fence" of precautions around the *mitzvot* themselves.

This *Sefirah* is exemplified by Isaac, who at the *Akeidah* (the Binding of Isaac) allowed himself to be bound on the altar, ready to offer his life in fulfillment of God's command. Thus he became the personification of the *Sefirah* of *Gevurah* (Power), the attribute of awe and fear of God as well as strict justice. In the *Shemoneh Esrei*,[14] the second *berachah* (in which God is addressed as "Master of powerful deeds") is identified with *Gevurah* (Power) and with Isaac.

The *Sefirah* of *Gevurah* is depicted as the left arm of the symbolic human body.

TIFERET (BEAUTY), THE SIXTH *SEFIRAH*

Tiferet (Beauty), the *Sefirah* of compassion, resolves the conflict between *Chesed* (Kindness) and *Gevurah* (Power). The essence of beauty is harmony in nature, music, or other art forms. Thus, *Tiferet* (Beauty) is the dimension that creates harmony between the love of *Chesed* on the one hand and the unmitigated stern justice of *Gevurah* on the other.

In human terms, *Tiferet* means following the middle road, the path of moderation, and shunning the extremes on either side. According to the Rambam (Maimonides), this is the ideal way of life. In his introduction to *Avot*, he sums up his ideas on this subject and defines the golden mean:

The middle course is the right way to follow in all human qualities. . . . Generosity is the happy medium between stinginess and wastefulness; courage, between recklessness and cowardice; dignity, between pridefulness and boorishness. Friendliness is the happy medium between aggressiveness and submissiveness, humility is the middle course between arrogance and self-abasement; contentedness, between greed and laziness; and goodheartedness is midway between meanness and extravagance.[15]

JACOB, SYMBOL OF *TIFERET*

The prototype of the *Sefirah* of *Tiferet* is Jacob, the *bechir ha'avot*, "the favorite of the Patriarch," for he symbolizes truth, as it says, "Grant truth to Jacob" (Micah 7:20). Truth implies the proper mix of opposing attributes. Since *Tiferet* stands for the perfect blend of *Chesed* and *Gevurah*, it is fitting that Jacob is associated with this *Sefirah*.

In the symbolic human body, *Tiferet* corresponds to the heart. Just as *Tiferet* (Beauty) creates unity and harmony out of the divergent forces of *Chesed* (Kindness) and *Gevurah* (Strictness), so does the heart unify and harmonize the variegated functions of all parts of the body.

NETZACH (ETERNITY), AND *HOD* (SPLENDOR), THE SEVENTH AND EIGHTH *SEFIROT*

Netzach (Eternity) and *Hod* (Splendor) are compared to "the two kidneys that give counsel." How is this to be understood? Having passed through the *Sefirah* of *Tiferet*, the Infinite Light is ready to enter the lower *Sefirot*. Before this can come about, advice must be sought as to how best to convey the flow of abundance. It can be compared to a teacher who wants to teach his student a difficult lesson. If he presents the lesson in its entire complexity, the student will not be able to grasp it. The teacher must reflect and deliberate on how best to explain the knotty problem.

Giving advice and counsel on how best to proceed is the function of the *Sefirot* of *Netzach* and *Hod*.

The word *Netzach* denotes eternity as well as triumph. Both meanings apply to this *Sefirah*, because one who overcomes adversity can endure.

In man, the *Sefirah* of *Netzach* signifies the triumph over all obstacles that stand in your way of serving God, whether external or internal. *Hod* stands for gratitude, thanking God for all His kindness.

Moses is the personification of *Netzach*; Aaron exemplifies *Hod*. In the model of the human body, *Netzach* and *Hod* are represented as *trein shokin*, "the two thighs," and together they are described as *trei palgei gufa*, "the two halves of the body." In kabbalistic writings, the thighs, which are the underpinnings of the body, are the reflection of *emunah*, faith, which is the foundation of Judaism.

Describing these two *Sefirot*, the *Degel Machaneh Efraim*[16] says, "*Netzach* and *Hod* are the two halves of the body, in other words, the two thighs. They are the mystery of *emunah* (faith), that is to say, they are the two pillars of truth: faith and attachment to God."

YESOD (FOUNDATION), THE NINTH *SEFIRAH*

Just as *Tiferet* mediates between *Chesed* and *Gevurah*, so does *Yesod* (Foundation) create a synthesis between the two opposing *Sefirot* of *Netzach* and *Hod*. *Yesod* is the *Sefirah* through which the flow of divine abundance is channeled and souls are routed to the physical world. In other words, *Yesod* is the tie that connects the giver and the receiver.

From the human perspective, the *Sefirah* of *Yesod* involves being bound and attached to God in thought, feeling, and deed. By the same token, *Yesod* expresses the idea that all Jews should be bound together in unity and harmony with the intention of serving God.

In the *Sefirah* model of the human body, *Yesod* is symbolized as the reproductive function, the organ that gives. Therefore, man's obligation not to abuse this function and the severity attached to the transgression of this obligation are related to this *Sefirah*. By extension, *Yesod* is associated with *brit*, the covenant of circumcision.

The sages of Kabbalah connect the *Sefirah* of *Yesod* (Foundation) with the quintessential *tzaddik* (righteous man). He is considered the *yesod* (foundation) of the world, as it is written, *Tzaddik yesod olam*, "The righteous man is the foundation of the world" (Proverbs 10:25).

The Rambam (Maimonides) explains the concept of the perfect *tzaddik* in the introduction to his commentary to the Mishnah: "The goal of Creation was to bring into being the perfect man who possesses both wisdom and good deeds."[17]

He goes on to explain that the perfect *tzaddik* cannot exist alone in the world. He needs the sun to warm him and the rain to quench his thirst. He needs a society of countless fellowmen to sustain him and cater to his needs: farmers, millers, and bakers to produce his bread, builders to provide shelter for him, tailors to make his clothes. Thus, although he is just one man, he requires the rest of the universe and, therefore, it exists for his sake. Consequently, the *tzaddik* is quite rightly called *tzaddik yesod olam*, the foundation of the universe, for the entire universe rests on him.

Yesod, the *Sefirah* of giving, is closely linked to Joseph, who is generally referred to as *Yosef Hatzaddik*, the *tzaddik* par excellence. It was he who gave grain to his brothers during the seven years of famine in Egypt, and it was he who provided grain for the Egyptian people, saying, "Take seed for yourselves" (Genesis 47:23).

Joseph's righteousness became evident when he spurned the seductive advances of his master Potiphar's wife (Genesis 9) and did not tarnish the covenant of circumcision (the organ of giving). As a result, Joseph the *tzaddik* is the epitome of the *Sefirah Yesod*.

THE BEAUTY OF POTIPHAR'S WIFE

In a discussion of the attempted seduction of Joseph, the *Gemara* relates that at the critical moment, "Joseph saw his father's image, and as a result, his passion left him by way of the nails of his hands" (*Sotah* 36b).

Jacob, Joseph's father, is the embodiment of the *Sefirah* of *Tiferet* (Beauty), which is the synthesis of the two antithetical *Sefirot* of *Chesed* (Kindness) and *Gevurah* (Power). Jacob thus represented the spiritual beauty that is inherent in harmony, reconciliation, and unity.

Seeing his father's image meant much more than conjuring up a mental image of Jacob's face and figure. Joseph beheld *Tiferet*, Jacob's *Sefirah*. He perceived the characteristic of spiritual beauty that was Jacob's hallmark. He suddenly realized that the physical beauty of Potiphar's wife was a reflection of the sublime spiritual beauty of the *Sefirah* of *Tiferet*.

This awareness immediately cooled his ardor, causing him "to run away and flee outside" (Genesis 39:12). He ran away from the allure of physical beauty and fled outside, to a higher world, to attach himself to higher, spiritual beauty.

The *Gemara* alludes to this when it says that "his passion left him by way of the nails of his hands." In other words, his desire abated when he reminded himself of his ten fingers, which are symbolic of the Ten *Sefirot*, as set forth in *Sefer Yetzirah*, "The *Sefirot* . . . are the number of the ten fingers, five opposite five" (*Sefer Yetzirah* 1:3).[18]

THE JOY OF *YESOD*

It cannot be stressed enough that the *Sefirot* are purely spiritual entities, and that all references to the human body and its organs are symbolic representations of abstract concepts.

In that spirit, Rabbi Yaakov Yosef of Polnoye[19] described the *midah* (attribute) of *Yesod*, which is embodied in the male organ, stating, "The *midah* of *Yesod* becomes manifest in man when serving the Creator is a source of incomparable pleasure to him. This spiritual enjoyment parallels the sublime physical pleasure the reproductive organ—[the embodiment of *Yesod*]—evokes in the union of the male and the female, as it says, 'In my flesh I see God' (Job 19:26)."

If you consider the immense pleasure that is generated by the physical union, you can imagine how much greater will be the joy you experience if you attach yourself to the Unity of God, who is the source of all pleasure.[20]

MALCHUT (KINGDOM), THE TENTH *SEFIRAH*

Malchut is the final *Sefirah*. It receives the flow of abundance from *Yesod* but does not pass it on to others. Therefore this *Sefirah* is generally associated with woman, who receives the seed.[21] In the *Zohar*, *Malchut* is often identified with the moon, which represents the female, personified by Eve.[22] For, like the female who receives the seed, the moon has no light of its own but is illuminated by the light of the sun. Of course, there is an obvious connection between the monthly lunar cycle of waxing and waning and the menstrual cycle of a woman.

King David is the prototype of the *Sefirah* of *Malchut* (Kingdom), which is likened to the moon. Just as the moon is reborn after a period of decline and total disappearance, so, too, the Davidic dynasty endures and will rise again with the coming of *Mashiach*. Confident of the restoration of the messianic monarchy, we say every month in *Kiddush Levanah*, the Sanctification of the Moon: David, *Melech Yisrael, chai vekayam*. "David, King of Israel, is alive and enduring."

Malchut, the *Sefirah* that only receives, is represented by the mouth, the organ through which man receives nourishment. *Malchut* has the further connotation of the Oral Torah, as it is stated in *Patach Eliyahu*, "Malchut is the mouth, that is called *Torah shebe'al Peh*, the Oral Torah."[23]

Malchut, the seventh of the lower *Sefirot*, is the emanation where the Infinite Light reaches its destination, and the divine flow of abundance is spread throughout our world. This seventh *Sefirah* is closely linked to *Shabbat*, for analogously, *Shabbat* is the seventh day of Creation, the day "on which God ceased from all the work that He had been creating" (Genesis 2:3), the time when God's glory becomes visible on earth.

The analogy can be extended to include King David. The *Zohar* speaks of the Seven Shepherds who are the prototypes of the seven *Sefirot*. They are the personalities who guided and shaped Israel's destiny: Abraham, Isaac, Jacob, Moses, Aaron, Joseph, and David. The seventh Shepherd is David, who stands for *Malchut* (Kingdom), and who as King of Israel represents God's majesty on earth.[24]

The symbols of the *Sefirah* of *Malchut* are mentioned in *Sefer Yetzirah* 4:1, the Book of Creation, attributed to the Patriarch Abraham. In that ancient book we read, "He formed the moon with [the Sefirah of Malchut] in the universe, the *Shabbat* day in the year, and the mouth in the soul."

✦

SHABBAT AND KING DAVID

A king is a ruler only when he has subjects who recognize him as their monarch and pay homage to him. Thus, *Shabbat* is an expression of God's *Malchut* (Kingship) because it is the day when God's glory becomes visible on earth; it is the culmination of the process by which He brings His Infinite Light from the highest regions to our world. The Jewish people, God's loyal subjects, accept Him as their King by keeping the *Shabbat* as an eternal covenant. Indeed, every Jew who observes *Shabbat* palpably senses the joy of God's Light that permeates his home and personal life on that day.

Like *Shabbat*, King David stands for *Malchut* (Kingship), for he is the human representation of God's majesty. The Davidic monarchy will come to fruition when an offspring of David, the son of Jesse, will usher in the messianic age, as it says, "A shoot shall grow out of the stump of Jesse, a twig shall sprout from his stock. . . . The land shall be filled with the knowledge of God as water covers the sea" (Isaiah 11:1, 9).

Shabbat and the messianic King, the twin manifestations of *Malchut* (Kingship), are movingly described in the *Shabbat* hymn *Lechah Dodi*:[25]

> Shake off the dust—arise!
> Don your splendid clothes, My people,
> Through the son of Jesse, the Bethlehemite!
> Draw near to my soul—redeem it!
> Come, my Beloved, to greet the bride—
> The *Shabbat* presence, let us welcome!

✿

THE GRATEFUL POOR MAN

Malchut, the lowest *Sefirah*, is the point of contact where our world touches the higher worlds, the channel through which the divine flow of plenty reaches man. It is the *Sefirah* that receives light but "that has nothing of her own."[26] *Malchut* thus represents the gratitude of a poor man toward his benefactor.

Man is the ultimate recipient of all of God's bounty. Therefore, emulating *Malchut* here on earth means recognizing that you possess nothing of your own and being aware that "it is God who gives you the power to become prosperous" (Deuteronomy 8:18). This realization arouses feelings of gratitude, deep humility, and submission to the will of God, the characteristics of *Malchut*.

WHERE IS THE PLACE OF HIS GLORY?

In the *Kedushah* of *Mussaf* we say that the ministering angels ask each other, *Ayeih mekom kevodo*, "Where is the place of His glory?" A puzzling question indeed, for surely the angels know that God's glory is infinite, transcends space, and is not confined to any one place.

The sages of Kabbalah point out the letters of איה *ayeih*, *where*, are the initials of את יום השבת *et yom haShabbat*, "the Shabbat day." Thus, *ayeh mekom kevodo* means that "the day of *Shabbat* is the 'place' of His glory," in the sense that God's glory is manifest on *Shabbat* for all who observe that day and keep it holy.

THE SPECIAL INGREDIENT

Although God's Presence in this world is hidden and not apparent to everyone, you can obtain a glimpse of His Light even here on earth. You can perceive it in the sweetness of *Shabbat*, for the *Shabbat* day is called "a semblance of the World to Come."[27] *Shabbat* is our link to the higher worlds.

In this connection, the *Gemara* (*Shabbat* 119a) records a fascinating conversation between the Roman emperor Hadrian and Rabbi Yehoshua:

The emperor asked Rabbi Yehoshua ben Chananiah, "Why does the food that you prepare for the Sabbath smell so good?"

Rabbi Yehoshua replied, "We have a special spice that we put into it, and its name is Sabbath."

"Give me some of it," demanded the emperor.

Said Rabbi Yehoshua, "It only works for those who observe the Sabbath, but for those who do not observe the Sabbath, it has no effect."

THE FIRST *MISHNAH* OF *SHABBAT*

The various symbols of the *Sefirah* of *Malchut*—the Oral Torah, the mouth, *Shabbat*, the poor man, and the act of receiving—all are concealed in the first *mishnah* of tractate *Shabbat*. This *mishnah* deals with the definition of the laws of *hotza'ah*, the act of transferring an object from your house into the street, and vice versa, which is prohibited on *Shabbat*.

In order to simplify the complexities of these laws, the *Mishnah* frames the various cases in terms of a householder who is standing inside and hands something to a poor man standing outside. To quote the first paragraph of this *mishnah*:

"If the poor man extended his hand inside and placed an object into the householder's hand, or he took an object from it and brought that object out, the poor man is liable and the householder is exempt."

Without going into the halachic details of *akirah* (picking up) and *hanachah* (putting down), we note that many of the symbols of *Malchut* converge in this *mishnah*:

The *Mishnah* itself comprises the words of the Oral Torah, which are transmitted by mouth; the subject of the *mishnah* is *Shabbat*; the focus is on the poor man, engaged in the act of receiving.[28]

This *mishnah* thus exemplifies the unity of *Halachah* and Kabbalah.

II

THE PARTS
AND ORGANS
OF THE BODY

Part I looked at man with a wide-angle lens, considering him in his relation to God, his place in the universe, and the purpose for which he was created. The concept emerged that the human form is a miniature world encompassing the entire cosmos as well as the infinite spiritual realm that lies beyond.

Part II takes a close-up view of man, focusing on the individual parts and organs of the human body. The sages meticulously examined the limbs and organs, but not from a clinical vantage point. They did not concentrate on the human anatomy, physiology, and pathology. Instead, they were concerned with the soul that inhabits the body and gives vitality to each of its parts. They discerned the *mitzvot* that connect each limb, vein, and nerve to its source in the higher worlds.

The underlying idea of all their insights is to tell us how to discover God in our flesh, how best to utilize a given organ in His service, and how to avoid the pitfalls associated with that organ, in the spirit of "In my flesh I see God" (Job 19:26). Their perceptive comments lift us to a higher plane and open our eyes to a wide range of new vistas. We see the human form, our head, face, mouth, tongue, and teeth in a totally different light. As we peruse the wisdom of the greatest minds of the Jewish people, we are dazzled by a profusion of original facets and symbolisms about such parts as the spinal column, the organs of digestion, the arms and legs, *milah* (circumcision), and many other members. The lessons we derive about our physical and spiritual health prove to be an invaluable treasure trove.

4

The Head

THE DUAL NATURE OF MAN

Man, the handiwork of God, was created in the divine mold. He is a blend of two contrasting elements, "the dust of the ground" and a divine spirit. In his carnal nature he resembles the earth, while his soul is rooted in the Throne of Glory.

The Arizal[1] finds an allusion to man's dual nature of body and soul in the word אדם *adam*, man. He notes that אדם *adam* is a fusion of the letters א *alef* and דם *dam*.

The letter א *alef*, which has the numeric value of 1, represents the unity of the Divine Creator. The word *dam*, meaning *blood*, symbolizes the physical aspect of man. Accordingly, אדם *adam* denotes man's two components: his immortal soul sheathed by his earthly form.

Notice that the *alef* in *adam* precedes *dam*. This tells you that the *alef*, your spiritual aspirations, should control and dominate your *dam*, your base instincts.

🌱

THE NAME ADAM

In the Hebrew there are four words that signify *man*: *enosh*, *gever*, *ish*, and *adam*. Of these, the word *adam* was chosen as the name for the first man. Why specifically *adam*, and none of the other terms?

Three of the words denoting *man* have a plural form: *enosh, anashim*; *gever, gevarim*; *ish, ishim*. The exception is *adam,* which has no plural form, the reason being that *adam* signifies man as a single unit encompassing many diverse elements. (Compare the English mankind.) The name Adam thus implies the unity of all mankind and the idea that all men are brothers.[2]

THE SHAPE OF THE *ALEF*

The letter *alef*, by its numeric value of 1, is symbolic of the oneness of God. Rabbi Moshe Cordovero[3] finds godliness hidden, not only in the numeric value but also in the graphic form of the letter א *alef*. He notes that the alef is composed of three parts: on the upper right there is a ׳ *yud*, and on the lower left there is a ׳ *yud*. These two letters are connected by a diagonal bar that is shaped like a ו *vav*.

The numeric value of a *yud* is 10; that of a *vav* is 6. By adding the three components of *alef* you obtain 10 + 10 + 6, a total of 26. This equals the numeric value of the four-letter Divine Name, *Yud-Hei-Vav-Hei* (*yud* = 10; *hei* = 5; *vav* = 6; *hei* = 5; 10 + 5 + 6 + 5 = 26). *Alef* thus symbolizes the oneness and the timeless nature of God.

(Unlike the divine appellations like the Merciful, Eternal, Almighty, and the Holy One, Blessed be He, which describe divine attributes, the four-letter Name, the Tetragrammaton, refers to the essence of God. For that reason, Y-H-V-H may not be pronounced under any circumstances, except during the Yom Kippur service in the *Bet Hamikdash* when the High Priest pronounced the Name on ten occasions.[4] When we read the Torah or during prayer, we pronounce the Name as *Adonai*, meaning "my Lord." On any other occasion, we do not even use this appellation but refer to God as *Hashem*, literally, the Name.)

KING OF THE LIMBS

The head is described as "king of the limbs"[5] because it is the seat of the brain and the intellect. In the microcosm that is man, the brain represents the three highest *Sefirot*: *Keter* (Crown), *Chochmah* (Intuitive Wisdom), and *Binah* (Understanding). These are called "*Sefirot* of the head" and are completely beyond the scope of human comprehension.

Let Your Mind Be the Ruler

[If you want to appoint a king] you must appoint the king whom God your Lord shall choose. You must appoint a king from among your brethren; you may not appoint a foreigner who is not one of your brethren (Deuteronomy 17:14).

Rabbi Yechezkel Rabinowitz of Radomsk (died 1910), comments in Kenesset Yechezkel: You must appoint a king. . . . You may not appoint a foreigner. The Hebrew word for king is מלך *melech*. The sages of Kabbalah note that מלך *melech* is an acronym of the initials of מוח *mo'ach* (brain, intellect), לב *lev* (heart), and כבד *kaved* (liver).

The brain is the seat of the soul, the intellect, and the mind. In a metaphoric sense, this verse is telling us to appoint our intellect as the ruler over the other parts of our body and not to allow ourselves to be dominated by the passions of the heart or the anger that is seated in the liver.[6]

Crown your mind king over your body. "You may not appoint a foreigner"—don't be seduced by the lusts and temperaments associated with any other organ of your body.

The Lofty Level of Moses' Prophecy

The Rambam: Moses tried to comprehend the essence of God in His true reality. Thus he prayed, "Please let me have a vision of Your Glory" (Exodus 33:8). But God let him know that this was impossible. Since he was a human being his intellect was still bound to physical matter. God said, in fact, "A man cannot have a vision of Me and live" (Exodus 33:20).

And so, there remained one transparent partition separating Moses from his grasp of the true essence of God, and this partition was his human intellect that was still connected to physical matter. God characterized the true comprehension of His essence as "beholding the divine face"[7] because when you see someone's face, his features become imprinted on your mind so that you will not confuse him with someone else. But when you see only his back, you may possibly recognize him, but then again, you may be unsure and take him for someone else. In the same way, the true comprehension of God is an understanding of the reality of His existence . . . so that the knower recognizes and understands that God's existence is unlike the existence of any other being. It is impossible, however, for a man to attain this high degree of understanding, although Moses came very close to reaching it. God expressed this in a figurative sense, saying, "You will see My back" (Exodus 33:23).[8]

Shaped like a Sphere

The shape of the head is round. This prompts the following interesting observation by Rabbi Yisrael of Rizhin:[9]

All of Creation has a circular shape: The firmament and the earth are spheres, and all fruits are round. All of life is cyclical, as it says, "One generation goes, another comes"

(Ecclesiastes 1:4). Time runs in cycles; as soon as one day ends, the next day begins. So it is with weeks, years, and the *yovel* (jubilee)[10] cycle. In a sense, the Torah is also like a circle; "its end is anchored in its beginning, and its beginning is anchored in its end."[11] For as soon as we end the reading of the Torah, we begin all over again.

The people of Israel, too, have the quality of a circle. When you run on a circular track, your starting point is the point where you end. The farther you move from your starting point, the closer you get to the finish line, which is also your starting point. So it is with the Jewish people. When they drift away from their origins and descend from their former glory, they sink to the lowest depths. But once they have hit bottom, they bounce back to their former eminence.

You can compare it to a man who has been lowered into a pit on a rope. If the rope is removed, he knows that he was left there to die. But if he remains attached to the rope he knows that he was lowered into the pit for a purpose, either to do some repairs or to retrieve a lost object. When he reaches bottom and fulfills his task, he is certain that he will be pulled up again. All he needs to do is tug with all his might at his end of the rope, and immediately he will be brought to daylight again. But if he forgets and unties himself from the rope he will stay in the dark forever. The Jewish people are tied to their Creator with a rope of Truth, as it says, "Jacob [the symbol of Truth] is the rope of His heritage [Israel]" (Deuteronomy 32:9). Through their faith and prayer the Jewish people will be lifted up from the darkness of suffering. All they need to do is tug at the rope of Truth and return to God. He will receive them with open arms, as it is stated, "Turn back to Me—and I will turn back to you" (Zechariah 1:3).[12]

The Head and the Body

The head, which is spherical, stands in sharp contrast to the body, which has a rectangular shape. There is a profound significance in this.

The circular form represents eternity and spirituality, "its end is anchored in its beginning, and its beginning is anchored in its end,"[13] like a never-ending cycle. For example, the circular wedding ring represents God's presence in marriage.

A square, on the other hand, has sides that end at its four corners. Rabbi Shimon ben Gamliel said, "Since the six days of Creation, there is no square shape in nature."[14] Thus, the shape of a square or rectangle suggests finitude, mortality, and death. This idea finds expression in the architecture of houses and buildings, prime examples of physicality, which are rectangular in shape. In fact, our entire existence is dominated by straight lines: roads, streets, cars, books, furniture, signs, flags, computers, all have a rectangular shape.

In man, the head is the seat of the intellect and the soul. Its spherical skull houses man's spiritual dimension, his divine spark. On the other hand, the human torso contains the organs that are needed to sustain physical life. It has a rectangular shape. Simply put, man's spiritual faculties and his immortal soul are enclosed in his head, a round container which is endless. His spirit lives on forever. Man's earthly components, that is to say, his circulatory, digestive, and procreative systems, are encased in his body, a rectangular chamber whose dimensions are finite. Indeed, his transitory physical body is here today and gone tomorrow. (These comments by Rabbi Chaim Finkel are based on *Maalot Hatorah* by Rabbi Avraham, the brother of the Vilna Gaon [Koenigsberg, 1851].)

Rosh, the Head

The Hebrew word for head is *rosh*; in Aramaic the head is called *reish*, (as in *Reish Galuta*, meaning Exilarch, Head of the Jews in the Babylonian Exile). *Reish* ר is also the Hebrew letter whose shape represents the head. Its horizontal top portrays a head bent over in prayer and submission to God's will. Its downward "leg" on the right represents the spinal column that supports the head.

Alternately, *rosh* means "a poor man," as in "The poor man [*rosh*] speaks beseechingly" (Proverbs 18:23). Assuming the inclined posture of the letter *reish*, the poor man meekly bows his head as he begs for alms. And in a way, we all are supplicants who are dependent on God's beneficence.

It is interesting to note that the letters in the *alef beit* that follow after ראש *rosh* are שבת *Shabbat*, the day of holiness (*shin* follows *reish*; *bet* follows *alef*; *tav* follows *shin*). This tells us that by adopting humility, the characteristic of *rosh/reish*, we attain a higher degree of *kedushah*.

THE NUMBER TWELVE

The conflict between the timeless cycle that is embodied in the roundness of the head and the finiteness of the rectangular shape of the body is, in essence, the ever-present struggle between spirit and corporeality, between the *yetzer tov* and the *yetzer hara*, the good and the evil tendency in man.

A quick examination of any cube or box-shaped object will tell you that it is has six sides and is bounded by twelve edges. In fact, all matter can be defined in terms of six sides (top, bottom, north, east, south, and west), and twelve edges.[15] Thus, it comes as no surprise that many things in the physical world come in sets of twelve: the twelve constellations of the Zodiac, the twelve sons of Jacob who were the progenitors of the twelve tribes of Israel, and the twelve months of the year.

It is our task to lift the physical world to the level of the spiritual. We therefore sanctify the moon every month by reciting *Kiddush Levanah*, lifting ourselves above our time-bound mundane existence.

In this connection, it should be mentioned that Moses was born and died in the month of *Adar*, the *twelfth* month of the year. Furthermore, if we calculate the numeric value of משה, Moshe, using the system of *mispar katan*, whereby all zeros are omitted, we obtain 12 (*mem* = 4; *shin* = 3; *hei* = 5; 4 + 3 + 5 = 12). This comes to tell you that Moses was firmly rooted in the physical world but overcame his carnal tendencies and became the *ish haElokim*, the man of God. To put it another way, he transformed the finite limitations of his twelve-edged rectangular body into the infinite circle of the spirit. (Rabbi Chaim Finkel's comments are based on *Pardes Rimonim* by Rabbi Moshe Cordovero [Salonica, 1552].)

The Smaller, the Better

Rabbi Shimon Shalom of Amshinov:[16] In nature we observe that the more precious something is, the less space it occupies. This is consistent with the way God created the universe, *yesh me'ayin*, ex nihilo, "something out of nothing." First there was absolute nothingness. Then a form of primeval matter was created that was ethereal and virtually insubstantial. Gradually, more substantial and bulky forms of matter came into being. And so we find that the closer something is to its source of *ayin*, "primordial nothingness," the less substance it has and the less space it takes up. For example, in the human body, the brain and the sensory organs, which are its most essential parts and nearest to man's spiritual origin, are small in size, whereas the organs that sustain his earthbound existence and are far removed from his spiritual roots are of massive proportions. Obviously, the stomach, the liver, and the digestive tract have a greater volume than the eye and the cerebrum. The same holds true for the earth. Precious gems and jewels are smaller than massive boulders. Similarly, in the thinking process we can differentiate between abstract and concrete forms of reasoning. Profound contemplation of God, man, and the world requires a higher form of abstract thinking that is completely detached from physicality, whereas earthbound thought, such as the study of physics, medicine, engineering, law, and economics, deals with tangible entities and is closely linked to the physical world.

The Remedy for Headaches and Other Ailments

The Talmud teaches: If a man has a headache, let him engage in the study of Torah, since it is written, "For [the words of the Torah] are a graceful wreath upon your head" (Proverbs 1:9).

If he feels pain in his throat, let him engage in the study of Torah, since it is said, "[they are] a necklace around your throat" (Proverbs 1:9).

If he feels pain in his bowels, let him engage in the study of Torah, since it is said, "[The Torah] will be a cure for your navel" (Proverbs 3:8).

If he feels pain in his bones, let him engage in the study of Torah, for it says, "and a tonic for your bones" (Proverbs 3:8).

If he feels pain in all his body, let him engage in the study of the Torah, for it says, "a healing for his whole body" (Proverbs 4:22). R. Yehudah, son of Rabbi Chiyah, remarked, "Come and see how the way of mortals is not like that of the Holy One, Blessed be He. In the way of mortals, when a man administers a drug to someone else it may be beneficial to one limb but harmful to another, but with the Holy One, Blessed be He, it is not so. He gave the Torah to Israel, and it is a drug of life for all his body, as it says, "a healing for his whole body" (Proverbs 4:22).[17]

He Had a Headache

A chasid complained to Rabbi Bunam of Pshis'cha[18] that he often suffered from severe headaches after praying.

"What has davening (praying) to do with the head?" the Rebbe exclaimed. "Prayer is characterized as avodah shebelev, serving God with the heart.[19] It is not a labor of the head!"

Midor Dor[20]

More about Headaches

Rav said, "I can tolerate any illness but not intestinal disease, any suffering but not stomach or heart trouble, any pain but not headache, any evil but not an evil wife."

Shabbat 11a

After drinking the four prescribed cups of wine on the night of the Passover *seder*, Rabbi Yehudah suffered such severe headaches that he had to bind his temples from *Pesach* to *Shavuot*.

Nedarim 49b

The Gnat in Titus's Brain

The Talmud relates: When Titus returned to Rome after having blasphemed God, ravaged Jerusalem, and burned the *Bet Hamikdash*, God sent a gnat that entered his nostril, climbed into his head, and knocked against his brain for seven years. One day, as he was passing a blacksmith's shop, the gnat heard the noise of the hammer and stopped knocking. He said: I see there is a remedy. So every day he brought a blacksmith who hammered before him. This went on for thirty days, but then the creature got used to it and again began to knock. When Titus died they opened his skull and found something like a one-year-old dove weighing two pounds. Abbaye said, "We have it on record that its beak was of brass and its claws of iron."[21]

Maharsha:[22] The punishment of a gnat entering his brain via his nostril was a fitting retribution, because Titus used his power of speech to blaspheme and revile God. The faculty of speech is one of the powers of the soul. The soul enters the brain by way of the nose, as it says, "God breathed into his nostrils a breath of life. Man [thus] became a living soul" (Genesis 2:7). The Targum translates "a living soul" as "a speaking spirit." For misusing the power of speech, the divine gift of the soul that enters through the nostril, Titus was tormented by a gnat that entered his brain through the nostril.

The dove that lodged in his brain is symbolic of the Jewish people, as it says, "Do not deliver Your dove to the wild beast" (Psalm 74:19). It tells us that ultimately, the Jewish people will overcome and outlive their enemies.

Jezebel's One Good Deed

Rabbi Chaim Shmulevitz:[23] The parts of the body that committed a sin are held responsible for that transgression and are punished for it. By the same token, the parts that performed a *mitzvah* are rewarded for the good deed. The following Scripture illustrates this concept:

[The evil Queen Jezebel was thrown out of the palace window,] and her blood spattered on the wall and on the horses, and they trampled her. . . . They went to bury her; but all they found of her were the skull, the feet, and the hands. [The dogs had devoured the flesh of Jezebel] (2 Kings 9:33, 35).

The *Midrash* says that only Jezebel's skull, her feet, and her hands remained intact because she had made it a practice to dance before the bride at weddings, therefore, her feet were not devoured. While dancing, she would clap her hands and gracefully shake her head, therefore her hands and her skull survived undamaged.[24]

The parts of the body that did the *mitzvah* of gladdening bride and groom were the ones that merited to be buried.

Sichot Mussar, Mishpatim, 5732

The Guardrail

Rabbi Shmelke of Nikolsburg[25] remarked: "It says, 'You must place a guardrail around your roof' (Deuteronomy 22:8). Erect a fence around your head to keep out evil thoughts. Don't think evil thoughts, because 'evil thought is worse than transgression'" (*Yoma* 29a).[26]

Tefillin *of the Head and Hand*

Rabbi Yehudah Halevi, in his classical work, the *Kuzari*, says:

A pious man realizes that all his limbs are placed in perfect wisdom and harmony and that they follow his will without his awareness of them. Being aware of the marvels of his body, a pious man will surely behave in such a way that all his movements are dedicated to the Creator who formed him and guides him toward perfection. It is as if the Divine Presence were constantly with him, and as if he were accompanied by angels. Thus he attaches his mind to God through a variety of actions, some of them prescribed by the Written Law, some by oral tradition. He wears *tefillin* on his head, the organ of thought, letting the straps fall down on his hands in order to see them; he wears *tefillin* on his arm opposite the heart, the source of his strength. He also wears the *tzitzit*, fringes, to remind him that he may not be misled by his senses, as it says, "You will then not stray after your heart and eyes" (Numbers 15:39). . . . Although our minds cannot grasp it in every detail, we can discern the general harmony within the universe and can conclude from its marvels that there is behind it the will and wisdom, purpose and power of an Almighty Creator.

The Purpose of the Tefillin

By putting on the *tefillin* we are fulfilling the commandment of "Bind them as a sign on your arm, and let them be *tefillin* between your eyes" (Deuteronomy 6:8). The *tefillin* are a constant reminder of the lesson of the Exodus that is spelled out in four sections from the Torah (Deuteronomy 6:4–9; Deuteronomy 11:13–21; Exodus 13:1–10; Exodus 13:11–16). Parchments containing these passages are inserted in the *tefillin*. They declare the absolute unity of God and remind us of the miracles He did with us when He brought us out of Egypt.

"God has commanded us to put *tefillin* on the arm to recall the 'outstretched arm' [of the Exodus], and that it be placed opposite the heart, to surrender the desires and thoughts of our heart to His service; and on the head, opposite the brain, so that the soul that is in the brain, together with the other senses, all be subjected to His service."[27]

Head, Hands, and Feet

Rabbi Pinchas of Koretz[28] said: You can compare mankind to the human form. Israel is the head, since its importance lies in the creativity of the Jewish mind. The nations of the world are the hands, since they stand out for their dexterity and manual achievements. Animals are the feet, since they are valuable because of their feet.

Furthermore, a man's life also can be compared to the human form. When he is young his strength is in his feet; in middle age, in his hands; in old age, in his head.[29]

The Human Brain

Make an ark of acacia wood, two and one-half cubits long, one and one-half cubits wide, and one and one-half cubits high (Exodus 25:10).

Malbim:[30] "Make an ark of acacia wood."—The measurements of the ark were such that it would contain the two Tablets of the Covenant. The two Tablets conform to the brain, which consists of two parts, the cerebrum in the front and behind it the cerebellum.

God's Tefillin

The concept that man was created in the image and likeness of God extends even to the *mitzvah* of *tefillin*, for God, too, wears *tefillin*. And so we read in *Berachot* 6a:

"Rabbi Avin said, 'How do you know that the Holy One, Blessed be He, puts on *tefillin*? For it says: The Lord has sworn by His right hand, by the arm of His strength' (Isaiah 62:8). '*By the arm of His strength*' refers to *tefillin*.

"Rabbi Nachman bar Yitzchak said: 'What is written in the *tefillin* of the Master of the Universe?' He replied, 'And who is like Your people Israel, a unique nation on earth'" (1 Chronicles 18:21).

The Maharsha[31] comments: By putting on *tefillin*, we show that we are attached to God with our heart, soul, and resources. By the same token, by donning His *tefillin*, God demonstrates His devotion to and oneness with the Jewish people, as it is stated, "I am my Beloved's, and my Beloved is mine" (Song of Songs 6:3).

THE HUMAN FACE

The Divine Imprint

The *Zohar* says: Man was created in the image of God. This is manifest in the human face, for the two eyes are shaped like two letters *yud*, and the nose is shaped like the letter *vav*. Bearing in mind that the numeric value of *yud* is 10 and that *vav* equals 6, we can say that the numeric value of two times *yud* (the two eyes) plus *vav* (the nose) equals 26. And 26 is the equivalent of the four-letter Divine Name *Yud-Hei-Vav-Hei* (10 + 5 + 6 + 5 = 26). Thus, the human face bears the divine imprint.

Looking at the human body in its entirety, we find another parallel between man and God. The head is shaped like a *yud* (10), the five fingers on each of the two hands represent two letters *hei* (2 x 5), and the elongated shape of the body resembles a *vav* (6). By adding these numbers we again obtain 26, the numeric value of the Tetragrammaton.

A third manifestation of the principle of "In my flesh I see God" (Job 19:26) comes to the fore in the crown of the male organ, which has the shape of the letter *yud* (10); the male organ itself, which is shaped like a *vav* (6); and the five toes on each of the two feet, which correspond to two letters *hei* (2 x 5). Again, by adding these values (10 + 6 + 10) we obtain a total of 26, the numeric value of the ineffable Divine Name.

Zohar, Vayeira

Panim *(Face)*

The Hebrew word for face is *panim*, a term related to *penim*, which means inside, interior, within. This is significant because it tells you that a Jewish face (*panim*) reflects the thoughts that revolve within (*penim*) you. A Jew is sincere and straightforward, *tocho kebaro*, "his inside is like his outside."[32] His face is a mirror of his inner thoughts and feelings.

The non-Jewish world takes a different view. The English word *face* means "surface" or "facade." The German word for face, *Gesicht*, and the French *visage*, both denote "that which is seen," in other words, "the exterior." Essentially, the word *face* means a mask, an outward show, a disguise of one's true sentiments.

Simply put, *panim* means a face that reveals the truth; the English word *face* suggests concealing the truth and putting up a front.

Aphorisms about the Face

Your frame of mind shows in your face.

Zohar, end of *Lech Lecha*

Moses's face resembled the sun; Joshua's face was like the moon.

Bava Batra 75a

The Radiance of Moses' Face

When Moses wrote the Torah, there was a drop of ink left on his pen. God applied this drop of ink to his head, and this became the brilliant light that illuminated his face, as it says, "Moses did not realize that the skin of his face had become luminous" (Exodus 34:29).

Tanchuma Hayashan, end of *Ki Tisa*

Different Faces, Different Tastes

The same way that every person's face differs from another, and no two are exactly alike, so too are their ideas different.

Berachot 58a[33]

If All People Looked Alike

God cast every person's face in the mold of Adam, yet no one looks exactly like anyone else. Why is it that people's faces differ from one another? To prevent a person who sees a beautiful house or a beautiful woman from claiming that the house or the woman is his. (If all people looked alike, no one could dispute a person's false claim to ownership) [Rashi].

Sanhedrin 38a

Keep Smiling

Receive everyone with a cheerful face (*Avot* 1:15).

The *Mishnah* text reads, *beseiver panim yafot*, "with a cheerful face." This wording presents a problem. The expression *panim yafot* means "cheerful face." But what is the meaning of the additional word *beseiver*?

The word *beseiver* is derived from *savar*, to suppose, believe, imagine. By inserting the word *beseiver* the *Mishnah* is telling you, "Receive everyone with a cheerful face, *even if you are not in a cheerful mood.* Just make believe, imagine, pretend that you are cheerful, and greet everyone with a smiling face."

The Reflection of God's Face

[The second of the Ten Commandments:] Do not have any other gods before Me (Exodus 20:3).

Tiferet Shmuel:[34] "Do not have any other gods before Me." The literal translation of this commandment is, "Do not have any other gods on My face." This rendering allows us to view this verse from a different vantage point.

We know that a person who conducts himself virtuously reflects the image of God in his face, as it says, "All the nations of the world will see that God's name is proclaimed over you, and they will be in awe of you" (Deuteronomy 28:10). Conversely, if a person strays from the right path he mars the divine image that is imprinted on his face. This is borne out by the fact that the Baal Shem Tov and many great *tzaddikim* could read a person's mind by looking at his face. And when a person was guilty of transgression, his divine image became blemished since the forces of evil affected his facial features.

The second commandment cautions against wrongdoing, stating, "Do not have any other gods on My face." In other words, "Do not transgress, since thereby you disfigure My image which is imprinted on your face. Do not displace My image with other gods."

Dog-Faced Leaders

The *Gemara* in *Sanhedrin* 97a enumerates the calamities that will occur in the days before the coming of *Mashiach*: the country will be ravaged, houses of Torah study will be turned into houses of prostitution, people who live near the borders of *Eretz Yisrael* will be displaced . . . and *penei hador kepenei hakelev*, "the leaders of the generation will resemble the face of a dog."

What is the meaning of this cryptic simile? The following original interpretation is suggested by the great Rabbi Chaim Volozhiner, foremost disciple of the Vilna Gaon and founder of the Volozhiner Yeshivah.

When a man walks his dog, the dog will always run out in front, but it will look back constantly to make sure that the master is following. Such are the rabbis and Jewish leaders of the premessianic times. They will march in front of their community, pretending to take the lead and teach the Torah way of life to the community. But instead of leading and admonishing, they look back and, being unprincipled pragmatists, take their cue from the people and design their message to please the audience. Like a dog, they run in front as if they were leading, but in reality they take their orders from their congregants. They are mere puppets, and it is the public that is pulling the strings.[35]

THE MOUTH

Aphorisms Concerning the Mouth

The mouth, hands, and legs are under man's control. If he wants, he can use them to study Torah. But if he wishes, he can use them to spread gossip and slander, or to blaspheme and revile God.

Bereishit Rabbah 67:3

Rabbi Shimon bar Yocha'i said: If I had been present at Mount Sinai when God gave the Torah to Israel, I would have asked the Almighty to give man two mouths: one with which to study Torah and another to use for all his other needs.

On second thought, I'm taking back what I said. Now that man has only one mouth, the world is brought to the brink of destruction by all the slander and gossip he spouts, imagine how bad things would be if he had two mouths!

Jerusalem Talmud, *Berachot* 2:1

When you open your mouth, your mouth tells the world who you are.

Zohar, Balak, 193a

The Mouth, Symbol of Malchut

The mouth symbolizes the *Sefirah* of *Malchut* (Kingdom). What is the connection between *Malchut* (Kingdom), which is spiritual, and the mouth, which is physical?

Malchut, the last of the lower seven *Sefirot,* is where God's Infinite Light reaches our world, the place where His will becomes actualized. God's will, which was an abstract entity, became a tangible reality through His spoken word. "By the word of God the heavens were made. . . . For He spoke and it came to be, He commanded and it stood firm" (Psalm 33:6, 9). The *Mishnah* specifically tells us, "With ten utterances the world was created" (*Avot* 5:1), a reference to the ten times the phrase "God said" is recorded in Genesis 1 and 2:18. Thus we can say that God's Kingdom (*Malchut*) was established through the word, which emanates from the mouth.

Man, a Speaking Spirit

Just as God's will became known through His word, so does man communicate his thoughts by means of the spoken word. In fact, the ability to speak is the quality that distinguishes man from animal. *Targum Onkelos,* an Aramaic translation of the Torah, renders the phrase "man became a living soul" (Genesis 2:7) as "man became a speaking spirit," meaning, an individual endowed with the ability to think and to articulate his thoughts in speech.

Rabbi Shimon Schwab in his work *Mayan Bet Hashoevah*[36] notes that when Adam was given the power of speech he was the only human being in the world. Eve had not yet been created.[37] To what purpose, then, was Adam granted this gift? What did he need it for? To whom could he talk? This proves that the primary reason that man was given the power of speech was to enable him to communicate with God, to speak to God in prayer.

Why Did Moses Have a Speech Defect?

When God appeared to Moses in the Burning Bush and gave him the mission to bring the Israelites out of Egypt, Moses demurred, claiming, "I am heavy of mouth and heavy of tongue" (Exodus 4:10). According to Rashi, this means that Moses had a speech defect.

Maharal:[38] How are we to understand that Moses, the man of absolute perfection, had a speech impairment?

In the timeless world of spirituality, eternity, and infinity, there is no change, whereas the physical world is timebound. Time is measured by the movement of physical objects in space; in fact, motion is the chief characteristic of our physical universe.

In man, the organs of speech—the mouth, the lips, the jaws, and the tongue—are associated with motion more than any sensory organ. You move your lips and your tongue in order to articulate speech; when your mouth is at rest no words can be formed. Thus, the faculty of speech, being linked to motion, is firmly rooted in physicality. By contrast, the senses of seeing and hearing are not dependent on motion. The eye and the ear perceive impressions passively. When you see and hear, your eyes and ears are completely at rest. Neither the eye nor the ear actively participates in the process of seeing and hearing.

Moses, a man of the spirit, was close to God and detached from the material world of motion. Therefore, Moses was "heavy of mouth and heavy of lips," since speech is contingent on the movements of the mouth, the tongue, and the lips. Moses, the man of God, had a speech impairment.[39]

His Tongue Was Burned

The *Midrash* says that Moses had a "heavy tongue" because his tongue was burned in his youth. When Pharaoh's daughter saved the child Moses, the astrologers said to Pharaoh: This is the one who will someday steal your crown. They urged him to kill Moses. Jethro (who later became the father-in-law of Moses), however, said: This is an ordinary child. Test him by placing before him a golden crown and a vessel containing burning coals and see which he takes. Moses reached for the shiny crown, but an angel pushed his hand, making him take the live coals. Like a child, he thrust his hand with the live coals into his mouth so that his tongue was burned.

Shemot Rabbah 1:26

Moses Was a Stutterer

Moses said: . . . I am heavy of mouth and heavy of tongue (Exodus 4:10).

Rabbi Yisrael of Rizhin: According to Rashi, this is an idiomatic phrase denoting that Moses had a speech defect. Moses was, in fact, a stutterer. Why indeed was it so ordained that Moses, the spokesman of God, should suffer from a speech defect?

It was essential for him to have a speech defect in order to establish the authenticity of his message of redemption.

The children of Israel had been given a sign by which to identify the true redeemer: he would address them with the words *pakod pakadeti*, "I have remembered you" (Exodus 3:16). But how could they be sure that the man uttering these words was not an impostor, purporting to be their savior?

Moses was known to be a stutterer, a person who is incapable of enunciating the letters *pei*, *kuf*, and *tav* without spasmodically repeating them, contorting his face. When Moses announced *pakod pakadeti*, uttering the *pei*, *kuf,* and *tav* in a normal fashion, they accepted this as miraculous evidence that he was indeed the true redeemer who had been sent by God.[40]

No Unclean Milk for Moses

[Pharaoh's daughter saw the box containing the infant Moses in the rushes and fetched it.] The infant's sister said to Pharaoh's daughter, "Shall I go and call a Hebrew woman to nurse the child for you?" (Exodus 2:7).

The *Gemara* comments: Why just "a Hebrew woman?" It teaches that they handed Moses to all the Egyptian women but he would not suck. God said, "Shall a mouth that will speak with the *Shechinah* suck what is unclean!" This is alluded to in the verse, "To whom would He give instruction? To whom expound a message? To whom will He teach knowledge and to whom will He make the message understandable? To those newly weaned from milk, just taken away from the breast" (Isaiah 28:9).

Sotah 12b

Lip Service

Rabbi Uri of Strelisk[41] asked, "In the *Shemoneh Esrei* (*Amidah*) we say, 'For You hear the prayer of every mouth.'[42] Why don't we simply say, 'For You hear every prayer'?"

He answered, "We praise God for hearing our prayers, even if they come only from the mouth, and not from the heart."[43]

Open My Lips

"O God, open my lips, and let my mouth declare Your praise" (Psalm 51:17).

This verse is the preamble to the *Shemoneh Esrei* (*Amidah*), the quintessential prayer that we recite three times each day. The Ramban[44] notes that the Hebrew word *sefatai* means not only lips but also riverbanks, that serve to prevent the river from overflowing, like, for example, *al sefat haye'or*, "on the banks of the Nile" (Genesis 41:3). According to this interpretation, when you utter this verse you plead with the Almighty to open your riverbanks—your lips—so that the torrent of emotions within you may burst forth in a mighty stream of praise.

Six Organs

Rabbi Levi said: There are six organs in the body that serve man; three are under his control and three are not. The eye, the ear, and the nose are independent of his will: he sees, hears, and smells even things he doesn't want to. The mouth, hand, and foot are subject to his will; he can speak decent things or slander and curse; his hands can fulfill the *mitzvot* of God or they can steal and kill; his feet can take him to the theater and the circus or to the house of worship and the house of study.

Bereishit Rabbah 67:3

The Mouth of the Embryo

Rabbi Simla'i expounded: When the embryo is in his mother's womb he is taught the entire Torah. The moment the baby is born, an angel comes and strikes it on the mouth so that it forgets the entire Torah it learned before birth (*Niddah* 30b).

What is the purpose of teaching the Torah to the unborn baby when he forgets everything the moment he is born? It is much easier to master a subject that you once knew but forgot than to grasp a subject that is totally new to you. When you study Torah you are bringing to the surface a body of knowledge you once were thoroughly familiar with, since you learned it before you were born. In fact, you are retrieving long-lost memories.

THE TONGUE

A Double Barrier

Speaking of the evils of slander and talebearing, the Talmud relates:

The Holy One, blessed be He, said to the tongue: All organs of the human body stand upright, only you are lying down; all parts of the human body are outside; you are guarded inside. What's more, I surrounded you with two walls, one of bone and one of flesh (the teeth and the lips).

Arachin 15b

The implication is that the tongue is more guarded and protected than all other parts of the body, yet the tongue's ambition is never satisfied.

Talkative Women

Ten measures of talk descended to the world; nine were taken by women, and only one measure was taken by the rest of the world (*Kiddushin* 49b).

The Bane of Slander

The Holy One, blessed be He, says about a person who slanders: He and I cannot live together in the world, as it is written, "He who slanders his friend in secret I will destroy, I cannot endure the haughty and proud man" (Psalm 101:5).

Arachin 15b

The Value of Silence

Rabbi Shimon ben Gamliel used to say: I have found nothing more beneficial for the body than silence (*Avot* 1:17).

The Ramchal[45] explains that evil and impurity cannot in and of themselves affect the human body. They are nonmaterial forces and have no way of physically affecting man and attaching themselves to him. However, a unique situation arises when a person speaks. Then his thoughts, which are of spiritual nature, are expressed through his physical organs of speech. Hence, speech is a blend of the spiritual and the material.

Therefore, when someone misuses his power of speech by slandering or lying, he allows the forces of evil and impurity to gain a foothold in him. Consequently, says our *Mishnah*, nothing can be more beneficial than silence, in terms of protecting the body from evil.

The Remedy for Slanderers

What is the remedy for a slanderer? If he is a Torah scholar, let him engage in Torah study, as it says, "The healing for a tongue is the tree of life" (Proverbs 15:4). And "the tree of life" means only the Torah, as it says, "It is a tree of life for those who grasp it" (Proverbs 3:18). If he is an ignorant person, let him become humble, as it says, "You can depart from it only through a broken spirit" (Proverbs 15:4).

Arachin 15b

Why Is Slander like an Arrow?

Scripture compares the tongue to an arrow: "You (the tongue) are like the sharp arrows of the mighty" (Psalm 120:4).

The tongue is compared to an arrow. Just as an arrow inflicts damage far from its source, so does the tongue spread slander, attacking its victim at a distance.

Bereishit Rabbah 98

Not like a Sword

Why is the tongue likened to an arrow and not to a sword? If a man draws his sword to kill someone, and the victim begs for mercy, the swordsman, moved by the plea, will replace his sword into its sheath. But if an archer has shot an arrow and then regrets it, he cannot recall the arrow. The damage inflicted by slander cannot be undone.

Shocher Tov 120

Like a Snake

According to the Talmud,[46] the snake only eats earth. Therefore, when it bites someone, it does not bite because it wants to eat human flesh, but it does so at God's command in order to exact retribution for the evil gossip the victim spoke.

Based on this thought, the Talmud says:

In time to come, all the animals will assemble and come to the snake and say: The lion attacks and devours; the wolf tears and consumes; but what benefit do you derive when you bite? But the snake will answer: What benefit does the person have who uses his tongue to slander? (Ecclesiastes 10:11).

Arachin 15b

The Punishment of the Spies

[The spies that Moses sent to explore the land returned and slandered the land.] The men who had given a bad report about the land thus died before God in a plague (Numbers 14:37).

Rabbi Chaninah bar Papa said: Their tongue became so long that they extended down to their navel, and maggots came out from their tongue and entered the navel and from their navel they penetrated their tongue.

Sotah 35a

Evil Gossip Kills Three

Evil gossip kills three: the one who tells it, the one who accepts it, and the one about whom it is told. But the one who accepts it is affected more than the one who tells it.[47]

Arachin 15b

The Best and the Worst

One day, Rabbi Shimon ben Gamliel told his servant Tobi, "Go to the market and buy the best dish you can find." Tobi went and bought a tongue for his master. The Rabbi then said to Tobi, "Go to the market and buy the worst dish you can find." Tobi went and again bought a tongue for his master.

Asked Rabbi Shimon: Why did you buy a tongue when I asked for the best food and again a tongue when I asked for the worst food?

Replied Tobi: A tongue can be both good and bad. When it is good, nothing in the world can surpass it, but when it is bad, nothing is worse than an evil tongue.

Vayikra Rabbah 33

A Dangerous Organ

There are 248 limbs in the human body. Some of them are lying down, others are erect. The tongue is arranged in many folds in the mouth, it is imprisoned between the two jaws, and a stream of water passes beneath it (i.e., saliva), but it still causes many conflagrations. Imagine the damage an erect tongue would cause!

Vayikra Rabbah 16:4

The Power of the Tongue

It happened that the king of Persia was suffering from a mysterious ailment and was near death.

"The only remedy that can save your life," said his doctor, "is for you to drink the milk of a lioness."

"Who will risk his life to obtain lion's milk for the king?"

"I volunteer to go, Your Majesty," one of the officers in the king's army said. "Just give me ten goats, and I'll bring you the lion's milk."

The officer made his way deep into the jungle, where he came upon a lion's den. Inside he found a lioness nursing her young whelps. From the distance he threw a goat to the lioness, which she eagerly devoured. The next day, he came a little closer and again hurled a goat into the lion's den. Each succesive day the ferocious beast became more gentle and acted more docile toward her benefactor. By the tenth day, the lioness allowed the officer to come close enough to enable him to milk her. Carrying the bottle with the precious lion's milk close to his heart, he immediately headed home.

On the way he fell asleep and dreamed that the limbs of his body were having a noisy argument.

Said the legs, "We are the most important parts of the body. If not for us, you would not have come close to the lioness to secure the milk."

Retorted the hands, "O no, if it had not been for us, you could not have milked the beast and carried the bottle. We are much more important."

Exclaimed the eyes, "Wrong. We are the most vital parts. Without us, you would never have found the lioness in the first place."

Said the heart, "I'm the one that dreamed up the whole idea. Without a doubt, I outrank all of you."

Then the tongue spoke up. "Quiet everyone! I am the most important part in the body. If not for the power of speech, where would you all be?"

The other parts were outraged. "How dare you compare yourself to us. You sit locked up in a dark place, and you don't even have bones in you."

"Just wait and see," replied the tongue. "I'll show you."

Early in the morning, the officer continued on his way back to the palace. Clutching the bottle with the precious fluid, he entered the king's chamber.

"Your Majesty," he said, handing the bottle to the king. "Here is the dog's milk I obtained for you."

"Dog's milk!" shouted the king angrily. "Is that what you brought me? You'll hang for this!"

As the officer was marched to the gallows, all parts of his body trembled with fear.

"Didn't I tell you that you don't amount to very much?" said the tongue to the other parts. "If I save you now, will you admit that I am the ruler over you?"

"Yes, we will," they all declared meekly.

"Stop the execution!" the tongue demanded convincingly. "Take me to the king immediately."

"Your Majesty, it was all a big mistake," the tongue argued eloquently. "Just a slip of the tongue. The milk you received was really lion's milk. Take one sip and you'll see."

The king drank the precious beverage, recovered, and generously rewarded the stalwart officer.

The moral of the story is summed up in the verse, "Death and life are in the power of the tongue" (Proverbs 18:21).

Yalkut Shimoni, Psalm 34

The Functions of the Organs

The Rabbis taught: The kidneys advise, the heart discerns, the tongue articulates the words, the gullet takes in food and conveys the food, the windpipe produces the voice . . . the liver is the seat of anger, the large intestines grind the food.

Berachot 61a

Not by Bread Alone

[The manna] was to teach you that it is not by bread alone that man lives but by all that comes out of God's mouth (Deuteronomy 8:3).

Rabbi Yehudah Leib Ashlag:[48] Man lives . . . by all that comes out of God's mouth. Man's mouth is a reflection of God's mouth. [And conversely, when the verse mentions God's mouth, this also means man's mouth]. Therefore, the delight you derive from the words that emanate from your mouth is infinitely greater than all the enjoyment you could ever gain from the food you put into your mouth.[49]

The Seven Moving Parts

When you speak, you cause seven organs to move simultaneously: the heart, the lungs, the windpipe, the tongue, the teeth, the lips, and the flesh of your cheeks. But when you are silent, they all stay in place and do not move. [A living person expresses thoughts through speech, and his entire body moves to enable him to speak. In death the mouth remains motionless, and the body is at rest.]

Zohar, Shelach 173

Aphorisms about the Tongue

The tongue has no bones, yet it destroys the mighty [The tongue, which appears to be powerless, can ruin the reputation of prominent leaders.] (*Meiri, Mishlei* 25).

The tongue is merely the translator between the heart and the listener (Ibn Ezra to Psalm 4:5).

The tongue is the pen of the heart and the messenger of the conscience (*Chovot Halevavot* 2:115). [Your words reflect the thoughts of your heart and your conscience.]

The tongue is of short stature but it can wreak powerful revenge.[50]

The tongue is the best of all sacrifices [By suppressing your desire to speak evil gossip, you are bringing the finest sacrifice.] (*Midrash Tehillim, Shochar Tov* 39:3).

❧

THE TEETH

The name of the letter ש *shin* is related to שן *shein*, tooth. Its shape resembles a molar, which grinds food. But *shein* (tooth) also is also used to characterize the sharpness of a word or a speech, *shanenu kacherev leshonam*, "who whet their tongues like swords" (Psalm 64:4).

Shein (tooth) is the root of the word *veshinantam*, meaning, "teach [these words] thoroughly to your children" (Deuteronomy 6:7). When we transmit the knowledge of the Torah to our children, we must implant in them their obligation to keep the *mitzvot* of the Torah with the whole sharpness of their definite orders and not let them be weakened by making allowances for so-called necessary considerations of the times we live in.[51]

Aphorisms about Teeth

Sixty (many) pains reach the teeth of him who hears the noise made by another man eating while he himself does not eat. (*Bava Kamma* 92b)

The man who [by smiling warmly] shows his teeth to his friend is better than one who gives him milk to drink. (*Ketubot* 111b)

Milt is good for the teeth but bad for the bowels; horsebeans are bad for the teeth but good for the bowels (*Berachot* 44b).

The Grinders Are Idle

King Solomon, the author of Ecclesiastes, paints an allegoric picture of the infirmities of old age. In Ecclesiastes he graphically describes the waning days of life:

The day when the guards of the house will tremble—the hands and the arms that protect the body from assault (*Ibn Ezra*);

and the powerful men will stoop—the legs that support the bodily frame (Rashi);

and the grinders are idle because they are few—the teeth have fallen out in old age (Rashi);

and the gazers through the windows are dimmed (the eyes).

Ecclesiastes 12:3

Thirty-two Teeth of Wisdom

Kabbalah teaches[52] that there are thirty-two Pathways of Wisdom. These pathways originate in God's Will, in the *Sefirah* of *Keter* (Crown), a *Sefirah* that is completely beyond human comprehension.

Man, who is created in the image of God, is a reflection of the *Sefirot*, whereby the *Sefirah* of *Keter* corresponds to the human brain, the seat of the soul. (*Keter* is also called *mochin*, brain.) The soul expresses itself through speech by means of the tongue, the lips, and the teeth. These instruments of speech are situated within the cavity of the mouth, immediately beneath the skull, which encloses the brain (*Keter*).

The thirty-two teeth in the mouth correspond precisely to the thirty-two Pathways of Wisdom that lead from *Keter* to the lower *Sefirot*.[53]

Astonishingly, this idea is embodied in the letters of the *alef-bet*. Consider the letter כ *kaf*. It is shaped like the cavity of the mouth. Since the cavity of the mouth is located beneath the brain (*Keter*) it symbolizes the lower worlds. Interestingly, the letter פ *pei*, which means mouth, is shaped like a כ *kaf* into which a tooth has been inserted. On a spiritual level, this means that the thirty-two Pathways of Wisdom (the thirty-two teeth) radiate into the cavity of the *kaf* (the lower world) to form a *peh* (mouth). Thus, when you articulate Torah thoughts, your mouth (*peh/pei*) gives voice to the thirty-two Pathways of Wisdom and proclaims the words that were spoken by the "mouth of God" (Isaiah 40:5). (Rabbi Chaim Finkel is commenting on the Vilna Gaon's commentary on *Sefer Yetzirah*.)

Thirty-two Pathways

The *Zohar*[54] states, "Wisdom is the beginning of all. Thirty-two pathways extend from it. And the Torah is filled with them, in twenty-two letters and ten utterances."

The above mentioned twenty-two letters are the letters of the *alef-bet*, and the ten utterances are the ten times the phrase "God said" occurs in the story of Creation.[55] These ten utterances correspond to the Ten *Sefirot*. Together, the twenty-two letters and the ten utterances are manifestations of the thirty-two Pathways of Wisdom that fill the Torah.

"And the Torah is filled with them." The Pathways of Wisdom encompass all that is written between the *bet* of *Bereishit*, the first letter of the Torah, and the *lamed* of *Yisrael*, the last letter of the Torah. Amazingly, the sum of the numeric values of *lamed* (30) and *bet* (2) amounts to 32.

The Vilna Gaon notes that 10 (the *Sefirot*) and 32 (the Pathways) are intimately related. A circle whose diameter is ten has a circumference that measures 32.

Furthermore, *lamed* and *bet* combine to form לב *lev*, the heart, and what's more, the human anatomy has thirty-two spinal nerves. Thus, the thirty-two Pathways of Wisdom represent the heart and the nerve center of Creation.

In the same vein, the *Sfat Emet*[56] remarks that each of the four *tzitzit* is composed of eight threads. The total of thirty-two threads is an allusion to לב *lev*, the heart, and the thirty-two Pathways of Wisdom.

THE EYE AND THE EAR

The Eyeball, a Microcosm

The eyeball is a miniature world: the white in the eye represents the ocean that surrounds the entire world, the iris is the earth, the pupil is Jerusalem, and the face in the pupil is the *Bet Hamikdash*.

Derech Eretz Zuta 9:13

The Pupil of the Eye

You do not see with the white part of your eyeball; you see with your pupil, the black part in the center of the eye. Similarly, the Holy One, Blessed be He, created for us light out of darkness.

Vayikra Rabbah, chap. 31

Ishon, *the Little Man*

The Hebrew word for pupil (the black of the eye) is *ishon*.[57] The Redak (Rabbi David Kimchi) in his *Sefer Hashorashim* explains that *ishon* means "a little upside-down man," *ishon* being a diminutive of *ish* (man).[58] The term becomes clear when we examine the anatomy of the eye. At the center of the iris is a circular opening, the pupil. Behind the pupil is the lens. Rays of light coming from the outside, passing through the lens, are focused on the retina to form an inverted image that is much smaller than the object that is viewed. It is for this reason that the pupil of the eye is called *ishon*, "a little upside-down man."

The Insatiable Eye

Abba Saul said: I was once a grave digger. On one occasion I entered an open burial cave and found myself standing in the eyeball of a corpse up to my nose. When I turned back I was told that it was the [voracious] eye of Absalom. (The *Gemara, Sotah* 9b, states that "Absalom set his eyes on that which was not proper for him; what he sought was not granted to him, and what he possessed was taken from him.")

Niddah 24b

Samson Followed His Eyes

Our Rabbis have taught: Samson rebelled against God through his eyes, as it says, "Samson said to his father, 'I noticed one of the Philistine women in Timnah. . . . Get her for me, for she is the one that pleases me'" (Judges 14:2, 3). Because of this the Philistines gouged out his eyes, as it says, "The Philistines seized him and gouged out his eyes" (Judges 16:21).

Sotah 9b

The Independent Eye and Ear

The ear that hears, the eye that sees—God made them both (Proverbs 20:12).

Midrash: Why does King Solomon single out the ear and the eye; didn't God make the entire body? Man will be held responsible for the actions of all parts of his body, except for the ear and the eye. The ear hears and the eye sees independently, whether man likes it or not; he has no control over them. Not so his hands and his feet; he can tell his hands to steal or not to steal; he can direct his feet to a sinful place or he can order them to go to a house of study.

Midrash Tanchuma, Mikeitz 5

A Shield for the Organs

All organs of the body are provided with a shield that prevents you from using them for improper purposes. For example, the lips are the shield that protects the tongue. When you are tempted to lie or slander, you simply close your lips. The ear is equipped with an earlobe designed to cover your ear so as to shut out unworthy talk. The eyelids shield your eye from viewing immoral scenes. The only thing that has no protective shield is your imagination, your power to think. It is free to create new thoughts that may be either beneficial or harmful. Therefore, special care is needed to channel your imagination in a positive direction.[59]

Agents of Sin

Rabbi Levi said: The heart and the eye are two agents of sin. And so it is written, "Give your heart to Me, My son; let your eyes watch My ways" (Proverbs 23:26). God is saying, in effect: If you give Me your heart and your eyes, I know that you belong to Me.

Jerusalem Talmud, Berachot 1:5

The Seven Gates

Appoint for yourselves judges and police in all your gates that the Lord your God is giving you, and make sure that they administer honest judgment for the people (Deuteronomy 16:18).

Shelah:[60] Appoint for yourselves judges and police in all your gates. Every person has seven "gates": two eyes, two ears, two nostrils, and his mouth. Through these gates we receive all our impressions of the outside world, or obtain nourishment from it. Our verse instructs us to "place judges and police in your gates"—be careful that no shameful or immoral images enter through these "gates" of yours, that no forbidden food enter your mouth and no gossip emanate from it. Let your eyes see no evil; let your ears hear no evil.

The Two Spies

When you see [the *tzitzit*] . . . you will not stray after your heart and eyes, which [in the past] have led you to immorality.

Numbers 15:39

Rashi: You will not stray after your heart and eyes. The heart and the eyes are the spies of the body; they are the agents of sin: the eye sees, then the heart desires, and the body commits the sin (*Tanchuma*).

The Beautiful Eyes of the Bride

The Talmud teaches that a bride whose eyes are beautiful does not need to be examined for imperfections. [Which means, if her eyes communicate kindness, you may assume that she is a good-hearted person, because the eyes are the windows of the soul.]

Ta'anit 24a

Three Things

There are three things that restore a person's good spirits: [beautiful] sounds, sights, and smells.

Berachot 57b

The Optic and Auditory Nerves

Make an Ark of acacia wood. . . . Cast four gold rings for the Ark, and place them on its four corners, two rings on one side, and two rings on the other side. Make two carrying poles of acacia wood and cover them with a layer of gold. Place the poles in the rings, so that the Ark can be carried with them. The poles must remain in the Ark's rings and not be removed. It is in this Ark that you will place the testimony (the Tablets) that I will give you.

Exodus 25:10–15

Malbim:[61] "Make an Ark of acacia wood . . . make two carrying poles. . . ." The Ark contained the two Tablets of the Covenant. The two Tablets correspond to the brain, which consists of two parts: the cerebrum in front, and behind it, the cerebellum.

The carrying poles of the Ark are analogous to the senses of sight and hearing. In order to receive the Torah, man needs eyes and ears, his eyes for reading and studying the Torah and for comprehending the greatness of God as it is revealed in nature. He needs his ears to receive the

Oral Law, which is transmitted from generation to generation.

The optic and auditory nerves connect the brain to the eyes and ears. These nerves convey the impressions from the outside world to the brain. The carrying poles of the Ark correspond to these sensory nerves. The rings in which the poles were placed stand for the sensory organs, the eyes and the ears. Thus, the rings, the poles, and the Ark are one indivisible unit. Accordingly, the Torah says, "The poles must not be removed from the Ark's rings."

After the poles have been inserted into the rings and the connection between the brain and the sensory organs is established, then, "It is in this Ark that you will place the testimony that I will give you" (Exodus 25:16).

The Seven Eyes

There are seven eyes of God ranging over the whole earth (Zechariah 4:10).

The eyes of God symbolize the divine *hashgachah*, providence or supervision, which oversees the world. The expression *seven eyes* alludes to the seven lower *Sefirot* through which God sees and supervises us.

It is remarkable that traditionally, the number seven is intimately related to Divine Providence. We know that the greatest manifestation of Divine Providence occurs in the month of *Tishrei*, the seventh month of the year (counting from *Nissan*), when God regards His children with special affection. In fact, the word *Tishrei* actually means "to look," as in the verse, *tashuri merosh amanah* (Song of Songs 4:8), "to look at the fruits of your faith."

The close relationship between *Tishrei*, the number seven, and the seeing eye is evident in an amazing numeric equation. The numeric value of תשרי, *Tishrei* equals 910, (*tav* = 400; *shin* = 300, *reish* = 200; *yud* = 10; 400 + 300 + 200 + 10 = 910). The value of עין, *ayin*, eye, equals 130 (*ayin* = 70; *yud* = 10; *nun* = 50; 70 + 10 + 50 = 130).

Thus, *Tishrei* equals seven times *ayin*, eye (910 = 7 ×

130). Furthermore, in *Tishrei* we celebrate Sukkot, when we dwell in the *sukkah* for seven days commemorating the seven clouds of glory that accompanied and protected Israel throughout their forty-year trek through the wilderness. We take the "four species" in hand (the three myrtle branches, two willows, one palm branch, and one *etrog*, for a total of seven), and wave them to the six directions of physical space (north, south, east, west, up, and down) and bring them to the heart, the seventh direction. On the seventh day of Sukkot, Hoshanah Rabbah, we make seven circuits around the *bimah* in the center of the synagogue, and on Simchat Torah, the month of *Tishrei* comes to a climax when we rejoice with the Torah, dancing seven *hakafot* with fervent exuberance.

Perception and Reality

Rabbi Yehudah Halevi:[62] Our intellect, limited as it is by the physical bounds of the body, cannot grasp the true knowledge of things except through the medium of the senses, which God granted all men to perceive various phenomena. Thus, there is no difference between my perception of the sun and yours. It appears to everyone as a disc that radiates light and emits heat. Even though the characteristics described by the senses are distortions of the true reality of the sun, they do no harm. On the contrary, they are helpful in providing certain proofs for our intellectual perception. For example: a person with perfect vision looking for his lost camel might be helped by someone who has poor vision and sees everything double. Should the weak-eyed person say that he saw two cranes in a certain place, the man with the perfect vision would immediately understand that the other had seen a camel but had mistaken it for a crane, due to his poor vision, and that his tendency to double vision had led him to think that there were two cranes. In this manner, the sharp-eyed person can make use of the report given by the weak-eyed one, taking into consideration his defective eyesight. A similar relationship exists between the senses and imagination on the one hand and the intellect on the other. The intellect is able to absorb the information provided by the senses, evaluate it, and reach the proper conclusion.[63]

The Eyes and the Nose

"This is the book of the chronicles of man. On the day that God created man, He made him in the likeness of God" (Genesis 5:1).

Klausenburger Rebbe: He made him in the likeness of God. This may be taken in a literal sense. The likeness of God is literally imprinted on the human face, since the human face is a reflection of the letters in the Divine Name. The eye looks like the letter *yud*, and the nose is shaped like a *vav*. Indeed, there is a widely held belief that Jews generally have long noses. In fact, the Talmud relates that when a Roman officer came looking for Rabban Gamliel in the *bet midrash* he called out, "The man with the big nose is wanted" (*Ta'anit* 29a).

The reason for this typically Jewish facial feature is that a long nose resembles the letter *vav*, the pivotal letter in the Divine Name.

The numeric value of *vav* equals 6; that of *yud* equals 10. Thus the two eyes that look like a *yud* amount to 20 (2 × 10 = 20). The nose that resembles a *vav* equals 6. If you add the two eyes and the nose you obtain 26, which is the numeric value of the four-letter Divine Name (*yud* = 10; *hei* = 5; *vav* = 6; *hei* = 5). In other words, the likeness of God is engraved on a Jew's face.

Shefa Chaim, p. 274

They Did Not See Eye to Eye

The eyes of both of them were opened and they realized that they were naked. They sewed together fig leaves and made loincloths (Genesis 3:7).

Rabbi Simchah Bunam of Pshis'cha:[64] The eyes of both of them were opened. This phraseology is somewhat awkward. We would have expected to read, "Their eyes were opened." The significance of the wording of "the eyes of both of them" is that before partaking of the Tree of Knowledge, Adam and Eve's personalities were fused into a perfect union of total identity of purpose and thought. They saw "eye to eye." After eating the forbidden fruit, they became egocentric. Thus, in a sense, their eyes were opened, and they realized that they were two separate individuals, each with his own distinct personality and self-interest. "The eyes of both of them were opened," they became two separate individuals, each viewing the world from his own selfish perspective.[65]

The Eyes of God

Rambam (Maimonides): The Hebrew word *ayin* means *fountain*, for example, "By a fountain (*eyn*) of water" (Genesis 16:7). It also denotes *eye*, as in, *ayin tachat ayin*, "an eye for an eye" (Exodus 21:24). Another meaning of the word *ayin* is providence, as it is said concerning Jeremiah, "Take him and look (*einecha*) after him" (Jeremiah 39:12). It is to be understood in this figurative sense when used in reference to God; for example, "My eyes and My heart shall always be there" (the *Bet Hamikdash*) (1 Kings 9:3); "The eyes (*einei*) [i.e., the Providence] of God your Lord are always upon it (*Eretz Yisrael*)" (Deuteronomy 11:12); "They are the eyes of God ranging over the whole world" (Zechariah 4:10), meaning His Providence is extended over everything that is on earth.[66]

The Tefillin

Rabbi Shem of Zaloshitz: In the entire *Tanach* (Bible), no part of the human body is described as "good." The only exceptions are the eye and the heart: "He who has a good eye is blessed" (Proverbs 22:9) [A "good eye" means an attitude of tolerance and benevolence toward others.] Also, "He that is of a good heart has a feast without end" (Proverbs 15:15).

Why are only the eye and the heart termed "good"? According to the Talmud,[67] "The eye and the heart are the two agents of sin: The eye sees, and the heart lusts." The things you see arouse your desire. To curb the excessive appetites of the eye and the heart we were given the *mitzvah* of *tefillin*. We place the arm *tefillin* on the left biceps, opposite the heart, and the head *tefillin* on the head, opposite the space between the eyes. We thereby curb the power of the eye and the heart, the two agents of sin, and transform them into agents of virtue.

Only the eye and the heart, having the potential of enticing a person to do evil, can be turned into a force for good. This thought is echoed in the verse, "Give your heart to Me, My son; let your eyes watch My ways" (Proverbs 23:26).

In the same vein, we say in the *Shacharit* prayer, "Enlighten our eyes in Your Torah and attach our hearts to Your commandments."[68]

Tzitzit

The *mitzvah* most closely associated with the eyes is the *mitzvah* of *tzitzit*,[69] the fringes that must be attached to a four-cornered garment. It is mentioned in Numbers 15:37–41, which is the third section of the *Shema*.

God spoke to Moses, telling him to speak to the Israelites and have them make *tzitzit* on the corners of their garments for all generations. They shall place a string of sky-blue wool in the corner *tzitzit*. These shall be your *tzitzit*, and when you see them, you shall remember all of God's commandments so as to keep them. You will then not stray after your heart and your eyes, which [in the past] have led you to immorality. You will thus remember all My commandments, and be holy to your God.

Numbers 15:37–40

Rabbi Samson Raphael Hirsch: Having eaten from the Tree of Knowledge, Adam and Eve became aware of their nakedness and felt a sense of shame for having succumbed to their physical nature. They had been misled by the sensuousness of their eyes. Thereupon God clothed them in leather garments.

Your eye sees only physical things. It tells you that only the tangible, material world is real. The *mitzvah* of *tzitzit* is a tangible instrument to remind you of a higher reality, one that cannot be seen by the eye. The *tzitzit* remind you of God and His *mitzvot*. In short, *tzitzit* direct your eye away from the visible and focus it on the invisible.

We are told to fasten this *tzitzit*-reminder to our garments. A reason for this is the fact that man received his first garment from God after his transgression to which he was driven by his sensuality. He sinned when he regarded the forbidden fruit as "good to eat and desirable to the *eyes*" (Genesis 3:6) (emphasis added). Thus, the *tzitzit* on our garments are a constant reminder "not to stray after our hearts and our eyes."[70]

Tzitzit = *613*

According to the sages, the human body is composed of 248 limbs, equal to the number of positive commandments (things you must do). The body contains 365 sinews, equal to the number of negative commandments (things that are forbidden). This teaches that man was created to carry out God's will as expressed in the *mitzvot*.

The total number of limbs and sinews in man equals the total number of *mitzvot*, both amounting to 613, a number symbolized by the *mitzvah* of *tzitzit*. The numeric value of the letters spelling out *tzitzit* is 600 (*tzadi* = 90; *yud* = 10; *tzadi* = 90; *yud* = 10; *tav* = 400); add to this the 5 knots and 8 strings which make up each *tzitzit*, for a total of 613.

Therefore, the sages say that the *mitzvah* of *tzitzit* is equal in importance to all the *mitzvot* in the Torah, as it

says, "When you see [the *tzitzit*] you will remember all of
God's commandments so as to keep them" (Numbers 15:39).

Rashi to Menachot 43b

The Heart and the Eye

When you see the *tzitzit* . . . you will then not stray after
your heart and eyes (Numbers 15:39).

"You will then not stray after your heart and eyes."
Shouldn't the order be reversed to read, "You will not stray
after your eyes and your heart"? After all, your desire is aroused
by the things you see; it is the eye that stimulates the heart.

The opposite is true. You only see the things your heart
desires. The things your heart does not crave, your eye does
not see.

Divrei Shmuel

An Eye for an Eye

[In the case where someone intentionally inflicted physical
wounds, the Torah mandates:] An eye for an eye, tooth for
tooth, hand for hand, foot for foot, burn for burn, wound
for wound, bruise for bruise (Exodus 21:24, 25).

The Talmud states that this cannot mean actual retali-
ation by putting out an eye of the offender. For what would
you do when a blind man put out the eye of a person who
was able to see, or where a cripple cut off the hand of another, or where a lame person broke the leg of another? How
can the principle of "an eye for an eye" be carried out, since
the Torah says, "There shall be one law for you" (Leviticus
24:22), which implies that the law should be the same in
all cases. This verse therefore must mean monetary compensation for the eye.

Bava Kamma 84a

The Mutilated Slave

If a person strikes his male or female [Canaanite] slave[71] in
the eye and blinds it, he shall set the slave free in compen-

sation for the eye. [Similarly,] if he knocks out the tooth of his male or female slave, he must set [the slave] free in compensation for his tooth (Exodus 21:26, 27).

The *Midrash* comments: Why is the Canaanite slave set free in lieu of the loss of his tooth or his eye? Said the Holy One, blessed be He, "Ham, [Canaan's father,] saw his father [Noah] naked and told it to his two brothers outside (Genesis 9:22)." That is why he was cursed to be a slave to his brothers. Now this Canaanite slave was mutilated in the organs [his ancestor] misused—his eyes and his teeth. Therefore he is set free because of them. [Ham debased his eyes when he saw his father naked and defiled his mouth and teeth when he told it to his brothers.]

Ba'alei Tosafot, Exodus 21:26

Kal Vachomer[72] *from "Tooth and Eye"*

[Referring to the law that states that a master who knocks out the tooth or eye of his slave has to set him free (Exodus 21:26, 27) the *Gemara* draws the following inference with regard to human suffering:] Tooth and eye are only one limb of the man, and still [if they are hurt], the slave obtains his freedom because of it. Surely, painful suffering that torments the whole body of a man [will atone for the sins he committed with all his limbs.]

Berachot 5a

Techeilet, *the Blue Thread*

They shall include a thread of sky-blue wool in the corner *tzitzit* (Numbers 15:38).

Techeilet refers to sky-blue wool. The blue dye was obtained from a rare kind of fish or snail, called *chilazon*,[73] that surfaced only once in seventy years. The identity of the *chilazon* has been unknown for many centuries. Therefore, our *tzitzit* do not contain the *techeilet* thread.

Rabbi Meir said (*Chullin* 89a):[74] Of all the different colors, why was blue chosen as the color for the *techeilet* thread in the *tzitzit*? The reason is that blue is reminiscent of the sea; the sea resembles the sky; the sky looks like a sapphire, and sapphire resembles the divine Throne of Glory, as noted in Ezekiel 1:26. [Which is to say that the sight of the *tzitzit* serves as a reminder of one's duties to God.]

The Maharsha comments that the various stages (the sea, the sky, and the sapphire) allude to the connection between the three lower worlds to the Throne of God. The sea represents our world, which consisted of only water when God said, "The waters shall be gathered to one place" (Genesis 1:9). Our world is connected to the sky, which symbolizes the intermediate world between the material and spiritual. The intermediate world, in turn, is bound up with the world of the angels, which is represented by a translucent sapphire. Finally, the world of the angels is linked to the divine Throne of Glory.

The underlying idea of the Maharsha's remarks is that by performing the *mitzvot* we are uniting the lower and the higher worlds and fulfilling the desired goal of Creation.

Green-Eyed Envy

The sages of the Talmud describe the Angel of Death as a creature that is "full of eyes" (*Avodah Zarah* 20b). Maharam Schiff[75] explains that the phrase "full of eyes" is a metaphor. The sages had in mind the envious eyes people cast on their neighbors' possessions and affluence. People harbor bitter resentment when fortune shines on others. They take it to heart, and the vexation shortens their lives. Indeed, jealousy is one of the main causes of premature death. Thus, the sages appropriately characterized the *Malach Hamavet* as an angel that is full of eyes.

Seeing Sound

All the people saw the sounds, the flames, the blasts of the ram's horn, and the mountain smoking. The people trembled when they saw it, keeping their distance. (Exodus 20:15).

Rabbi Menachem Mendel of Kossov: All the people saw the sounds. How can you see sound? With his physical eye man sees everything that surrounds him, from a tiny blade of grass growing at his foot to the immense stars at a distance of countless light-years. But man also "sees" with his intellect. Proof of this is that when you understand something, you say, "I see." There is, however, a fundamental difference. Seeing with a physical eye is a direct process. On the other hand, intellectually you can "see" only by means of hearing. You must hear a concept before you understand it. Why can't we see with our mind's eye as directly and clearly as we do with our physical eye? It is our corporeality, our physical nature, that forms the barrier that prevents our intellectual "eye" from directly perceiving the truth of the Torah.

When the people of Israel were standing at Mount Sinai, their physical nature departed from them, and for a short time, they were capable of seeing with their mind's eye concepts and ideas that normally can be understood only after they are heard. They "saw the sounds" means that their minds apprehended the Torah intuitively, without it passing through the process of hearing.[76]

The Pupil of God's Eye

Rabbi Shlomoh of Lutzk: We see with our eyes, but we perceive with our intellect. Thus, the intellect is more important than the eyes. Nevertheless, the intellect itself is unable to see. Proof of this is the fact that when you close your eyes or are in the dark, even though your intellect is alert, you cannot see anything. The reason is that your intellect is of a spiritual nature, whereas the things you see are physical, and your spiritual intellect cannot apprehend a physical object. However, the eyes are composed of a refined substance and have an ethereal and translucent quality. The intellect is drawn into the rarified environment of the eye, where it concentrates itself and "congeals," and by means of light rays it can perceive an object even though that object is physical in nature.

Similarly, the light of God's intellect is revealed in the human body. In the body, too, there are organs that have a refined, lucid, and transparent quality. These organs, such as the heart, the brain, and the nerves, are the quintessential parts of the body because they are the seat of the divine spark of life. It is through these organs that the divine intellect manifests itself.

The same holds true for all creation. The single element that is the purest and closest to spirituality in all of creation is the Jewish people. They are the channel through which God's Presence is revealed. Therefore, the Jewish people is characterized as the apple of God's eye, as it says, ". . . protecting [the Jewish people] like the pupil of His eye" (Deuteronomy 32:10). Just as the human intellect perceives the world by means of the eyes, so does God's Presence extend to the universe by way of the Jewish people.[77]

Sight Interferes with Sound

[Announcing the Giving of the Ten Commandments], God said to Moses, "I will come to you in a thick cloud so that all the people will hear when I speak to you" (Exodus 19:9).

Rabbi Chanoch of Alexander asks: How would God's coming in a cloud be conducive to make the people hear His words?

We all know from personal experience that our senses interfere with one another and disrupt each other's function. Our sense of vision inhibits our ability to use our hearing to the fullest. When you are listening to a lecture or a symphony, your mind is distracted by images or scenes that intrude. If you want to concentrate on what you are hearing you close your eyes. This, then, was the reason God came "in a thick cloud." He wanted to shut out any visual diversion, so that all Israel would listen with undivided attention and total concentration. They would be "all ears."[78]

Ayin Hara, *the Evil Eye*

The *Mishnah* states, "Rabbi Yehoshua says: An evil eye, the evil inclination, and hatred of other people remove a person from the world" (*Avot* 2:16).

The *Bartinura* explains that "evil eye" refers to envy, greed, and discontent, in general, being dissatisfied with one's lot.

Why Not Evil Eyes?

Why do the sages speak of the evil eye in the singular? Why is it never "evil eyes"?

If a person looks with both his eyes he cannot cause any harm. When his eyes are open he is a reflection of the divine image; thus no evil can flow from him. However, this is not so when he closes one eye. That is why the evil eye is mentioned always in the singular.

Chasdei Avot

Immunity from Ayin Hara

In the *Gemara* we find the following revealing discussion about *ayin hara* (the evil eye).

[As a reward for obeying His laws], God will take away from you all sickness (Deuteronomy 7:15).

Rav comments, "This verse refers to the evil eye [i.e., God will remove the evil eye]." For the evil eye is the single factor that is at the root of "all sickness" (Rashi).

Continuing in this vein, Rav says, "Ninety-nine percent of all people die through the evil eye, and only one percent die of natural causes."

Bava Metzia 107b

The One-Eyed Prophet

The concept of the evil eye is mentioned by the Torah commentators in connection with Balaam, the heathen prophet, who wanted to cast an evil eye on the children of Israel. But God turned his curse into a blessing. We read in the Torah that Balaam opened his imprecation as follows:

[Balaam] proclaimed his oracle and said, "This is the word of Balaam, son of Be'or, the word of the man with *the blinded eye*" (Numbers 24:3, 15, emphasis added).

Rashi comments that "Balaam's eye was perforated and taken out, and its socket appeared open. . . . In fact, he was blind in one of his eyes" (*Sanhedrin* 105a).

The *Zohar* (1:68b) translates "the blinded eye" as "the evil eye."

The Netziv[79] in his commentary *Ha'amek Davar* explains the blindness of Balaam's eye, stating: Balaam brought the blindness of his eye upon himself. He was struck sightless because he tried to cast an evil eye on Israel.

Like Fish

Jacob blessed his son Joseph, "May He bless the lads, and let them carry my name, along with the names of my fathers, Abraham and Isaac. *Veyidgu larov bekerev haaretz*, May they increase in the land like fish" (Genesis 48:16).

Rabbi Jose ben Rabbi Chaninah expounded: Just as fish under water are concealed from the sight of others, and the evil eye has no power over them, so the evil eye has no power over Joseph's descendants, even though they live on earth where they are exposed to envy.

Berachot 55b; Rashi

A Remedy for the Evil Eye

The Talmud says: If you enter a town and are afraid of an evil eye, place the thumb of your right hand in your left hand and the thumb of your left hand in your right hand, and say: I, so-and-so, am an offspring of Joseph over whom the evil eye has no power, as it says, "Joseph is a fruitful son, [like] a fruitful vine by the fountain (Genesis 49:22). Do not read '*alei*' *ayin* [by the fountain] but '*olei*' *ayin* [rising above the power of the evil eye]."

Berachot 55b

The Anatomy of the Ear

The Talmud[80] teaches: Why do the fingers have a pointed shape? To enable you to put your fingers into your ear to shut out indecent talk.

Why is the entire ear hard and only the earlobe soft? So that, when you hear something that is improper you should fold your lobe up and close your ear with it.

Don't allow your ears to listen to empty chatter, because your ears are the most impressionable of all the sensory organs.

The Maharsha explains that the bony cartilage of the outer ear is hard, so as to enable the ear to receive sound. From a scientific point of view, the soft earlobe serves no useful purpose. Therefore, the only function of the earlobe is to shut out improper speech.

Beyond Man's Control

The ear is not in the power of man; he must hear even the things he does not want to hear.

Bereishit Rabbah 67:3

The Greedy Camel

[Why does a camel have small ears?] When the camel went to demand horns, they cut off his ears. [The lesson: Don't be greedy.]

Sanhedrin 106a

The Ear Is like a Grate

Rabbi Levi said: The ear is like a grate on which garments have been placed. If you burn incense under the grate, then, no matter how many garments you placed on it, they will all smell good. It is the same with the 248 limbs of the body; they all are vivified by the ear. From where do we know this? Because it says, "Incline your ear and come to Me; listen, and you shall be revived" (Isaiah 55:3). The Holy One, Blessed be He, said, "If you bend your ear to hear the Torah you will inherit life."

Devarim Rabbah 10

Scriptures about Hearing

He who stops his ears at the cry of the wretched, he too will call and not be answered (Proverbs 21:29).

Don't revile a king even among your intimates. Don't revile a rich man even in your bedchamber. For a bird of the air may carry the utterance, and a winged creature may report the word (Ecclesiastes 10:20).

Comments the *Midrash*: The walls have ears (*Vayikra Rabbah* 32, *Berachot* 8b).

The Life-Giving Ear

Midrash: If someone falls off the roof, his entire body is mutilated. When the doctor comes, he bandages his head, his hands, his legs, and all his parts so that the patient winds up bandaged from head to toe.

God says: I heal in a different manner. A man has 248 limbs including the ear, and his body is marred with transgressions. Now, if only his ear listens, his entire body is infused with life, as it is stated, "Listen and you shall be revived" (Isaiah 55:3).

Shemot Rabbah, end of chapter 27

Why Was His Ear Pierced?

A Hebrew slave who was sold for robbery had to serve for six years and was set free in the seventh year. If the slave declared that he is fond of his master and does not want to go free, his master must bring him to the courts. Standing the slave next to the door or the doorpost, his master had to pierce the ear with an awl. The slave would then serve his master until the year of the Jubilee (Exodus 20:2–5).[81]

The *Gemara* (*Kiddushin* 22b) comments: Why was the ear, of all the organs of the body, selected to be pierced? Rabban Yochanan ben Zakkai answered, "The ear that heard the divine utterance, 'For the children of Israel are actually My slaves. They are My slaves because I brought them out of Egypt' (Leviticus 25:55), and yet he preferred a human master—let that ear be pierced."

Rabbeinu Bachya remarks: Why must the slave stand next to the door? The Hebrew word *delet* (door) is identical to the letter *dalet*. Standing at the *delet* (door) he is reminded of the outsize *dalet* of *echad*, the last word of the *Shema Yisrael*, which is the keynote of all Judaism. It is the "gateway to God, the righteous shall enter through it" (Psalm 118:20). But this slave does not understand this; he preferred an earthly master over his heavenly Lord.[82]

Four Are Considered as Dead

The Talmud says: Four are considered as dead: A poor man, a leper, a blind person, and one who is childless.

Nedarim 64b

Rabbi Chaim Shmulevitz: These are not four unrelated cases. They have a common denominator.

The power of sight enables a person to sympathize with someone else. Only when you see your neighbor's distress can you commiserate with him. The things you see affect your heart and your emotions. Hearing about a great disaster does not move you as much as witnessing the suffering of the victims. Without eyesight a person cannot feel the pain of others. He is isolated, alone in the world. And a lonely person is considered as dead. The same is true for a leper. The Torah decrees that a leper must remain in isolation, outside the camp (Leviticus 13:46). Since he has no contact with other people he is considered as dead.

Then there is the famous story of the two women who appeared before King Solomon (1 Kings 3:16–28). The one whose baby son had died had stolen the other woman's baby. What did she hope to achieve by stealing the infant? After all, she would always know that this was not her child. The answer is that, merely having a baby on whom she could shower her motherly instincts of caring and giving satisfied her emotional needs. Driven by an overpowering innate desire to benefit others she stole her neighbor's baby, with total disregard of the pain she inflicted on the unfortunate mother.

The poor man is considered as dead because he, too, cannot give anything to his fellowman. Thus, there is a common thread that binds the four categories: the inability to fulfill man's inborn desire to do good to others.

Sichot Mussar, Beha'alotecha, 5732

The Blessing of the Blind Scholar

The Talmud relates: When Rabbi and Rav Chiya came to a town, they were told: There is a rabbinical scholar here who is blind. Said Rav Chiya to Rabbi: Stay here, you must not lower your princely dignity [Rabbi was the *Nasi*, Prince, i.e., the president of the Sanhedrin]. I will go and visit him. But Rabbi went with him. When they were taking leave of the blind scholar, he said to them: You have visited one who is seen but does not see; may you be granted to visit Him who sees but is not seen [i.e., God]. Said Rabbi to Rav Chiya: If I had listened to you, you would have deprived me of this blessing.

Chagigah 5b

Eat Only When It Is Light

"[God] who fed you in the wilderness with manna . . . in order to test you" (Deuteronomy 8:16). Why was eating the manna a test? You cannot compare a person who sees what he eats with one who does not see what he eats. [The manna had the flavor of any food one imagined, but it looked like manna. (Rashi)]. This is an indication the blind may eat all they want but they are never satisfied. Said Abbaye: Therefore, when you want to have a meal, make sure you have it only when it is light, [so that you can see what you are eating.]

Yoma 74b

TEARS

Six Kinds of Tears

The *Gemara* teaches: There are six kinds of tears; three are beneficial and three are harmful. The tears caused by smoke, tears of mourning, and tears of the bathroom (from stomach cramps) are harmful. But tears brought on by a medicine or by a pungent condiment (like mustard, horseradish, or onion) or by an eye ointment are beneficial, but tears of joy are best of all.

Shabbat 151b, *Eichah Rabbah* 2:15

The Wells of the Face

The *Midrash* says: The face that God gave to man is no bigger than the distance between the tips of the thumb and the index finger. In it there are several wells, yet they do not blend into one. The secretion of the eyes is salty, that of the ears is oily. The discharge of the nose is offensive, and saliva in the mouth is sweet. The reason why saliva is sweet is that a person sometimes eats a food that his stomach does not accept. If not for the sweet saliva of the mouth, the person would vomit, and his soul would not return (his life would be in danger).

Bamidbar Rabbah 18:22

Why Did Adam Cry?

Rabbi Yehoshua ben Levi said: When the Holy One, Blessed be He, said to Adam: "[The earth] will bring forth thorns and thistles for you, and you will eat the grass of the field" (Genesis 3:18), tears streamed from his eyes. Said Adam, "Master of the Universe, does this mean that I and my donkey will eat from the same trough?" (He feared that his intellect would sink to the level of a donkey, for the donkey's mentality is generated by the food it eats [Maharsha].)

But when God told Adam, "By the sweat of your brow you will eat bread," his mind was set at ease. (Eating bread increases knowledge, as stated in *Sukkah* 42b [Maharsha].)

Esau's Tears

[When Esau heard that Isaac had blessed Jacob] he raised his voice and began to weep (Genesis 27:38).

Midrash Tanchuma: Esau shed three tears. Said the Holy One, Blessed be He, "The evil Esau is crying. How can I send him away empty-handed?"

However, Israel retorts, "Master of the Universe, when the evil Esau shed three tears You immediately took pity on him. You made him the ruler over the entire world and granted him tranquility in this world. How much more should You show compassion toward us who weep continuously, day and night. Isn't it about time that You should have pity on us and put an end to our suffering?" (*Midrash Tanchuma, Toledot* 169).

This *Midrash* suggests the following idea: Esau, the embodiment of evil, had fulfilled only one *mitzvah*, that of honoring his father by bringing him a tasty dish, as he had been told to do (Genesis 27:3, 4). As a reward for this single good deed he was given dominion over the entire world for himself and his offspring. Imagine how infinitely greater will be the reward that is in store for the Jewish people who observe the 613 *mitzvot*, not just once, but each and every day!

Rabbi Shmelke of Nikolsburg asks: Why indeed hasn't God paid attention to the tears the Jews are shedding? Why don't Jewish tears outweigh the tears of Esau's children? The answer is this: Esau shed tears pleading for material gain and worldly goods. Unfortunately, Jews are also crying "Esau's tears," weeping for mundane values and earthly possessions. Instead, a Jew must shed "Jewish tears," bewail the exile of the *Shechinah*, bemoan his own shortcomings in the spiritual realm. Only then will *Mashiach* arrive.[83]

The Impaired Vision of the Elderly

The Gemara interprets the phrase "The clouds come back again after the rain" (Ecclesiastes 12:2) as the clouding over of the eyes in old age due to constant crying over all the grief a person experiences. Shmuel, a teacher of the Talmud who was a physician, said: Crying in a person past forty years of age causes irreparable harm to the eyes. To illustrate this remark, the *Gemara* relates that when Rabbi Chaninah's daughter died, he suppressed his tears. His wife reproached him for his apparent insensitivity: "Have you just sent out a chicken from your home?" she asked. He answered, "Shall I suffer two losses? The loss of a child and the loss of my eyesight [due to crying]?"

Shabbat 151b

A Voiceless Cry

[The infant Moses was hidden by his mother in a wicker basket and placed in the Nile, where the basket was found by Pharaoh's daughter.] When she opened it, she saw that it was a child, a boy crying. She took pity on it and said, "This must be a Hebrew child" (Exodus 2:6).

Rabbi Simchah Bunam of Pshis'cha: She saw that it was a child, a boy crying. She saw him cry but did not hear him. Then she said, "This must be a Hebrew child." Only a Jew can weep in silence, with a voiceless cry, from the depth of his heart.

Rabbi Aharon Halberstam of Sanz remarked: How could she be certain that it was a Jewish child? When you meet someone, your own sentiments evoke similar feelings in the other person. Affection inspires affection; animosity arouses animosity.

Pharaoh's daughter knew that the Jewish people are compassionate by nature, whereas Egyptians have a cruel and ruthless character. When, upon seeing the baby, she felt compassion welling up in her heart, she knew that this emotion was triggered by a child of the *rachamanim*, the compassionate people—a Jewish child.

The Gates of Tears

Zohar: Even if all gates are tightly shut, the Gates of Tears are always open (*Zohar*, *Terumah* 165).

Talmud: Rabbi Eleazar said, "Since the day on which the *Bet Hamikdash* was destroyed, the Gates of Prayer have been closed. But although the Gates of Prayer are closed, the Gates of Weeping are not closed, as it says, 'Hear my prayer, O God; give ear to my cry; do not disregard my tears'" (Psalm 39:13).

Berachot 32b

Commenting on the above *Gemara*, the Yid Hakadosh[84] said, "All Heavenly Gates are closed except the Gates of Tears. Why are they the exception? Because tears are a sign of grief, and grief cannot open gates that are closed. That's why the Gates of Tears are kept open. The other heavenly portals, however, can be opened wide by joyful prayer."

Rabbi Baruch of Medzhibozh remarked: "The Gemara[85] teaches that the Gates of Tears are not closed, which means that tearful pleas for mercy are accepted by God. Now you may ask, since the Gates of Tears are not closed, what purpose do they serve? The answer is: If you plead tearfully but without intelligence, then the gates are closed."[86]

Weeping for Joy

Said the Ba'al Shem Tov: Weeping is indeed evil, because
man should serve God with joy. But if a person weeps for
joy, tears are commendable.

For These Things I Weep

The Talmud relates: It happened that the son and daughter of Rabbi Yishmael ben Elisha were sold as captives to
two Roman masters. One day, the two masters happened
to be in the same place. One said: "I have the most beautiful slave in the world." The other said, "I have a female slave
whose beauty is unmatched anywhere in the world." They
then said to each other, "Let us marry them to each other
and share the children." They put them in the same room.
The boy sat in one corner, and the girl in another. He said,
"I am a *kohen*, a descendant from High Priests, and I shall
marry a maidservant?" She said, "I am the daughter of a
kohen, the descendant of High Priests, and I shall be married to a slave?" So they passed the entire night in tears.
When the day dawned they recognized each other and fell
into each other's arms, weeping bitterly until they died. For
them Jeremiah lamented, "For these I weep, my eyes run
with tears" (Lamentations 1:16).

Gittin 58a

The Altar Weeps

Rabbi Eliezer said: If a man divorces his first wife, the very
altar pours forth tears over him (*Sanhedrin* 22a).

Maharsha, expounding on the theme of this *Gemara*,
notes that if man and wife are happily married, God's Name
is anchored among them (*Sotah* 17a). However, if their
marriage fails they are consumed by fire.

The Maharsha explains: The word אִישׁ *ish* (man) contains
a *yud*, and the word אִשָּׁה *ishah* (woman) contains a *hei*. To-

gether, *yud* and *hei* form a Divine Name. In other words, a harmonious marriage is blessed by God's Presence. However, God withdraws His Presence if the marriage fails; His Name of *Yud-Hei* departs. The partners are consumed by the fires of hatred and animosity. For if you delete the *yud* from איש *ish*, all that remains is אש *eish*, fire. Similarly, if you delete the *hei* from אשה *ishah*, only אש *eish*, fire, remains.

The Different Natures of Men and Women

If husband and wife deserve it, the *Shechinah* dwells among them—if they don't, fire consumes them.

Sotah 17a[87]

As we probe the theme of איש *ish* (man) containing the *yud*, and אשה *ishah* (woman) containing the *hei* of the Divine Name, a revealing thought emerges.

The words איש *ish* and אשה *ishah*, (man and woman), have in common the letters *alef* and *shin* which form אש *eish*, fire, an indication of the fire of human emotion and passion. At the same time, both *ish* and *ishah* possess one of the letters of the Divine Name. There is, however, a glaring difference. In איש *ish* (man), the *yud*—the divine element—is wedged between the *alef* and the *shin* of *eish* (fire). Thus, the components of fire are separated by the *yud*, which means that in man the emotions (*eish*) are firmly controlled and kept from erupting by the reasoning intellect (*yud*). By contrast, in אשה *ishah* (woman) the divine letter *hei* is externally attached to the *eish* (fire). Hence, in the female, the אש *eish* (fire) of emotion remains intact and is fanned at the slightest provocation.

Rabbi Chaim Finkel

MOUTH AND LIPS

The Lips of the Dead Are Moving

Rabbi Yochanan said: The lips of a scholar move even in the grave if his Torah thoughts are quoted in this world (*Yevamot* 97a). This beautiful metaphor suggests that the departed live on after death when their writings are studied, their wisdom is retold, and their good deeds are emulated.

This idea is expressed in the following *Gemara* (*Yevamot* 96b): King David prayed, "O that I might dwell in Your tent in both worlds" (Psalm 61:5). The *Gemara* asks: How can anyone live in both worlds at the same time? The *Gemara* answers: David pleaded that people would quote his sayings in this world (so that his lips would be moving in the grave as though he were alive [Rashi]).

Moses Is Speaking Even Today

The dead are living on, not only in the world to come; they continue to live even in this world. This idea is suggested by the following commentary: [Shortly before his death,] Moses went and spoke the following words to all Israel (Deuteronomy 31:1).

Tiferet Shlomoh:[88] The commentators are mystified by the words "Moses went." Where did he go? For what purpose? The Torah does not provide an answer.

Moses went to *Gan Eden*, the Garden of Eden, but although he departed this life and is no longer with us, he is still speaking his words of Torah wisdom to the Jewish people. Throughout the ages, whenever the Torah is being studied, the sound of Moses' voice is heard as it resonates in the *yeshivot* and houses of learning. He continues to speak to us from the pages of the *Chumash*, the *Gemara*, the commentaries, through the mouth of the myriads of *lomdei* Torah (students of Torah), both young and old.

Like a Crimson Thread

Your lips are like a crimson thread . . . (Song of Songs 4:3).

On Yom Kippur, in the days when the *Bet Hamikdash* stood, a scarlet thread was strung across the entrance of the Sanctuary. If God granted the Jewish people forgiveness, the red string turned white. When the people in the court saw this miraculous sign of forgiveness, they felt an indescribable joy.

In the Song of Songs, an allegorical book that describes God's love of the Jewish people, God alludes to this red thread when He says to Israel, "Your lips are like a crimson thread."

The *Midrash* explains the dialogue between Israel and God:

The Jewish people said, "Sadly, we have today neither the *Bet Hamikdash* nor the red thread."

God replies, "Your lips are like a crimson thread. The lips of the Jewish people uttering their prayers to Me are as dear to Me as was the red thread in the times of the *Bet Hamikdash*" (*Shir Hashirim Rabbah* 4:3).

Lips instead of Bulls

Take words with you and return to God. Say to Him: 'Forgive all guilt and accept what is good. Instead of bulls we will pay [the offerings of] our lips' (Hosea 14:3).

The *Midrash* explains: The Jewish people said to God, "When the *Bet Hamikdash* stood we brought sacrifices as an atonement for our sins. Now all we have to offer are our prayers. Therefore, please "forgive all guilt and accept what is good." The word טוב, *tov* (*good*) has the numeric value of 17 (*tet* = 9; *vav* = 6; *bet* = 2), and 17 is also the number of *berachot* in the weekday *Amidah* (which originally consisted of seventeen blessings[89]). In other words, Israel is asking God, "Please accept our *Amidah* prayer."

Bamidbar Rabbah 18

Greater than Sacrifices

Rabbi Eleazar said: Prayer is more effective than sacrifices.

Berachot 32b

Hannah's Prayer

In Jewish thought, the lips are closely associated with prayer. For example, we preface the *Shemoneh Esreih* (*Amidah*) with the words, "My Lord, open my lips, that my mouth may declare Your praise" (Psalm 51:17). Furthermore, we read, "You have granted him the desire of his heart, have not denied the request of his lips [prayer]" (Psalm 21:3).

The sages present Hannah's prayer as the model of prayer to be emulated. Briefly, this is the story. Despite fervent prayers, Hannah, the wife of Elkanah, was childless. One Rosh Hashanah she went to the *Bet Hamikdash* and poured out her anguished heart to God. Her prayers were answered, and she gave birth to the prophet Samuel. And so we read: "Now Hannah was praying with all her heart; only her lips moved, but her voice could not be heard" (1 Samuel 1:13).

Discussing this passage, the *Gemara* says: How many important laws can be learned from the story of Hannah's prayer. "Now Hannah was praying in her heart"—from this we learn that when you pray you must concentrate your thoughts. "Only her lips moved"—from this we learn that when you pray you must articulate the words distinctly with your lips. "But her voice could not be heard"—from this we learn that it is forbidden to raise your voice in the *tefillah*.

Berachot 31b

She Prayed for a Son

The *Gemara* expounds the verse, "Now Hannah was praying in her heart" (1 Samuel 1:13). Rabbi Eleazar said: This means, "She spoke about her heart." She said to God, "Master of the Universe, of all the things You have created in a woman, You have not created anything without a purpose, eyes to see, ears to hear, a nose to smell, a mouth to speak, hands to do work, legs to walk with, breasts to nurse a baby. These breasts that You have put on my heart, are they not meant for nursing? Give me a son, so that I may nurse with them."

Berachot 31b

Selected Sayings about Prayer

The Holy One, Blessed be He, craves the prayer of the righteous (*Yevamot* 64a).

Prayer without *kavanah* (concentration) is like a body without a soul (*Yeshuot Meshicho* 14:1).[90]

When you pray, know before whom you are standing (*Berachot* 28b).

Rabbi Yochanan said: Even if a sharp sword rests on a man's neck he should not desist from prayer, as it says, "Though He slay me, yet I will trust in Him" (Job 13:15).

Berachot 10a

When you pray, direct your eyes downward and your heart upward.

Yevamot 108b

He who prays for his neighbor while he himself needs the same thing, will be answered first.

Bava Kamma 92a

The Distance from Mouth to Heart

Rabbi Yisrael Salanter[91] said: Your mouth is as far removed from your heart as heaven is from earth. Nevertheless, when rain falls from heaven, things begin to grow on earth.

Which means to say that often our prayers are articulated routinely, only with our mouths, without involvement of our hearts and emotions. However, when our hearts are stirred and our feelings are ignited, then our prayers become words of meaningful communication with God.

Mouth-to-Heart Resuscitation

[The Torah] is something that is very close to you. It is in your mouth and in your heart, so that you can keep it. (Deuteronomy 30:14).

Rabbi Elazar of Koznitz: It is in your mouth and in your heart. Shouldn't the heart precede the mouth, since whatever you say originates in your heart? The point is that if you begin by performing *mitzvot* just with your mouth, externally, outwardly, and for ulterior motives, gradually your heart will become aroused, and you will end up observing the Torah with deep feeling and sincere emotion.[92]

The Shechinah *Enters*

The Ba'al Shem Tov said: When you begin the *Shemoneh Esrei* (*Amidah*) and say the introductory verse, "My Lord, open my lips," (Psalm 51:17), the *Shechinah* immediately enters you and speaks with your voice. If you firmly believe this, you will pray with *kavanah* (concentration of thought).
Likutei Amarim 1b

The Lips of the Righteous

> By the mouth of the upright shall You be exalted;
> By the lips of the righteous shall You be blessed;
> By the tongue of the pious shall You be sanctified;
> and by the inner core of the holy shall You be praised.
> *Shacharit* for Shabbat and *Yom Tov*—Nusach Sefarad

Each of the four categories of worshipers mentioned in this prayer (the upright, the righteous, the pious, and the holy) is on a higher scale of devoutness than the preceding one. This is reflected in the way they praise God. While the upright exalts God with his mouth, and the righteous blesses Him with his lips, the pious uses his tongue. His prayer emanates from a deeper source. The highest praise, that attained by the holy person, stems from the depth of his heart, from the inner core of his being.[93]

THE VOICE

A Woman's Voice

Rav Chisda said: A harsh voice in a woman is considered a blemish, since it is written, "Let me hear your voice; for your voice is sweet, and your face is comely" (Song of Songs 2:14).

Ketubot 75a

Why Is a Woman's Voice Sweet?

The students asked: Why is a woman's voice sweet and a man's voice is not sweet? [Rabbi Dostai replied:] A man derives his voice from the place from which he was created, [the earth, and when you strike the earth no tone is produced]. A woman derives her voice from the place from which she was created [a bone, and when a bone is struck it produces resonant sound].

Niddah 31b

Were They Jealous of the Choirboys?

The *Gemara* tells us that young boys were admitted to the service in the *Bet Hamikdash* to join the Levites in the singing. They were called assistants to the Levites, but some called them tormentors of the Levites because their voices were high-pitched, and the voices of the adult Levites were low. The choirboys could sing high, whereas the men could not.

Arachin 13b

Speaking with One Voice

If a man has an incorrigible and wayward son who does not
obey the voice of his father and the voice of his mother, and
though they chastise him, he does not listen to them, then
his father and mother must grasp him and bring him to the
elders of the city . . . all the men of his city shall then stone
him to death. . . .

Deuteronomy 21:18–21

What is the significance of the redundancy, "Who does
not obey the voice of his father and the voice of his mother"?
Wouldn't "the voice of his father and mother" have been
sufficient?

The *Gemara* (*Sanhedrin* 14a) derives from the repeti-
tion of the phrase "the voice," that for a "rebellious son" to
be sentenced to death, it is required that the voices of the
parents be identical.

Rabbi Samson Raphael Hirsch elaborates on this
theme, enumerating the conditions that must exist before
a child can be declared a "rebellious son."

1. The child must have both a father and a mother.
2. The father and mother alike must play a part in
   bringing up their son.
3. Both parents must speak in one and the same voice.
   They must speak as one, as it says in verse 20, "he
   does not listen to our voice" (not "our voices").

Speaking in one and the same voice means that both parents must relate to the child with equal seriousness; that
both must convey to the child an equal commitment to
Torah values.

Furthermore, it means that both parents must impress
the child with equal authority and dignity; both must evoke
in him the same sense of awe and respect. And most important, both parents must be as one in their thoughts and
aspirations with regard to the child's education. Only if parents have met all these criteria can they tell themselves that

they are not to blame if their child turns out to be an incorrigibly rebellious son. If even one of the factors is absent, if the parents have not worked together in complete harmony in bringing up their child, then the fact that the child has become stubbornly unruly is not in itself proof of his innate depravity. Perhaps if his parents had given him a better, more genuine education, the child might have turned out different. [Indeed, these requirements made the application of the law of the rebellious son impossible (*Sanhedrin* 71a)].

Rabbi Samson Raphael Hirsch, Deuteronomy 21:18

THE NOSE

The Etymology of Af, *the Nose*

God formed man out of the dust of the ground and breathed into his nostrils a breath of life. Man thus became a living creature (Genesis 2:7).

Rabbi Samson Raphael Hirsch: "He breathed into his nostrils a breath of life." The Hebrew words *af* and *apayim*, nose and nostrils, denote the opening of the body through which man greedily draws in the stream of life necessary for the maintenance of life. In a broader sense, *apayim* means a striving, wishing, longing facial expression. Thus, *erech apayim*—literally, a long face—means patience. *K'tzar apayim*—a short face—means impatience. And *af* signifies unsatisfied desire, anger.

The phrase *bezei'at apecha tochal lechem*, "By the sweat of your brow you will eat bread" (Genesis 3:19) literally translated means, "by the sweat of your nose you will eat bread." The nose, the organ that inhales, signifies the effort to absorb the world into oneself, to gain a little piece of the universe for oneself, which is the purpose of all work.

Rabbi Samson Raphael Hirsch,
commentary on Genesis 2:7

The Shape of the Nostrils

God formed man out of the dust of the ground, and breathed into his nostrils a breath of life. Man thus became a living creature (Genesis 2:7).

Rabbeinu Bachya: The nose is the organ through which the soul enters and leaves the body, and it is through his soul that man rises above the animal and becomes an image of God. Amazingly, man's divine image is evident in the human body:

One of the marvels of creation is that the letter ש *shin* is etched on the nostrils, which are shaped like a ש *shin*, whereby the bottom of the *shin* represents the tip of the nose (see illustration).

This ש *shin* is the first letter of the Divine Name שדי *Shaddai*, written ש *shin*, ד *dalet*, י *yud*. The ד *dalet*, the second letter of the name *Shaddai*, is also manifest in the human form. When you stretch out your hand, your body and arm take on the shape of a *dalet*. The י *yud* of *Shaddai* is apparent in the corona of the male organ, which is shaped like a *yud*.

Indeed, the human body is a reflection of the divine, as it says, "In my flesh I see God" (Job 19:26).

Guard Your Senses

Rabbi Nachman of Bratzlav: Knowledge can be acquired through arduous labor and protracted study, or it can come in one God-given instantaneous flash of intuition.

We know that ardor of the heart is aroused by the vibrations of the brain waves, since motion produces heat. The faster the brain waves vibrate, the more heated is the fervor that is ignited in the heart. Thus, when the mind receives a flow of divinely inspired instantaneous intuition, the heart catches fire immediately and burns with glowing enthusiasm.

The only way you can be receptive to this flow of divine inspiration is by sanctifying your mouth, nose, eyes, and ears, for these are the channels that convey this divine flow of light to your mind. You sanctify your *mouth* by avoiding to speak untruth. You should be God-fearing, for the awe of God is associated with the *nose*, as it says, "[*Mashiach*] will exude an aroma of reverence of God" (Isaiah 11:3). Furthermore, you should trust the teachings of the sages, which are transmitted to you through your *ear*. And you sanctify your *eyes* by averting them from immorality. Briefly, your mouth, nose, eyes, and ears are linked to your brain. If you guard them, your mind is open to receiving the divine flow of enlightenment.[94]

A Berachah *over Fragrance*

The *Gemara* teaches: From where do we learn that a *berachah* should be said over sweet smells?[95] From the verse, "Let every soul praise God" (Psalm 150:6). What is it that gives enjoyment to the soul and not to the body? You must say that this is fragrant smell.

Berachot 43b

The Rebbe Wanted to Take Snuff

It happened that Rabbi Yitzchak of Vorki woke up in the middle of the night and felt a desire to take snuff, but the snuffbox was on the table in the adjacent study. He pondered the alternatives. To get out of bed, go to the study, and get the snuffbox would mean giving in to his *yetzer hara*, his tendency to seek pleasure. On the other hand, if he did not get up he would be surrendering to his tendency toward laziness. At last he reached a decision: "I'll get up, go into the study to get the snuffbox, but I won't take the snuff."[96]

A Bizarre Dream

Bar Kappara said to Rabbi: "I dreamt that my nose fell off." Rabbi replied: "[This means] that blazing anger has been removed from you."

Berachot 56b

(Rabbi's interpretation of the dream is based on the double meaning of the word *af*, which denotes both nose and anger. Examples for *af* meaning anger are found in the verse, "God's anger (*af*) will be directed against you" (Deuteronomy 11:17), and in the description of the fury of the behemoth, when God says to Job, "Out of his nostrils comes smoke as from a steaming boiling cauldron" (Job 41:12). Thus the dreamed removal of Bar Kappara's nose is an indication of the elimination of his anger.)

Don't Compound Your Mistake

Rabbi Chiya was asked: If a person has eaten and drunk without saying a *berachah* (blessing), should he say the *berachah* afterwards? He replied: If one has eaten garlic so that his breath smells, should he eat more garlic so that his breath should go on smelling?

Berachot 51a

Maharshah explains: Having made one mistake, should he make another by not saying a *berachah* over the part he still has to eat?

A Stuffed Nose

The *Midrash* tells a parable: A lion that had not eaten in a long time developed a severe case of bad breath. He met a donkey and said to him: "Put your head near my mouth, and tell me if my breath is sweet."

The donkey followed suit and said, "I'm sorry, but your breath has an offensive odor."

"How dare you insult me?" roared the lion, and he promptly ate the donkey.

A few days later, he met a wolf and asked the same question of him. The wolf replied favorably.

"How dare you lie to me?" bellowed the lion and devoured him too.

Later he questioned a fox, but the clever animal avoided falling into the trap.

"I am sorry," said the fox to the lion. "I have a bad cold. My nose is stuffed, and I cannot smell."

Yalkut Hatorah

The lesson: A stuffed nose at the proper time can get you out of a tough spot.

Sneezing

The *Midrash* says: Until the days of Jacob, when a person's time to die had arrived, he sneezed, and his soul left him through the nose. Jacob appealed to God for mercy. That is why, when someone sneezes, you call out: *Chayim tovim!* ("Good life!") Proof that in earlier times he would have died.

Midrash Yelamdeinu

A Favorable Sign

Rabbi Zeira said: If you sneeze while praying, it is a good omen for you. It means that just as you are given relief here on earth [since sneezing gives relief (Rashi)], so too, you will receive relief from heaven, [and your wishes will be fulfilled (Rashi)].

Berachot 24b

Six Good Signs for a Sick Person

Six things are a good sign for a sick person: sneezing, perspiration, open bowels, seminal emission, sleep, and a dream. Sneezing, as it is written, "His sneezings flash light [of healing]" (Job 41:10).

Berachot 57b

He Sneezed Seven Times

The *Tanach* (Bible) relates that the kind Shunammite woman's son had died suddenly. The prophet Elisha was notified, and when he arrived at the bedside he prayed to God.

"Then he mounted the bed and placed himself over the child. He put his mouth on the child's mouth, his eyes on his eyes, and his hands on its hands, as he bent over him. And the body of the child became warm. . . . Thereupon the boy sneezed seven times, and the boy opened his eyes" (2 Kings 4:33–35).

HAIR

Heads You Win, Tails I Lose

The Talmud relates: When R. Ammi and R. Assi were sitting before R. Isaac, one of them said to him, "Will you please tell us some legal points?" The other said, "Will you please give us some homiletical instruction?" When he began a homiletical discourse he was prevented by the one, and when he started a legal discourse he was prevented by the other. So he said to them, "I will tell you a parable: This is like a man who had two wives, one young and one old. The young one used to pluck out his white hair, whereas the old one used to pluck out his black hair. Thus he finally became bald on both sides." [Either way I lose].

Bava Kamma 60b

The Nazir's *Hair*

There are devout persons who are not content with observing what the Torah requires. They seek a more strict, abstemious way of life. To such a person the Torah affords the opportunity to become a *nazir*. If one takes a vow to become a *nazir* he must abstain from wine, grape juice, grapes, and any alcoholic beverage. He is forbidden to cut his hair. Finally, he must avoid contact, or being under the same roof, with a corpse.[97]

Rabbi Samson Raphael Hirsch analyzes the law that requires a *nazir* to leave his hair to grow untrimmed. He explains that hair represents a protection of the skin that shields it from the outside world and reduces its receptiveness to outside influences. "The law that requires a *nazir* to allow the hair to grow unrestricted thus indicates that a *nazir* should be in isolation and focus on himself for the period of his *nezirut*. He is to strive to be closer to God, His Sanctuary, and His teachings. The insulating growth of his hair admonishes him to fulfill this assignment. Accordingly, his head bears the sign of holy resolution, 'the uncut hair that grows on his head is sacred, kadosh'" (Numbers 6:5).

Rabbi Samson Raphael Hirsch,
Commentary to the Pentateuch

A Man's Crowning Glory

"As long as he is under his nazirite oath, no cutting instrument shall touch [the hair on] his head. Until he completes his term as a nazirite to God, the uncut hair that grows on his head is sacred" (Numbers 6:5).

Tzeror Hamor: The person's holiness is directly linked to the growth of his hair. The hair represents the crowning glory of a man's appearance. It evokes man's resemblance to God, his "image of God" (Genesis 1:26). It calls to mind the words of the prophet Daniel in his vision of God, "His garment was like white snow, and the hair of His head was [white] like pure wool" (Daniel 7:9). So also with Samson: his hair was his strength. When he sinned, he lost the magnificence of his hair.[98]

Not to Be Emulated

Rabbi Elie Munk: The *nazir* is like one of an elite group who strives to come nearer to God through renunciation of ordinary life but who risks withdrawing permanently from the struggle that is man's ultimate means of consecration. It is important to note that the *nazir* will never be an example for others to follow. Quite the contrary, when his period of withdrawal comes to an end, he brings an atonement sacrifice because, to a certain extent, he is at fault.

The history of the monastic Essenes [the people of Massadah and the Dead Sea scrolls] proves that Judaism, with all its vitality, was not able to integrate that sect, whose purity of thought was beyond question. For Judaism needs life, and the Jew can reach fulfillment only by dominating the material aspects of existence, not by repressing or denying them.[99]

The Commendable Nazir

At the completion of the term of *nezirut*,[100] the *nazir* must shave off the hair on his head, as it says, "The *nazir* shall shave off the crown of hair on his head" (Numbers 6:18).

The *Gemara* relates: Shimon Hatzaddik (Simeon the Just) once met a *nazir* who came from the South country [at the conclusion of his *nezirut* term]. He saw that the *nazir* had beautiful eyes, a handsome appearance, and his thick locks of hair were arranged in jet-black ringlets.

He said to him, "My son, what made you decide to destroy this beautiful hair of yours?"

The *nazir* replied, "Back home, I was a shepherd for my father. Once when I went to draw water from a well I gazed at my reflection in the water. At that moment my evil desires seized me and tried to drive me from the world [through the sin of pride]. But I said to [my lust], 'Evil creature! Why do you boastfully intrude into a world that is not yours, with one who is destined to become dust, worms, and maggots? I swear that I will [become a *nazir* so that I will be forced to] shave off [this beautiful hair] for the sake of heaven.'"

Shimon Hatzaddik immediately arose and kissed his head, saying, "My son, may there be many *nezirim* (nazirites) like you in Israel!"

Nedarim 9b

Shimon Hatzaddik implied that many people, motivated by pride and ambition, take the nazirite vow out of a desire to gain recognition for their exceptional piety. The shepherd, however, took the vow for the right reason. He wanted to overcome his innate haughtiness by eliminating its source, his beautiful hair, which he would have to shave off at the end of the period of *nezirut*.

Absalom's Hair

Absalom boasted of his hair, therefore he was hanged by his hair (*Sotah* 10b).

The Talmud says: Absalom rebelled against his father [King David] through his hair, as it says, "No one in all Israel was so admired for his beauty as Absalom. . . . When he cut his hair—he had to cut it every year, for it grew too heavy for him—the hair of his head weighed two hundred shekels by the royal weight" (2 Samuel 14:25, 26). [Through his beautiful hair and handsome appearance, he gained popularity and lured the people away from his father, King David.]

Therefore he was hanged by his hair, as it says, "Absalom encountered some of David's followers. Absalom was riding on a mule, and as the mule passed under the tangled branches of a great oak, his hair got caught in the oak, and he was left hanging between heaven and earth as the mule kept going" (2 Samuel 18:9).

[The *Gemara* remarks:] He took a sword and wanted to cut himself loose, but at that moment Sheol was split open under him [so that if he had cut through his hair he would have fallen into the nether world.] Joab then took three darts and drove them into Absalom's chest.

Sotah 10b

His Beard Turned White

The Talmud relates: [When the rabbis came to appoint the youthful Rabbi Eleazar ben Azariah, as head of the Academy], he replied: I will go and consult the members of my family. He went and consulted his wife. . . . She said to him: You have no white hair [you are too young for this elevated post]. He was eighteen years old that day, and a miracle happened to him. Eighteen rows of hair [on his beard] turned white. That is why Rabbi Eleazar ben Azariah said: "Behold, I look like *one* who is seventy years old,"[101] and he did not say simply, "I am seventy years old."

Berachot 28a

How Does Hair Grow?

The *Gemara* wants to determine whether the hair grows from the roots or at the tips.

The *Gemara* answers: Judge by the red paint [with which the tenth animals were marked during tithing]. The wool grows fresh again underneath the markings. Furthermore, when old men dye their beards they grow white again at the roots (*Nazir* 39a).

The Beautiful Woman Prisoner

If you see a beautiful woman among the prisoners and desire her, you may take her as a wife. In such a case, when you bring her home, she must shave off her hair and let her fingernails grow.

Deuteronomy 21:12

Ibn Ezra: He was attracted to her because of her hair, that is why she must shave it off.

Rabbi Samson Raphael Hirsch: The object is to make her less attractive, so that he sees her in homely surroundings and has time to judge her character. For a marriage based solely on the dictates of passion leads to discord and disappointments in the raising of children.

5

The 248 Limbs

THE HUMAN FORM IS PERFECT

The *Midrash* offers a beautiful analogy about the limbs of
the human body:

Visitors on a guided tour through the king's new palace invariably will find fault with something. Some will say,
"The pillars are not tall enough," or "The walls are not
straight." Others will say, "The ceiling should have been
higher." But you will never hear anyone complain about the
palace that is the human body. No one has ever said, "I wish
I had three eyes," or "If only I had three legs my body would
be perfect!" Isn't it strange! The King of kings counts every
limb in your body, puts it in its proper place, and builds
you to perfection, as it says, "Is He not your Father, who
created you, the One who fashioned and established you?"

Bereishit Rabbah 12

ADAM WAS COSMOPOLITAN

Rabbi Meir said: The dust of the first man was gathered from all parts of the earth. Adam's body came from Babylon, his head from *Eretz Yisrael*, his limbs from other lands, and his private parts from Akra di Agan (a town near Pumbeditha, Babylonia).

Sanhedrin 38a, b

Maharsha comments: It makes sense that the head, which is the seat of the soul and the intellect, should be from *Eretz Yisrael*, the land that is particularly conducive to wisdom, as it says, "The very air of *Eretz Yisrael* makes you wise" (*Bava Batra* 158b).

THE TALMUD SPANS THE GLOBE

When Adam was created, his body came from Babylonia, his head came from *Eretz Yisrael*, and his limbs from other lands (*Sanhedrin* 38a, b).

Rabbi Meir Shapiro of Lublin[1] made a penetrating observation: Now let us look at a page in the Talmud: the *Mishnah*, the earlier part, was compiled by Rabbi Yehudah Hanassi in *Eretz Yisrael*; so we have a parallel to Adam, the first created man: his head derived from *Eretz Yisrael*. Now the *Gemara*, the later, major part of the Talmud, was put together by the Babylonian sage Rav Ashi. Again we have a parallel: Adam's body came from Babylonia.

Now further: the commentaries of Rashi and Tosafot, printed alongside the *Gemara* text, originated in France. In the back of each printed tractate we have more commentaries: Rabbeinu Asher (the Rosh), from Germany, the Rambam on the *Mishnah*, from Egypt, and then the last ones: Maharshal, Maharsha, Maharam, and so on—all produced in Poland. Thus the analogy continues: Adam's limbs came from other lands. . . . The Talmud was composed and formed in the same way as Adam.[2]

TEN MIGHTY RULERS

Wisdom strengthens the wise more than ten mighty rulers that are in the city (Ecclesiastes 7:19).

The *Gemara* expounds: The adage "Wisdom strengthens the wise" refers to repentance and good deeds; the phrase "more than ten mighty rulers" refers to the two eyes, two ears, two hands, two feet, the reproductive organ, and the mouth. [The proverb teaches that by repentance and good deeds one can conquer the evil desires of these ten limbs].

Nedarim 32b

Maharsha notes that the ten limbs comprise the senses: the two eyes—sight; the two ears—hearing; the two hands, feet, and the reproductive organ—touch; the mouth—taste. All human activity is accomplished by means of these senses. That is why the ten limbs are called chiefs. The sense of smell does not play an important part in providing man's needs and is, therefore, not mentioned.

THE COMPUTATION OF THE 248 LIMBS

The *Mishnah* in *Ohalot* 1:8 lists the 248 limbs, whereby a limb is defined as a member that includes flesh, sinews, and bones. There are:

30 in the foot, *pissat haregel* (6 in each toe, 5 x 6)

10 in the ankle, *karsol* (the bone that connects the foot to the lower leg)

2 in the lower leg, *shok* (the lower leg to the knee [*Vilna Gaon*]

5 in the knee, *arkuva* (two bones on each side and the kneecap in the center [*Tosefta*])

1 in the upper leg, *yerech*

3 in the *katlit* (the top of the upper leg that abuts the hips)

11 ribs

30 in the hand, *pissat hayad*, (6 in each finger, 5 x 6)

2 in the forearm, *kaneh*

2 in the elbow, *marpeik*

1 in the upper arm, *zeroa*

4 in the shoulder, *kateif*

101 for each side; for both sides 202.

18 vertebrae, *chuliyot bashedrah*

9 in the head, *rosh* (including the jaw [*Tosefta*])

8 in the neck, *tzavor*

6 in the key to the heart, *mafte'ach halev* (the bones of the chest that enclose the heart [*Tiferet Yisrael*])

5 in the openings, *nekavim*[3] (pelvic bones [*Tiferet Yisrael*])

46 plus the above-mentioned 202, for a total of 248 limbs.

Encyclopedia Talmudit cites Dr. Kazenelson, a contemporary scientist, who offers a theory to prove the accuracy of the talmudic count of 248 limbs of the body. He explains the discrepancy with the findings of modern anatomy, which counts only 211 bones, by the fact that the talmudic sages counted the parts of the corpse of a sixteen-year-old.[4] We know that at birth a child has many more parts because the cartilage between the bones has not hardened yet. As the child grows older, the cartilage hardens, becomes ossified, and the bones are unified. As a result, the number of limbs decreases, so that the body of a sixteen-year-old contains precisely 248 limbs.[5]

THREE PARTNERS

Our Rabbis taught: There are three partners in man: The Holy One, Blessed be He, his father, and his mother. His father supplies the white substance out of which are formed the child's bones, sinews, nails, the brain, and the white in his eye; his mother supplies red substance out of which is formed his skin, flesh, hair, blood, and the black of his eye; and the Holy One, Blessed be He, gives him the spirit and the soul, beauty of features, eyesight, the power of hearing, and the ability to speak and to walk.

Niddah 31a

THE PROCESS OF PROCREATION

Honor your father and mother. You will then live long on the land that God your Lord is giving you (Exodus 20:12).

Malbim:[6] Honor your father and mother. This commandment follows immediately after the commandment to keep the *Shabbat*. The close connection of these two *mitzvot* is evident also in the verse, "Every person must respect his mother and father and keep My *Shabbat*" (Leviticus 19:3). What is the link that binds these two *mitzvot*?

During the six days of Creation, God brought into being a proto-type of each species, including man. If God had not stopped the process of Creation, He would have continued to create new individuals, just as He had done during the first six days, and the system of procreation whereby parents beget children would not exist. However, when, on *Shabbat*, God ceased to create, He ensured the continuance of life on earth by instituting the process of reproduction. Hence, we may say that parents are partners of God. They beget the child's body while God gives it the soul and breathes life into it.

Thus, the fact that a person is born of a father and a mother is the direct result of God's resting on *Shabbat*. This is the key to understanding the juxtaposition of "honoring father and mother" and *Shabbat*.

A BODY WITHOUT A HEAD

[After Jacob's death,] Joseph comforted his brothers and tried to make up.

(Genesis 50:21)

The *Midrash* says: Joseph told them, "You are the body and I am the head. If you remove the body, what good is the head? By the same token, if you remove the head, what good is the body?"

Bereishit Rabbah 100

MASTERY OVER HIS LIMBS

Rabbi Ammi said: Originally, his name was אברם Abram, whose numeric value is 243 (*alef* = 1; *bet* = 2; *reish* = 200; *mem* = 40). After his *brit milah*, God changed it to אברהם Abraham, with a numeric value of 248 (*alef* = 1; *bet* = 2; *reish* = 200; *hei* = 5; *mem* = 40) which corresponds to the number of parts of a man's body.

At first God gave him mastery over 243 limbs, and later over 248. The additional five are the two eyes, two ears, and the reproductive organ.

The Ran[7] comments that man has no power over his eyes and ears. He can direct his hands and feet to do his bidding, but he cannot control the things he sees and hears. However, as a reward for undergoing the *milah*, God gave Abraham mastery over his eyes and ears, the organs that entice man to immorality. He was now able by his own will-power to forbid them to gaze upon or listen to immorality.

ABRAHAM'S LIMBS OBEYED GOD

Abraham stretched out his hand and took the slaughter knife to slay his son (Genesis 22:10).

Rabbi Avraham Borenstein of Sochatchov: Abraham stretched out his hand and took the slaughter knife. The verse could have simply stated, "Abraham took the slaughter knife." The uncharacteristic wordiness suggests that Abraham applied a degree of force in order to take the slaughter knife. How are we to understand this? Abraham had trained his limbs to perform nothing but *mitzvot*, to the point that his limbs were capable of doing only the will of God. But slaughtering Isaac did not constitute a *mitzvah* at all. God had commanded Abraham only to "bring Isaac as an offering" (Genesis 22:2). Abraham, however, mistakenly interpreted this to mean that he was to slaughter his son. This was not God's intent. Therefore, when Abraham tried to take the knife, his hand refused to obey him, and he had to use force to coerce his defiant limb. [8]

ABRAHAM'S HOSPITALITY

[God visited Abraham during his indisposition in the aftermath of his circumcision. When three passersby appeared, and the opportunity arose to offer them his hospitality, Abraham said to God:] "My Lord, if You would, do not go away, [but wait until I have taken care of my guests (Rashi)]" (Genesis 18:3).

Rabbi Meir of Premyshlan:[9] Abraham asked God to wait while he received the three wayfarers. The Talmud[10] derives from Abraham's conduct that hospitality is greater than welcoming the *Shechinah*. This leaves us with the question: How did Abraham know that this is so? We know that Abraham observed all *mitzvot*, even though the Torah had not yet been given.[11] He reached the point that his 248 limbs and 365 sinews were dedicated to serving God. Each member was drawn to the *mitzvah* that pertained to it and refused to transgress any prohibition. For example, on Pesach his mouth refused to eat *chametz*, and on Sukkot, Abraham's limbs dragged him to a *sukkah*. Now, when Abraham saw the wayfarers, he noticed that his legs were racing toward them, and no matter how hard he tried, he simply could not stop them. This told him that hospitality takes precedence over welcoming the *Shechinah*.

Divrei Meir[12]

THE 613 *MITZVOT*

The 248 limbs correspond to the number of positive commandments (things you must do), while the 365 sinews equal the number of negative commandments (things you may not do), for a total of 613 *mitzvot*. This conveys the idea that man was given his body—his limbs and sinews—to fulfill God's will.

Rabbi Simla'i expounded: Moses received 613 *mitzvot*—365 negative commandments parallelling the days of the solar year and 248 positive commandments corresponding to the limbs of the body.

Makkot 23b

THE *MITZVAH* OF THE HEART

The *Midrash* says that the Almighty is the heart of the Jewish people. What does that mean? The 248 limbs of the body correspond to the 248 positive *mitzvot*. The heart matches the commandment of "I am God your Lord" (Exodus 20:2). This is the commandment to believe in God.[13] Just as the heart is the paramount organ, the member that imparts life to the entire body, so is the *mitzvah* to believe in God the premise and first principle on which all the 248 positive commandments are based.

Maharsha to *Makkot* 23b

THE TORAH CORRESPONDS TO THE HUMAN BODY

The Rambam (Maimonides), in his epistle to his son, writes that the Torah comprises the entire human body. Moses is an allusion to the intellect, Aaron is a metaphor for the heart, the children of Israel represent the limbs of the body, and Pharaoh exemplifies the *yetzer hara*, the evil urge in man.

MITZVOT WITHIN MITZVOT

Vilna Gaon: Every *mitzvah* may be compared to a tree. It is a living organism that has roots, a trunk, branches, and leaves. It produces a rich harvest of fruit that contains seeds, and each seed holds inside its core a future tree that will produce fruit containing seeds, ad infinitum. Like a small seed that contains a potential tree, each *mitzvah* comprises all of the 613 *mitzvot*.

Maalot Hatorah[14]

This thought is a reflection of the essential relationships in the universe, both in the spiritual and the physical realm. In the system of *Sefirot*, each *Sefirah* comprises all other *Sefirot* to form a link between the higher and lower worlds that is almost infinite in its immensity and complexity. Analogously, in the physical universe, our planet is one unit of the vast solar system. The solar system in turn is only a small component of our galaxy, which is a flat, rotating spiral system containing myriad stars. Our galaxy, again, is just one of millions of other galaxies that have been revealed by telescopes. The system of worlds within worlds that dominates the macrocosm of the universe has a parallel in the microcosm that is man. Each microscopic cell in the human body contains a DNA molecule that is the carrier of the genetic information of that person. Thus, in a way, a man's entire body is present in each cell, and, theoretically, an entire human being could be cloned from one single cell.

The sages of the Talmud teach that the 613 limbs and sinews of the body correspond to the 613 *mitzvot*. The parallel between *mitzvot* and the body is quite striking. Just as each cell contains the genetic code of the entire body, so does each *mitzvah* comprise all other *mitzvot*. Man is only an infinitesimally small particle in the vast expanse of the universe, yet he has a direct line of communication to the loftiest heights of the spiritual realm, reaching far beyond the galaxies. By performing a *mitzvah*, he influences the world of the *Sefirot*, restores the world, communicates with God, and causes great divine abundance to descend.

Rabbi Chaim Finkel

THE HEART

A Good Heart

The *Mishnah* teaches: [Rabban Yochanan ben Zakkai] said to his disciples: Go out and discover which is the proper way to which a man should cling. Rabbi Eliezer said: A good eye. Rabbi Yehoshua said: a good friend. Rabbi Yose said: a good neighbor. Rabbi Shimon said: One who considers the outcome of a deed. Rabbi Elazar [ben Arach] said: a good heart.

Rabban Yochanan ben Zakkai said to them: I prefer the words of Elazar ben Arach, for your words are included in his words (*Avot* 2:13).

Rabbi Samson Raphael Hirsch: The term *lev*, heart, denotes a typically Jewish concept. The heart is the wellspring of every emotion, every aspiration, every endeavor. It is the source of every moral and spiritual impulse, even of all thought and character. If the heart is "good," the entire person will be guided by the rule of the good. He will not be capable of desiring evil. [15]

Wise of Heart

Speak to everyone who is wise of heart, to whom I have granted a spirit of wisdom, and let them make Aaron's vestments (Exodus 28:3).

Rabbi Chaim Shmulevitz: What does the designation "wise of heart" mean? For an answer, let us look at King Solomon, the wisest man who ever lived. How did Solomon attain his extraordinary wisdom? We are told that at the beginning of his reign, God appeared to the young and inexperienced king and said, "What shall I grant you?" To which Solomon replied, "Grant Your servant an understanding heart to judge Your people, to distinguish between good and bad; for who can judge this vast people of Yours?" God said to him, "Because you asked for this—you did not ask for long life, you did not ask for riches, you did not ask for the lives of your enemies, but you asked for discernment in dispensing justice—I now do as you have spoken. I grant you a wise and discerning heart" (1 Kings 3:5–12).

Solomon was granted wisdom because he exhibited an overriding desire for wisdom. He valued wisdom more than riches and long life. He knew that life without the wisdom of Torah is worthless. Thus, "a wise heart" means a craving for wisdom. You must have a supreme yearning for wisdom to be called "wise of heart," and God responds by granting wisdom, as it says, "I have granted wisdom to all those who are wise of heart" (Exodus 31:6).

Sichot Mussar, 5731:10

Broken Vessels

The *Midrash* says: If an ordinary person uses broken vessels he is ashamed, but God prefers broken vessels, for it says, "God is close to the brokenhearted" (Psalm 34:19); "God, You will not despise a broken and crushed heart" (Psalm 51:19).

Vayikra Rabbah 7

A Poor Man's Broken Heart

The Rambam says: It is forbidden to scold a poor man or to raise your voice and yell at him because he is brokenhearted and crushed. Remember, it says, "God will not despise a broken and crushed heart" (Psalm 51:19).

Rambam, *Laws of Gifts to the Poor* 10:5

Diminishing Intellectual Powers

Rabbi Yochanan said: The heart (intellectual power) of the ancients was like the door to the *Ulam*[16] [which was twenty cubits wide], but that of the last generation was like the door of the *Heichal* [which was only ten cubits wide], and ours is like the eye of a fine needle. . . . And we, said Abaye, are like a peg in a wall with regard to *Gemara*. (It was as difficult for them to master their studies as it is to force a peg into a wall [Rashi].) And we, said Rava, are like a finger in wax with regard to logical arguments (A finger cannot penetrate through hard wax. It only depresses it slightly [Rashi].) We, said Rav Ashi, are like a finger in a pit when it comes to forgetfulness. (As easy as it is to insert a finger into the mouth of a well, so easy was it for them to forget what they learned [Rashi].)

Eruvin 53a

It should be understood that all these personalities were towering scholars of unfathomable greatness. For example, Rav Ashi (died in 427 c.e.) was the leading talmudic authority who compiled the Babylonian Talmud. Their statements are a reflection of their modesty and the deep respect they felt toward the sages of the preceding generations. In a broader sense, the comparisons of these sages are indicative of the gradual decrease of *ruach hakodesh* (holy spirit) from the spiritual primacy of Moses to the prophets, *Tannaim*, *Amoraim*, *Geonim*, *Rishonim*, and *Acharonim*. Later authorities will always bow to the greater wisdom of earlier sages. Thus, an *Acharon* (later authority) will not dispute a decision of a *Rishon* (early authority), any more than an *Amora* (teacher of the *Gemara*) will disagree with a ruling by a *Tanna* (teacher of the *Mishnah*). Similarly, the rabbis of our generations, eminent scholars though they may be, treat the rulings of earlier sages as inviolate.

Descendants of Saints or of Apes?

In Judaism it is axiomatic that rabbis and laymen accord the greatest respect to the opinions and writings of earlier authorities. This attitude of veneration of the sages of the past has ensured the preservation of our tradition in its pristine form. The following well-known anecdote provides an eloquent illustration.

On a flight from Israel to New York, Rabbi Yaakov Kamenetzky,[17] the venerable *rosh yeshivah*, found himself seated next to Yerucham Meshel, an Israeli labor leader and an avowed atheist. While the two men were engaged in an animated discussion about certain passages in the Book of Ruth, Reb Yaakov's son and granddaughter periodically came to check on his well-being.

"How wonderful that you have such close contact with your children and grandchildren," marveled the Histadrut official. "I seldom see my children, and the grandchildren— never."

"That should not surprise you," smiled the *rosh yeshivah*. "Permit me to explain. We religious Jews have our own understanding of the passing of generations. We see Jewry's face-to-face encounter with God on Sinai as the spiritual high point of world history. The generations immediately after Sinai viewed their parents with awe: 'They actually heard God speak!' And their children after them looked at their parents with a similar deference: 'Imagine! They actually lived with people who were present at Sinai!' And so it has been throughout the generations, to the point that my children and grandchildren respect me, thinking that my relative closeness to Sinai endows me with a wisdom and spiritual sensitivity that they do not possess.

"But you believe in the Darwinian view of life. You believe that man is in constant evolutionary ascent from the apes. Why should your children or grandchildren respect you? All your age and your generation represent to them is one step closer to the apes!"

The Heart of the World

Amshinover Rebbe: The *gematria* (numeric value) of לב *lev*, heart, is 32 (*lamed* = 30; *bet* = 2). The *gematria* of the Divine Name is 26 (*yud* = 10; *hei* = 5; *vav* = 6; *hei* = 5). The multiplication of 32 x 26 yields 832. Interestingly, the *gematria* of ארץ ישראל *Eretz Yisrael* also equals 832 (1 + 200 + 90 + 10 + 300 + 200 + 1 + 30 = 832). This equation tells us that just as the heart is the center of the body, so is *Eretz Yisrael* the center of the world. Pursuing this line of thought, we may say that Jerusalem is the heart of *Eretz Yisrael*, as it says, "Speak to the *heart* of Jerusalem" (Isaiah 40:2). Furthermore, the *Bet Hamikdash* is the heart of Jerusalem, and the Holy of Holies, the heart of the Bet Hamikdash. That is why, when King Solomon completed the building of the *Bet Hamikdash*, God appeared to him and said, "My *heart* shall forever be there" (1 Kings 9:3). Thus we may say that "My heart" (God's heart) is 26 x 32 = 832 (*Hashem* = 26, *lev* = 32), which "shall forever be there," in *Eretz Yisrael* = 832.

Two Donations

A poor man came to Rabbi Bunam of Pshis'cha to beg for alms. The Rebbe gave him a respectable donation, which the poor man gratefully accepted. As he turned to leave, the Rebbe called him back and gave him more money. Surprised and curious, the poor man asked the Rebbe for his reason.

"The first *nedavah* (donation)," replied the Rebbe, "was because, having a Jewish heart, I took pity on you. The second was because I wanted to fulfill the *mitzvah* of giving *tzedakah*."

Siach Sarfei Kodesh 2:279

Rabbi Bunam of Pshis'cha expressed a fundamental Jewish idea. The laws of the Torah distinguish us from every other nation. The value systems of other nations stem from noble sentiments of the heart such as compassion, mercy, and love. But an ethic that is based on sentiment is transitory and unstable. When the sentiment has passed, the ethical impulse evaporates. Torah ethics are rooted in law and justice. To a Jew, charity is *tzedakah*, which means justice. We give charity, not because we are motivated by a momentary, fleeting emotion of pity and compassion, but because it is *tzedakah*, a divinely ordained law of justice.

The Three Sections of the Body

Rabbi Shimon Shalom of Amshinov: The *Gemara* in *Chagigah* 16a states, "Man has six main functions. Three of these he has in common with the angels: his understanding, his power of speech, and his erect posture. Three other functions he shares with the animals: his eating and drinking; his excretion; and his procreation."

In all Creation, man is the only creature that thinks, speaks, and walks erect. With his upright posture he points upward toward heaven, the source of his existence.

The human body that aims upward is a combination of three segments: an upper, a lower, and an intermediate section. The upper section is the head, the seat of his spiritual faculties, whereas the lower portion contains his animalistic organs, which perform his digestive and excretory functions, as it says, "[T]he spirit of man is the one that ascends on high, while the spirit of the beast is the one that descends down to the earth" (Ecclesiastes 3:21). Situated between the upper and lower parts is the heart, which radiates warmth. It is surrounded by the lungs that cool it, and together they keep the temperature of the body in balance.

On a spiritual level we may say that the head is the seat of the intellect, wisdom, and knowledge of God. "The spirit of the beast" is situated in the lower part. The moderator between the two extremes is the heart, which gives life to both parts.

Mashmia Shalom, p. 160

The Heart and the Lungs

Rabbi Shimon Shalom of Amshinov: The central organs of the human body are the heart and the lungs, in Hebrew לב *lev* (heart) and ריאה *rei'ah* (lungs). The numeric value of לב *lev* is 32 (*lamed* = 30; *bet* = 2), that of ריאה *rei'ah* is 216 (*reish* = 200; *yud* = 10; *alef* = 1; *heiu* = 5). Adding *lev* (32) and *rei'ah* (216) yields 248, which is precisely the number of limbs in the body. The equation thus confirms that the combination of the heart and the lungs (248) gives vitality and energy to the 248 organs of the body.

On a deeper level, the heart and the lungs represent two profound concepts. The heart is the source of burning love of God, as it says, "burning with a fire that reached the heart of heaven" (Deuteronomy 4:11). It is the seat of the overwhelming desire of the soul to be united with its root, the *En Sof*, the Infinite. If this desire remained unchecked, the soul would leave the body to be reunited with its Maker. The lungs, which hover over the heart, perform the function of cooling the blazing ardor of the heart and preventing the soul from leaving the body. Now we can rearrange the letters ריאה *rei'ah*, to form יראה *yir'ah*, which means fear or awe. Indeed, it is the *yir'at.Hashem*, awe of God, embodied by the lungs, that restrains the unbridled *ahavat Hashem*, love of God, personified by the heart.

Mashmia Shalom, p. 156

The above commentary touches on a profound kabbalistic concept, the principle of *ratzoh vashov*, "run and return," of the "to and fro," the "up and back" that pervades all of Creation as it is described in the prophecy of Ezekiel 1:14. This principle of fluctuation dominates man's existence and is evident in the pulse of his heartbeat and the rhythm of the breath in his lungs. It is apparent in the twin emotions of *ahavat Hashem* and *yirat Hashem*, the love and awe of God. And it comes to the fore in man's desire to free himself from the bonds of physicality and unite with the Creator and the opposing urge to remain in this world and partake of life.

The Heart as a Metaphor

Rambam (Maimonides): In Scripture, of all the inner parts of the human body only the heart is figuratively applied to God. It denotes intellect. The shoulder is never used as a figure in reference to God, because it is known as a mere instrument of transport, and it comes into close contact with the thing it carries. For an even greater reason, the organs of nutrition are never attributed to God; they are immediately recognized as signs of imperfection. . . . But why are the senses of hearing, sight, and smell applied to God, but not those of taste and touch? We find in the Scriptures, "God saw" (Genesis 6:5); "God heard" (Numbers 11:1); "God smelled" (Genesis 8:21); but we do not come across the expressions "God tasted," "God touched." I think the reason for this is that God does not come into contact with a body in the same way one body comes into contact with another, since He cannot even be seen by the eye. While the senses of taste and touch act only when in close contact with the object, the senses of sight, hearing, and smell perceive even distant objects. . . .

In the same way, you can easily see that imagination has greater shortcomings than thinking and reasoning. Therefore, imagination (*ra'ayon*) is never used as a figure of speech in speaking of God, whereas thought and reason are figuratively ascribed to Him. For example, "The thoughts that God thought" (Jeremiah 49:20); "By his understanding He stretches out the skies" (Jeremiah 49:12).

Moreh Nevuchim, Guide for the Perplexed I:46, 47

Your Heart Is an Altar

The Ba'al Shem Tov said: It is written, "There shall be a constant fire burning on the altar, not to go out" (Leviticus 6:6). Your heart is the altar. In whatever you are doing let a spark of the holy fire remain inside you, so that you can fan it into a flame.

Sefer Ba'al Shem Tov

What Is Heart-Service?

If you are careful to obey My commandments, which I am prescribing to you today, and if you love God your Lord and serve Him with all your heart and soul, [then God made this promise].

Deuteronomy 11:13

The *Gemara* asks: It says, "to serve Him with all your heart." What is heart-service? Service of the heart is prayer.

Ta'anit 2a

With Both Your Inclinations

Love God your Lord with all your heart, with all your soul, and with all your might. (Deuteronomy 6:3).

The rabbis of the *Gemara* are puzzled by the word *levavecha*, "your heart," which is written with a double *bet*; why not the more common *libecha*, with one *bet*? The double *bet* of *levavecha* tells you to love God "with both your inclinations, with the good inclination and with the evil inclination" (*Berachot* 57a).

The Torah does not demand that we crush our natural instincts, but rather that we subdue them and make them instruments in the service of God. The *yetzer hara*, the allure of evil, says Rabbi Samson Raphael Hirsch, is as much a gift of God as the *yetzer tov*, our attraction to goodness. Our nobility and moral worth stem from the allure that vice holds for us. Without it we would not be human beings, there would be no morality and no virtue. The good that we did would not be a morally free-willed human act. With the absence of the *yetzer hara*, our whole moral worth would collapse.

A Double Lamed

The Hebrew word for heart is לב *lev*, spelled *lamed*, *bet*. The sages of Kabbalah note that since numerically *bet* equals two, the word *lev* can be read as "*lamed* times two" or "two *lamed*s." The shape of the ל *lamed* is a *kaf* with a *vav* on its roof. Amazingly, if you place two *lamed*s face-to-face, like this כל, you obtain a shape of a human heart, whereby the two *vav*s represent the two coronary arteries. Thus we can say that *lev* is "two *lamed*s" in the most literal sense. But there is more. The letter *lamed* also means "to teach." Accordingly, the two *lamed*s of *lev* (heart) symbolize the teaching contained in the two Tablets of the Covenant—the Ten Commandments—which is the heart of the entire Torah.[18]

The Coronary Arteries

Kabbalah teaches that the divine blessings pour down on our world in an abundant flow of goodness. This flow descends through the Ten *Sefirot* that are connected by channels that are disrupted or repaired through human actions. Transgression of God's will clogs the channels, whereas the performance of *mitzvot* restores the flow of divine plenty. The task of the Jew is to restore the world, in a process called *tikkun*, by living according to the laws of the Torah. Every *mitzvah* a Jew performs has enormous cosmic consequences, for a good deed helps to clear the blocked channels and allows the current of God's beneficence to flow freely to this world.

A striking analogy is a human heart whose coronary arteries have become clogged by deposits of cholesterol. The accumulation of this substance impedes the vital flow of blood to the heart and the brain and may lead to heart attacks, strokes, and other diseases of the blood vessels. However, strict adherence to a proper diet will dissolve the obstructions, permit the blood to resume its normal flow, and restore the heart to good health. Analogously, adherence to Torah and *mitzvot* will remove all obstacles and restore the cascading stream of divine bounty.

6

Organs of Digestion

THE LIVER

Talmudic Sayings about the Liver

The liver is the main source of the blood (*Bechorot* 55a).
The liver is the seat of anger (*Berachot* 61b).
If a drop of gall falls into the liver, the anger is placated (*Berachot* 61b).

An Arrow Pierced His Liver

In Proverbs we read an allegory about a young man who is enticed by a harlot. "Thoughtlessly he follows her, like an ox going to the slaughter . . . until the arrow pierces his liver. He is like a bird rushing into a trap, not knowing his life is at stake" (Proverbs 7:23).

Metzudat David: For the momentary pleasure of eating a few seeds the bird enters the trap, not realizing that it will lose its life. Similarly, the young man loses his life in the World to Come for a few fleeting moments of sensual enjoyment.

The Unifying Force of the Liver

Kabbalah teaches that the unity of the worlds is reflected in the function of the liver. Of the three major organs of the body—the brain, the heart, and the liver—the liver controls the natural processes of life. Thus, it unifies the body, and in that capacity symbolizes the unity of God.

It is interesting to note that the numeric value of כבד *kaved*, liver, amounts to 26 (*kaf* = 20; *bet* = 2; *dalet* = 4), which is also the value of the four-letter Divine Name (*Yud* = 10; *hei* = 5; *vav* = 6; *hei* = 5). In other words, the unifying function of the liver is indicative of the oneness of God.

Liver, Heart, and Brain

[The mixed multitude among the Israelites demanded meat to eat, saying,] But now our spirits are dried up, with nothing but the manna before our eyes.

Numbers 11:6

Rabbi Yehudah of Stutchin: "But now our spirits are dried up, with nothing but the manna before our eyes." The kabbalists teach that man has three major organs that impart vitality to all parts of the body: the liver, the heart, and the brain. These organs are the seats of the three levels of the soul: *nefesh*, the animalistic life force, rests in the liver; *ruach*, the spirit, dwells in the heart; and *neshamah*, the divine soul, is centered in the brain. Thus, the brain is the seat of spirituality, godliness, and the *yetzer tov* (the good inclination.) Conversely, the liver is the seat of the *yetzer hara* (the evil inclination) and the carnal instincts. The heart, midway between the brain and the liver, houses the *ruach* (spirit). It is the moderator between the brain and the liver, between the *yetzer tov* and the *yetzer hara*.

After the Israelites left Egypt, where their spirituality

was suppressed, they were given the manna—the heavenly food—to cleanse them of the defilement and lusts of Egypt. However, the mixed multitude had physical cravings stemming from their *nefesh*, which is seated in the liver. That is why they said *nafsheinu yeveisha*, "our *nefesh*, our carnal instinct, is dried up with nothing but the manna—this spiritual food that appeals only to the *neshamah* in the brain—before our eyes."[1]

The Liver, Symbol of the Serpent

The above-mentioned commentary to the effect that the liver is the seat of man's *yetzer hara*, his carnal instinct, helps us understand a kabbalistic insight according to which Adam corresponds to the brain, Eve parallels the heart, and the serpent, the personification of the *yetzer hara*, is equated with the liver.

In this connection it is noteworthy that, when you count the letters of the Torah, you find that the exact center of the Torah is the *vav* of the word גחון *gachon* (belly) in the verse, "Thus, you may not eat any creature that crawls on its belly" (Leviticus 11:42). Rashi explains that "the creature that crawls on his belly" refers to a snake. This presents the paradox that the middle letter, the focal point of the entire Torah, is part of a word that denotes the lowest organ of the lowliest and most despicable creature, the serpent. More astonishing yet, this middle letter of the Torah is a *vav*, one of the letters of the four-letter Name of God. How can God's name be associated with the serpent? There is a lesson in this. The pivotal vav of *gachon* (the belly of the snake) teaches us that absolute evil does not exist but that a spark of holiness resides even in the *yetzer hara*. Without an evil impulse, man would have no freedom of choice, he could not earn a reward for doing good, and morality would be meaningless. If a person is virtuous and subdues his *yetzer hara*, his evil impulse will have helped him to attain the ultimate good.

The Spleen

The Talmud teaches: If the spleen is gone, the animal is *kosher*, but if the spleen was pierced, the animal is *trefah*.

Chullin 42b

On a spiritual level, this *halachah* teaches us a moral lesson. A person can live a normal life without a spleen, but if his spleen is diseased it will endanger his entire body. Thus, it is better to remove a failing spleen before the disease spreads. Similarly, it is better to expel a bad student before he influences the entire class. Simply put, one rotten apple will spoil the bunch.

Rabbi Issur Furst,
dean of Yeshivah Mesivta of Montreal

The Gall

God will take all the sickness from you (Deuteronomy 7:15).
Rabbi Eleazar said: This refers to the diseases of the gall, because diseases of the gall make the entire body sick. In fact, eighty-three illnesses are caused by the gall, and all of them are neutralized by eating a breakfast consisting of bread with salt and drinking a jugful of water.

Bava Metzia 107b

THE STOMACH; NUTRITION; DIGESTION

Don't Talk While Eating

Rabbi Yochanan said: You should not speak while you are eating, because the windpipe might get in front of the foodpipe, and the speaker might choke. [When a person uses his voice, the cover on the windpipe opens, and food particles may lodge in it, causing the person to choke (Rashi).]

Ta'anit 5b

The Miracle of Saliva

The *Midrash* says: Look how many miracles the Holy One, Blessed be He, performs for us, and we don't even realize it. If not for God's miracles, when you eat bread, the rough crumbs would wear away and erode your digestive organs. But the Almighty built a wellspring of mucus in your throat [and saliva in your mouth], which make the bread go down smoothly.

Shemot Rabbah 24:1

An Early Breakfast

Have an early breakfast in the summer because of the heat, and in the winter because of the cold. People say that sixty men may pursue a man who has meals early in the morning and will not overtake him.

Bava Metzia 92b

Bread for Breakfast

The *Gemara* says: Thirteen things were said about eating bread for breakfast: It is an antidote against heat and cold, winds and demons; it instills wisdom into the simple, causes you to triumph in a lawsuit,[2] enables you to study and teach the Torah, to have your words heeded, and retain what you learned. He who has bread in the morning does not perspire, lives with his wife, and does not lust after other women; and it kills worms in one's intestines. Some say it also banishes envy and induces love.[3]

Bava Metzia 107b

Overindulgence Leads to Sin

The *Gemara* gives a vivid illustration of the detrimental effects of pampering and overindulging.

Rabbi Chiya said: A man had a son; he bathed him, anointed him, gave him plenty to eat and drink, hung a purse around his neck and set him down in front of the door of a house of prostitution. How could the boy help sinning?

Rabbi Acha said: This bears out the popular saying, "A full stomach is a bad thing," as it says, "When they grazed they were satisfied; when they were satisfied they grew haughty; and so they forgot Me" (Hosea 13:6).

Berachot 32a

Selected Aphorisms about Eating

The belly carries the legs (*Bereishit Rabbah* 70). If a person's stomach is full, he feels robust and steps lively.

A donkey steps according to the barley it eats (*Shabbat* 51b).

Eat in moderation. More people die at the cooking pot than are victims of starvation (*Shabbat* 33a).

In a meal that you enjoy indulge not too freely (*Gittin* 70a).

If someone says, "With what shall I eat my bread?" take the bread away from him too (*Sanhedrin* 100b).

Drawing out a meal prolongs a man's days and years (*Berachot* 54b). [If you draw out your meal, poor people will have an opportunity to come and join your table. As a reward, you will be granted long life (Rashi).]

At the time when the *Bet Hamikdash* stood, the altar used to make atonement for a person; now a person's table makes atonement for him [through the hospitality he shows to poor guests] (*Chagigah* 27a).

Bread and wine are the main courses of the meal. All other dishes are secondary (*Zohar, Balak* 189b).

If you want to invite twenty guests, prepare a meal for twenty-five. If you want to invite twenty-five guests, prepare for thirty (*Esther Rabbah* 2).

You cannot compare a man who has bread in his basket to one whose basket is empty (*Yoma* 18b). [The latter frets about where his next meal is coming from, and the worry does not let him enjoy his present meal.]

Chew well with your teeth, and you will find it in your steps [If you thoroughly chew your food, you will feel buoyant and your step will be bouncy.] (*Shabbat* 152a).

Two Sick Men

On the subject of forbidden foods, the *Midrash* relates the following fitting allegory:

There once was a doctor who had two patients, one of whom was going to live, whereas the other was going to die. To the one who was going to live he prescribed a strict regimen, telling him what foods to eat and what foods to avoid. To the incurable patient he said, "Go ahead, eat anything you like."

So it is with the nations of the world who will not partake of the life of the world to come. To them God said, "Every creature that lives shall be yours to eat; like the green grasses, I give you all these" (Genesis 9:3). But to Israel, who are destined to live, He said, "Of all the animals in the world, these are the ones that you may eat" (Leviticus 11:2).

Vayikra Rabbah 13

Forbidden Foods Are Harmful to the Soul

Rabbi Simchah Zissel Ziv of Kelm, one of the great masters of the *Mussar* movement, said: The gentiles suffer no ill effects and do not ruin their health in the least by eating nonkosher meat. The reason that Jews are harmed by such food is that they have a refined and saintly nature. Their spiritual makeup is pure and unclouded. A holy and unblemished soul is repelled by anything loathsome.[4]

Two Donkeys and a Pig

The Midrash tells a parable: A farmer had two donkeys and a pig. To the donkeys he gave measured amounts of food; the pig he fattened up, giving it all it could eat.

Said the younger donkey to the older one: It's not fair! The pig that does not do any work gets all it wants!

Replied the older donkey: Just wait a while. Soon you will see the pig come to a bitter end. The farmer is stuffing it only to bring about its downfall.

Esther Rabbah 7

The Way of the Torah

This is the way of the Torah: Eat bread with salt, drink water in a small measure, sleep on the ground, live a life of deprivation—but toil in the Torah! If you do this, "You are praiseworthy, and all is well with you" (Psalm 128:2). "You are praiseworthy" in this world; "and all is well with you"— in the world to come.

Avot 6:4

The Bread and the Rod

Rabbi Shimon bar Yocha'i said: The bread and the rod came down from heaven tied together. Said the Almighty: If you engross yourselves in the Torah, I am giving you bread to eat. If you don't, here is the rod to punish you.

Sifrei, Eikev 40

Serving God by Eating

The Ba'al Shem Tov said: "When you eat and enjoy the taste and the sweetness of the food, remember that it is God who put taste and sweetness into the food. Then you will truly be serving Him by your eating."

Sefer Ba'al Shem Tov

Sound Advice

Rabbah bar Bar Chanah told the following pun: Eat an onion (*batzeil*) and dwell in the protection (*betzeil*) [of your house]. [Do not splurge on food, then you won't have to sell your house (Rashbam[5]).] Do not eat geese and chicken lest you develop a craving for them [and you will want to eat them all the time (Rashi)]. Reduce your intake of food and drink, then you will be able to afford to build an extension to your house.

Pesachim 114a

The Manna

The taste of the manna varied according to the tastes of the people who ate it. To young men it tasted like bread, to the aged it tasted like honey wafers. To babies it tasted like the milk from their mother's breast, and to the sick it was like fine flour mixed with honey (*Shemot Rabbah* 5:9).

Nourished by Osmosis

The manna was absorbed directly into the 248 limbs; [it did not pass through the digestive tract (Rashi)] (*Sifrei, Beha'alotecha*).

Not like a Balloon

Rabbi Tanchum said: If you puncture a balloon all the air escapes. Surprisingly, man is full of cavities and openings, yet his spirit does not escape. Who made man like this? "For You are great and perform wonders; You alone are God" (Psalm 86:10).

Bereishit Rabbah 1

Eat in Moderation

Rabbi Pinchas of Koretz said: Eating in moderation tends to lengthen life. We find among animals and reptiles that those who eat the least live the longest.

Nofet Tzufim

The Cure for Rabbi Tzadok's Stomach

The *Gemara* relates that Rabbi Tzadok fasted for forty years in order that Jerusalem should not be destroyed. He was so gaunt that when he would eat something between his fasts, the food he swallowed could be seen descending into his stomach. When he ended his fast, he sucked the juice from dried figs and discarded the figs.

The *Gemara* asks: How did the physicians heal Rabbi Tzadok? On the first day they gave him water in which bran had been soaked; the next day thay gave him water with coarse bran and flour. The next day they gave him water with flour. They continued the treatment until his stomach slowly expanded.

Gittin 56b

A Craving for Manna

[God] made life difficult for you [in the desert], letting you go hungry, and then He fed you the manna that neither you nor your ancestors had ever experienced. This was to teach you that it is not by bread alone that man lives but by all that comes out of God's mouth (Deuteronomy 8:3).

Rabbi Mendel of Rymanov: "[God] made life difficult for you, letting you go hungry." This paragraph enumerates all the blessings God showered on the Israelites during their forty-year sojourn in the wilderness. A question arises: How can letting them go hungry be considered a blessing? Ordinarily, when a person craves a certain food, once he receives that food his hunger is stilled, even before he actually tastes it. In spiritual matters the opposite is true. The more your yearning for knowledge is satisfied, the thirstier you are for more knowledge. The more you learn, the more eager you are to increase your wisdom. That was the blessing inherent in the manna. Although everyone received an abundant quantity of manna each day, due to its spiritual quality, they were always hungry for more and did not grow tired of it.[6]

Not by Bread Alone

It is not by bread alone that man lives but by all that comes out of God's mouth (Deuteronomy 8:3).

The Arizal: How are we to understand that the soul, which is purely spiritual, is nourished by food that is a material substance? All Creation exists only by dint of God's words that He uttered when He brought the world into being. The energy of the divine utterances is hidden inside the food. It is this spark of divine power in the food that sustains the soul. When a Jew takes a fruit in hand and says the *berachah*, "Blessed are You, God, our Lord, King of the Universe, who creates the fruit of the tree," the spiritual potency of God's utterance that is inherent in the fruit is awakened. This spiritual energy is the food for the soul.

Our verse hints at this. "Man does not live by bread alone"—he does not live by the tangible, physical bread—"but by all that comes out of God's mouth"—he lives by virtue of God's utterances at the time of Creation that are the hidden life force inside the bread. This spiritual power is the nourishment for the soul.[7]

Treat Bread with Respect

Our Rabbis taught: Four things have been said in reference to bread: Raw meat should not be placed on bread [since the bread would become unappetizing]; a full cup should not be passed along over bread [for fear some should spill on the bread and make it unappealing]; bread may not be thrown [for the act of throwing is a degrading act]; and you should not use bread to prop up a plate.

Berachot 50b

Food and Drink

The law of the Torah requires you to eat more than you drink. (The burnt offering of Rosh Chodesh, which was entirely consumed on the altar, consisted of three *esronim* of flour, and one-half *hin* of wine (Numbers 28:12, 14). Thus, the amount of solid foodstuff (the bull and the flour) easily exceeded the amount of liquid (the wine) (Rashi) (*Megillah* 12a).

If you let your food float in water, you will be protected from intestinal disorders. How much water should you drink? Rav Chisda said: A cupful per loaf of bread (*Berachot* 40b).

Overdraw Your Account

The *Gemara* recommends: On your food and drink you should spend less than your income allows. On your clothes you should spend as much as you can afford [so that you will be dressed according to your status and will not be humiliated (Rashi)]. However, on the support of your wife and children you should spend more than you have because they depend on you, and you can depend on the Almighty [to provide for your needs].

Chullin 84b

He Can't Stand a Stomachache

Rav said: "I can tolerate any illness, but not a stomachache; any pain, but not heartache; any ache, but not a headache; any evil, but not an evil wife" (*Shabbat* 11a).

Rav's statement about an evil wife may have been prompted by personal experience. We are told that his wife used to torment him: "When he asked her to prepare a dish of lentils, out of spite, she prepared beans. When he asked for beans, she cooked lentils" (*Yevamot* 63a).

Like a Pig's Stomach

The *Gemara* teaches: A pig's stomach resembles that of a human.

(Taanit 21b)

This statement may be interpreted to mean that a man whose soul is suppressed, and whose only interest is the pursuit of pleasure, is no more than an animal. Like a pig, such a person's entire existence revolves around filling his stomach and gratifying his hunger. Hence it may be said that the stomachs of man and pig resemble each other. However, with the help of the Torah, a Jew has the ability to subdue his stomach-oriented physical nature and attain a purity of soul that ranks him higher than the angels.

A Pig Has No Neck

Expanding on this theme, Kabbalah teaches that before Creation, God's Presence filled all existence. In order to bring the universe into being, God made "room" for the world by withdrawing into Himself in a process called *tzimtzum*, stricture. We find a parallel to this in man, as it is written, "In my flesh I see God" (Job 19:26). The head represents the spirit of God, the body is congruent with the universe, and the narrowing of the neck corresponds to *tzimtzum*, the process of divine contraction that preceded Creation. A pig has no neck; its massive body virtually swallows up its small head; its physicality has usurped its spirituality. The absence of the pig's neck symbolizes the total mastery of body over spirit. That is why a pig is the epitome of the forbidden food, the antithesis of holiness (Rabbi Chaim Finkel commenting on *Maalot Hatorah*).

When Jews Eat and Drink

Rava said: When Jews eat and drink, they begin discussing Torah insights and say words of praise to God. But when idolators eat and drink, they talk only about only indecent things.

Megillah 12a

The Angels Are Not Hungry

Rabbi Leib Chasman, one of the great teachers of the *Mussar* movement, once was invited to the Friday-night meal at the home of the saintly Chafetz Chaim[8] in Radin. Upon returning home from the Friday night service, Rabbi Leib noted with surprise that the Chafetz Chaim did not recite the customary *Shalom Aleichem*, the hymn welcoming the *Shabbat* angels. Instead, he immediately recited the *Kiddush*, whereupon the fish course was served. Only after this course did the Chafetz Chaim intone the *Shalom Aleichem*. Rabbi Leib was unable to contain his curiosity.

"Why is it," he asked, "that you deviated from the traditional order?"

"I was sure you were hungry," the Chafetz Chaim replied with a twinkle in his eye, "so I wanted you to have a bite to eat first. The angels are not hungry; they can wait."

Hameorot Hagedolim

You Eat for Yourself

You will serve God your Lord, and He will bless your bread and your water. I will banish sickness from among you (Exodus 23:25).

The Kotzker Rebbe[9] asks: *Va'avdetem*, "You will serve," is written in the plural, in contrast to *lachmecha*, "your bread," which is written in the singular. What could be the reason for this anomaly?

Prayer, the service of God, even if it is performed by an

individual, is joined in heaven with the prayers of many others into a service of a multitude. Thus, the prayer of one person becomes the prayer of many and has the same powerful effect.

However, when it comes to eating, even if many people are having a meal at the same table, each person eats only for himself.[10]

There's Always Room for Dessert

Abbaye said: There are two popular sayings: "A poor man does not know when he is hungry" [an ignorant person does not know his own ignorance], and "You can always find room in your stomach for sweet things" [the wisdom of the Torah is infinite; you can always discover new and original insights].

Megillah 7b

Abundance for the Living

We read in the Talmud: In the days of Rabbi Shmuel bar Nachman the land was stricken with a famine and an epidemic.

The people asked, "What shall we do? We cannot pray for mercy for two things at the same time. So let's pray for relief from the epidemic and let's suffer the famine."

"On the contrary," said Rabbi Shmuel bar Nachman. "Let's pray for relief from the famine. For when the Merciful One sends abundance, He sends it for the living, [and He will keep us alive]."

Ta'anit 8b

KIDNEYS

Scriptures about the Kidneys

I shall rejoice with all my kidneys when your lips speak the right things (Proverbs 23:16).

His bowmen surrounded me; He pierced my kidneys; He showed no mercy; He spilled my bile onto the ground (Job 16:13).

I myself, not another, would behold Him; would see with my own eyes: my kidneys pine within me (Job 19:27).

Who put wisdom in the kidneys? Who gave understanding to the mind? (Job 38:36).

O God of Hosts, O just Judge, who tests the kidneys and the heart. Let me see Your retribution upon them, for I lay my case before You (Jeremiah 11:20).

Kidneys, Advisors to the Heart

Our Rabbis taught: The kidneys advise, the heart understands, the tongue shapes the words, the mouth articulates, the gullet takes in and lets out all kinds of food, the windpipe produces the voice, the lungs absorb all kinds of liquids, the liver is the seat of anger, the gall lets drops fall into it and soothes the anger, the spleen produces laughter, the large intestine grinds the food, the stomach brings sleep, and the nose awakens.

Berachot 61a, b

Abraham's Two Kidneys

Rabbi Shimon said: Abraham's father did not teach him to believe in God, neither did he have a teacher. How then did he learn the Torah? The Holy One, Blessed be He, provided him with two kidneys that played the role of teachers. They gushed forth and taught him Torah and wisdom. [He recognized the truth about God and the Torah within himself.]

Bereishit Rabbah 61:1

7

The Spinal Column, the Ribs, and the Skin

A BONE CALLED *LUZ*

The *Midrash* identifies a bone, called *luz*, that is indestructible. It is a vertebra at the end of the spinal column that resembles an almond.

Relates the *Midrash*: The Roman emperor Hadrian once asked Rabbi Yehoshua ben Chananiah, "From which part of the body will God make man sprout forth when the dead are revived?"

He replied, "From the *luz* bone of the spinal column."

"What evidence do you have," asked Hadrian, "that this bone does not disintegrate like all other bones?"

As proof, Rabbi Yehoshua placed a *luz* in water, and it did not dissolve; he let it pass through millstones, but it was not ground; he put it in a fire, but it was not incinerated; he placed it on an anvil and struck it with a hammer; the anvil was flattened out and the hammer split, but the *luz* remained undamaged.

Vayikra Rabbah 18:1

A City Where Death Has No Hold

The Talmud mentions a city named Luz against which "Sennacherib marched without disturbing it, against which Nebuchadnezzar marched without destroying it, and even the Angel of Death has no permission to pass through it. When the old men there become tired of life they go outside the wall and die."

Sotah 46b

The Modim *Prayer and the Spine*

The Talmud states: If a person does not bow when reciting the *Modim* prayer, his spine will turn into a snake at the end of seven years (*Bava Kamma* 16a).

This statement is an allegory and should not be taken literally. The underlying idea is that *Modim* is the *berachah* in the *Shemoneh Esrei* (*Amidah*) in which we express our thanks to God for the many good things He has done for us. When we stand erect, our proud bearing demonstrates our independence and self-esteem. By bowing, we show that we surrender to God's will and that we recognize that He is the Source of our lives.

When someone refuses to bend to the will of God, his spine becomes like the snake in the Garden of Eden. That snake symbolizes the evil tendency and the arrogance that made Adam disobey God's command. By his unwillingness to bow at *Modim*, a person exhibits the arrogance and ingratitude that are the mark of the serpent. The *Gemara* is saying that after seven years, this haughty attitude will become fully ingrained in his character; the spine that refuses to bow will turn into a snake.

We find an amazing correlation between *Modim* and the spinal column. *Modim* is the eighteenth *berachah* in the *Shemoneh Esrei*, and the spinal column consists of eighteen vertebrae.[1] Thus, we thank God and subjugate our will to Him in the eighteenth *berachah* by bowing to Him with the eighteen vertebrae of our spine.

BOWING WHILE STANDING ERECT

Said Rabbi Baruch of Medzhibozh: We say in the *Nishmat* prayer: "Every erect spine shall prostrate itself before You." You must bow to God even while you are standing erect. Bowing is not only a physical action; it must also be done in the heart and mind. [2]

THE LETTER *DALET*

The shape of the letter *dalet* is that of a man whose spine is bent over, a symbol of total submission. The root of the word *dalet* is *dal*, "a poor man," the pauper who meekly bows to his benefactor.

THE BROKEN WELL

Before the silver cord snaps, and the golden bowl is shattered, and the pitcher is broken at the fountain, and the wheel is smashed at the pit. And the dust returns to the ground as it was, and the spirit returns to God who bestowed it (Ecclesiastes 12:6,7).

This metaphor compares the infirmities of old age to the breakdown in the machinery of a well. The silver cord (the spine) snaps, the golden bowl (the skull) is shattered, the pitcher (the stomach) breaks, and the wheel (the body) is smashed.

The dust refers to the human body, which was formed of dust. It returns to the earth from which it came, and the spirit (the soul) returns to its Maker.

Rashi, Ibn Ezra

THE REVIVAL OF THE DRY BONES

The Rabbis of the *Midrash* explain: The development of an embryo begins with the skin and the flesh and ends with formation of the sinews and the bones. Conversely, when the dead will be revived, their resuscitation will begin with the regeneration of the sinews and the bones and conclude with the skin and the flesh. That was the order in which the dry bones in Ezekiel's vision were brought to life, as it says, "Suddenly there was a sound of rattling, and the bones came together, bone to matching bone. I looked, and there were sinews on them, and flesh had grown, and skin had formed over them" (Ezekiel 37:7, 8).

To what can the revival of the dry bones of Ezekiel be compared? To a man who visits a bathhouse and gets undressed. The clothes he takes off first are the ones he puts on last.

Bereishit Rabbah 14

THE NECK

Rabbi Simchah Bunam of Pshis'cha said: The neck connects the head, the seat of man's spirituality, to the body, the physical part of man. It is for this reason that the Jewish people, the people of the Torah, are called "the neck of the world," for the Torah connects God with all the worlds, even the lowliest ones.

Ramatayim Tzofim, Eliahu Rabbah 8

Esau's Kiss

"[When Jacob met his brother Esau after their long separation], Esau ran to meet him. He hugged Jacob and, throwing himself on his shoulders, kissed him. They both wept" (Genesis 33:4).

Sefat Emet:[3] "Esau hugged Jacob . . . and kissed him." According to the *Midrash*,[4] Esau tried to bite his brother's neck, but Jacob's neck turned to marble.

A question arises: How can the *Midrash* say that Esau wanted to bite Jacob, when the Torah expressly states that he kissed him? Esau's kiss is tantamount to a deadly bite. Esau's embrace, meaning the spirit of assimilation, represents a mortal menace to the existence of the Jewish people.

Moses' Neck Turned to Marble

When Pharaoh heard [that Moses had slain the Egyptian who had killed one of the Hebrews], he tried to put Moses to death (Exodus 2:15).

The *Midrash* comments: Pharaoh ordered the deadliest sword in all Egypt to be brought to the palace. Ten times the executioner swung the sword trying to sever Moses' head, but his neck turned into a marble column, and the sword did him no harm.

Shemot Rabbah 1

No Scarves

The Kotzker Rebbe insisted that his *chasidim* not wear scarves or ties around their neck while praying. Said he, "So that there be no separation between the mind and the heart."

Siach Sarfei Kodesh

Never Give Up Hope

Even if a sharp sword is at a man's neck, he should not restrain himself from seeking mercy (*Berachot* 10a).

A Stiff-Necked People

[Moses] said, "If I have gained Your favor, O God, let my Lord go among us, because this is a stiff-necked people. Forgive us our sins and errors, and make us Your own" (Exodus 34:9).

Rabbi Meir of Premyshlan: "Because this is a stiff-necked people." Moses contended that the Jewish people are the most stubborn of all nations. They will tenaciously cling to God and His Torah in spite of all persecutions. They will remain unyieldingly faithful to the *mitzvot* and sacrifice their lives rather than submit to forced conversion. Indeed, through their innate stiff-necked quality they have survived the tortures of the Inquisition and withstood pogroms, oppression, and tyranny. Moses said to God, "Make us Your own—our stiff-necked nature ensures that we will remain faithful to you forever."

Divrei Meir

Eighteen Vertebrae

The *Gemara* asks: To what do the eighteen *berachot* in the *Shemoneh Esrei* (*Amidah*) correspond? Rabbi Joseph said: To the eighteen vertebrae in the spinal column.

Berachot 28b

Praying with All His Bones

King David said, "All my bones shall say, 'God, who is like You?'" (Psalm 35:10). When a Jew prays, he sways and shakes because all the limbs of his body are joining him in singing God's praises.

Said the Ba'al Shem Tov: When you see a drowning man

thrashing about, flailing his arms trying to save himself from the churning river, you certainly will not laugh at his bizarre motions. Likewise, when you see someone moving his body and gesticulating wildly while he is praying, don't ridicule him. He is trying to save himself from drowning in the distraction that is threatening his prayerful concentration.

Sefer Ba'al Shem Tov, chapter on prayer

The Rot of the Bones

The Talmud says: It is written, "Envy is rot to the bones" (Proverbs 14:30). The bones of a person who has envy in his heart will rot, but the bones of a person whose heart is free of envy will not rot.

Shabbat 152a

Jacob's Dislocated Hip Joint

[Before his encounter with Esau, a stranger appeared and wrestled with Jacob.] When the stranger saw that he could not defeat him, he touched the upper joint of Jacob's thigh. Jacob's thigh became dislocated as he wrestled with the stranger (Genesis 32:26).

According to the *Midrash* (Bereishit Rabbah 77), the stranger was the guardian angel of Esau and the incarnation of evil. Rabbeinu Bachya remarks that Jacob's wrestling with Esau's guardian angel symbolized the struggle with evil he and his descendants would have from this time on.

Quotes about the Internal Organs

Bless the Lord, O my soul, and all the organs within me, bless His holy name (Psalm 103:1).

The Holy One, Blessed be He, created in man every organ on a fixed basis, so that if any one organ is twisted man cannot live (*Chullin* 56b).

How long does it take to digest a meal? Rabbi Yochanan said: Until you become hungry again (*Berachot* 53b).

THE RIBS

Adam's Rib

God then made the man fall into a deep sleep, and he slept. He took one of his ribs and closed the flesh in its place. God built the rib that He took from man into a woman, and He brought her to the man. The man said, "Now this is bone from my bones and flesh from my flesh. She shall be called woman [*ishah*] because she was taken from man [*ish*]" (Genesis 2:21–23).

Rabbi Samson Raphael Hirsch: Unlike in the case of the creation of man, the material for the woman's body was not taken from the earth. God formed one side of man into woman, so that what was previously one human being became now two. Thereby, the equality of man and woman is conclusively demonstrated. The name *ishah* (woman) does not imply dependence of woman on man but rather equality, the two belonging together. It means one human destiny shared by the two sexes.

Rabbi Samson Raphael Hirsch,
commentary to the Torah

A Woman Has More Understanding

"God built the rib . . . into a woman" (Genesis 2:22). The word *vayiven*, "He built," is from the same root as *binah*, "understanding." This teaches that God gave woman more understanding than man.

Niddah 45b

Why Was Eve Created from the Rib?

The *Midrash* says: God said, "I will not create her from man's head, lest she be light-headed and frivolous; nor from the eye, lest she be flirtatious; nor from the ear, lest she be an eavesdropper; nor from the mouth, lest she be a gossip; nor from the heart, lest she tend to be jealous; nor from the hand, lest she be thievish; nor from the foot, lest she be a gadabout; but from the modest part of man, [the rib,] for even when he stands unclothed, that part is covered."

Bereishit Rabbah 18:3;
Midrash Tanchuma, Vayeishev)

Is God a Thief?

The Talmud relates that the emperor once said to Rabban Gamliel: Your God is a thief, because it is written, "God made Adam fall into a deep sleep, and he slept. He took one of his ribs and closed flesh in its place" (Genesis 2:21). Thereupon the emperor's daughter said to Rabban Gamliel: "Leave him to me, and I will answer him."

Turning to the emperor, she said: "Get me a police officer."

"What for?" he asked.

"Thieves broke in last night and robbed a silver pitcher, leaving a gold one in its place."

"I wish we had thieves like that every day!" the emperor exclaimed.

"Ah!" she shot back. "Didn't Adam gain when his rib was taken and he was given a wife to serve him?" (*Sanhedrin* 39a).

The Worst Punishment for Evildoers

[After the creation of Adam and Eve,] God saw all that He had made, and behold, it was very good. It was evening and it was morning, the sixth day (Genesis 1:31).

Rabbi Yaakov Yosef of Polnoye: "It was very good." The *Midrash*, in a puzzling commentary, interprets the phrase "it was very good" to be a reference to *Gehinnom* (Gehenna, hell, purgatory). What could be the meaning of this curious statement?

The *Gemara* says, "In the messianic days there will be no Gehinnom" (*Nedarim* 8b). Asks Rabbi Yaakov Yosef: Without Gehinnom, how will the wicked be punished for their evil deeds? His answer: The wicked will go straight to *Gan Eden* (the Garden of Eden). There they will be in the company of the great *tzaddikim* who pray fervently and study the Torah diligently all day. Being unaccustomed to spiritual enjoyment, the wicked will feel intensely miserable in a place where there is no eating and drinking and where they are surrounded by people they despised all their lives. Every moment in paradise will be sheer torture for them. Indeed, to the wicked, being permitted to enter *Gan Eden* is a punishment worse than Gehinnom. The *Midrash* is quite apropos; the place "that is very good" means Gehinnom for evildoers.[5]

THE SKIN

The Clouds of Glory

Rabbi Yisrael of Rizhin: The *Gemara* [*Rosh Hashanah* 3a] relates that when Aaron died, the Clouds of Glory that accompanied the Israelites in the wilderness departed. What is the connection between Aaron and the Clouds of Glory? The Rizhiner answers with an apt metaphor.

We know that vapors rise from the pores in the skin. If many people stand close to each other, the vapors emanating from their pores coalesce. However, if people are far apart, the vapors dissipate.

Aaron was known as the leader who reconciled feuding adversaries and established peace between husband and wife. When he was alive, the entire nation clung together in harmony. The vapors rising from the pores of the vast throng of the 600,000 Israelites blended into one and rose up to become the Clouds of Glory. Thus, the Clouds of Glory were a testimony to the spirit of unity and brotherhood that encompassed the Jewish people.

When Aaron died, the ardent love that bound the people evaporated. The huge crowd dispersed as each went his own way. The vapors that rose from their pores vanished, and the Clouds of Glory that earlier had formed from these vapors departed.

Nachalat Yisrael, Chukat

Garments of Skin

[After Adam and Eve transgressed and ate from the Tree of Knowledge,] God made garments of skin for Adam and his wife and He clothed them (Genesis 2:21).

In the *Gemara* (*Sotah* 14a) we read that Rav and Shmuel differ regarding the nature of these garments. According to one, "garments of skin" means material that grows from the skin, meaning wool. According to the other, the garments were made from material from which the human skin derives pleasure, meaning linen [which is pleasant to the touch and feels good on the skin].

Pursuing this line of thought, we can say that wool is the fabric that keeps the body warm. Thus, it symbolizes inwardness, which is to say, the garments made of wool focused on the spiritual. Linen, the cloth that gives pleasure to the skin, represents externality and a concern with the superficial; the garments made of linen are symbolic of material things.

Continuing in this vein, the *Midrash* tells us that when Cain and Abel each brought an offering, Cain's offering consisted of flax (from which linen is made). He was motivated by the external, material values epitomized by linen. Abel, on the other hand, offered sheep (the source of wool). He gave of his inner self, aspired to closeness to God, to internality exemplified by wool.

Taking this theme one step further, we note that the Torah forbids wearing a garment that contains a mixture of wool and linen: "Do not wear a forbidden mixture [shaatnez], where wool and linen are together [in a single garment]" (Deuteronomy 22:11). This translates into the idea that internality and externality—spirit and matter— should be kept separate, that altruism and selfishness are two antithetical concepts that do not mix (Rabbi Chaim Finkel, commenting on *Maalot Hatorah*).

Tzora'at: Leprosy

Tzora'at is a disease that is discussed extensively in the Torah. Although many of its symptoms resemble those of leprosy, *tzora'at* is an affliction of the skin that is caused by a spiritual defect. The sages of the Talmud tell us that *tzora'at* is a divine punishment for slander and talebearing. The *metzora* (leper) was isolated for a period of time and was compelled to live outside the camp, for the slanderer was considered a moral leper who has no place in the camp of Israel.

A Leper Counts as Dead

Rabbi Yehoshua ben Levi said: Four are counted as dead: A poor man, a leper, a blind person, and a person who is childless. A leper, because it is written, "[When Miriam was stricken with *tzora'at* (leprosy), Aaron asked Moses to pray for her recovery.] Aaron said to Moses, let her not be as one dead" (Numbers 12:12).

Nedarim 64a

Why Must a Leper Be Isolated?

The *Gemara* asks: Why is a leper different that the Torah said, "He must live alone, and his place shall be outside the camp? (Leviticus 13:46). By slandering and maligning he separated a husband from his wife, a man from his neighbor, therefore the Torah says: "He must live alone."

Rabbi Yehoshua ben Levi said: Why is a leper different that the Torah said: ["He should bring] two live kosher birds" (Leviticus 14:2), so that he may become pure again? The Holy One, Blessed be He, said: [The slanderer] was guilty of babbling, therefore let him offer a babbler (a bird that babbles constantly) as a sacrifice.

Arachin 16b

8

The Extremities

THE HANDS

The Merit of Honest Labor

When you eat the labor of your hands, you are praiseworthy, and it is well with you (Psalm 128:2).

You bless the fruit of the labor of his hands (Job 1:10).

When man labors and produces with his hands, God will send His blessing (*Tanchuma, Vayeitzei* 13).

The Clenched Fist and the Open Hand

Rabbi Meir said: "When a person enters the world, his hands are clenched as if to say, 'The whole world is mine, I shall conquer it'; but when he departs from the world, his hands are spread open as if to say, 'I have acquired nothing from this world.'"

Kohelet Rabbah 5:14

His Fingers Testified

At the time of his passing, Rabbi raised his ten fingers toward heaven and said, "Master of the Universe, You know full well that I have toiled in the study of the Torah with my ten fingers and that I did not enjoy any worldly benefits, even with my little finger. May it be Your will that I will have peace in my last resting place."

Ketubot 104a

The Long Arm of Pharaoh's Daughter

The *Gemara* (*Sotah* 12b) tells us that when Pharaoh's daughter went to bathe in the Nile and saw the box containing the child Moses in the rushes, she stretched out her arm to fetch it. Miraculously, her arm became lengthened so that she was able to reach the box, and thereby the course of history was changed.

According to Rabbi Chaim Shmulevitz, this is an allegory. Why did she stretch out her arm? Didn't she see that she could not possibly reach across the river? We are told here that she was not discouraged by the great distance between herself and the box. She stretched out her arm and made a mighty effort to reach for the box and rescue the child, although this must have seemed impossible to accomplish. And with single-minded determination she attained the unreachable goal. This teaches us that with firm resolve, total dedication, and an iron will we can achieve superhuman feats.

Don't say, "How can I possibly reach the level of scholarship of the students of Rabbi Akiva Eiger or the Vilna Gaon?" That's a mistake. It all depends on your willpower. If you have a burning desire to achieve greatness in Torah, the enormous spiritual resources that lie dormant in your soul will flare up, and you will reach undreamed-of heights of understanding.[1]

Twenty-two Objects in Our Bodies

Sefer Yetzirah, the kabbalistic book attributed to Abraham, establishes a parallel between the twenty-two letters of the *alef-bet* and "twenty-two objects in our bodies" (2:6). The objects are the ten fingers, ten toes, the tongue, and the reproductive organ.

In a superficial way, these profound concepts can be explained by saying that the Ten *Sefirot* in the higher worlds are represented by the fingers of the hand. The Ten *Sefirot* in the lower world correspond to the ten toes. Kabbalah teaches that there are *Sefirot* of the left and of the right side. The right side is the side of God's love and kindness (*chesed*); the left side is the divine force that restrains the abundant love through strict justice (*din*). The *Sefirot* of the center mediate between the two extremes. The *Sefirot* of the higher worlds are reflected in the human form as the fingers of the right and the left hands, which are united above through the tongue. Those of the lower worlds are mirrored in the toes of the right and the left feet, which are united through the reproductive organ.

The Vilna Gaon explains that the fingers correspond to the first Tablets of the Ten Commandments and the toes to the second Tablets. Like the fingers on each hand, each Tablet had five commandments inscribed on it. The Torah is transmitted orally, a process symbolized by the tongue; it is conveyed from generation to generation, a process represented by the reproductive organ.

The Dance of the Tzaddikim

The *Gemara* says: In the world to come, the *tzaddikim* (righteous) will dance in a circle, and the Holy One, Blessed be He, will sit in the center, in *Gan Eden*. Each *tzaddik* joyfully will point his finger at God, as it says, "In that day they shall say: This is our God; we trusted in Him, and He delivered us. This is God in whom we trusted; let us rejoice and exult in His deliverance!" (Isaiah 25:9).

Ta'anit 31a

The Ring on the Bride's Forefinger

The Torah of God is perfect, renewing life;
The testimony of God is sure, making the simple wise;
The precepts of God are just, rejoicing the heart;
The commandments of God are clear, making the eyes light up;
The fear of God is pure, abiding forever;
The judgments of God are true, righteous altogether.

Psalm 19:8–10

The *Midrash* (*Midrash Tehillim* 19:14) teaches that these six verses, all expressing the divine origin of the Torah, allude to the six orders of the *Mishnah*, the Oral Law.

In the Hebrew text, each of these verses is composed of five words. Thus, for example, the first verse reads, *Torat Hashem temimah meshivat nafesh.* The five words are an allusion to the five fingers of the right hand. Furthermore, God's name appears as the second word in each of the six passages. Thus, the Divine Name corresponds to the second finger, the finger on which the bride receives her wedding ring. The bride points her forefinger upward to receive the ring, symbolically pledging to uphold the God-given Torah in the couple's newly founded home, both in its written and oral form.

The 28 Bones of Ko'ach

The Vilna Gaon finds amazing insights in the interchange of letters and numbers relating to the word *yad*, hand. The Hebrew word for hand ד, *yad*, has a numeric value of 14, (*yud* = 10; *dalet* = 4). This coincides with the fourteen bones (phalanges) in the fingers of each hand.[2] Thus, in the two hands there are twenty-eight (2 x 14) such bones, so that

when two Jews shake hands they create a bond of 28, which
is to say that they fortify each other, 28 being the numeric
value of כח, *ko'ach*, power.

Pursuing this trend of thought, we are reminded of the
fact that God revealed Himself on two occasions: once
through nature, at the beginning of Creation, when He
brought the world into being by means of Ten Utterances,[3]
the second time through the Torah, when He gave us the Ten
Commandments. (Notice the recurrent theme of the number ten: Ten *Sefirot*, Ten Utterances, Ten Commandments.
In man, these mystical concepts are clothed in human form
as the ten fingers and toes.)

Comparing the two verses that introduce those two
divine revelations, we find that the opening verse of the story
of Creation, בראשית ברא אלקים את השמים ואת הארץ, *Bereishit bara
Elokim et hashamayim ve'et ha'aretz*, "In the beginning God
created heaven and earth" (Genesis 1:1), contains 7 words
and 28 letters.

Now let us examine the introductory verse to the Ten
Commandments, וידבר אלקים את כל הדברים האלה לאמר, *Vayedabbeir
Elokim et kol hadevarim ha'eileh leimor*, "God spoke all these
words, saying" (Exodus 20:1). Surprisingly, this passage
also contains 7 words and 28 letters. Thus, Creation and
the Giving of the Torah, the two revelations of the divine
Will through nature and Torah, are equivalent.

Continuing in this vein, the week has seven days, and
each day is composed of four segments, the four phases
mentioned in the *Shema*: "(1) while you sit in your home;
(2) while you walk on the way; (3) when you retire; and (4)
when you arise" (Deuteronomy 6:7). Consequently, a week
comprises twenty-eight (7 x 4) such segments.

To summarize, the meaning that emerges from these
permutations is that if we dedicate our hands (28 bones)
to living each day (28 phases of the week) according to the
Torah (28 letters in the two crucial verses), we will receive
renewed strength, *ko'ach* (28), as the prophet says, "They
who trust in God shall renew their strength [*yachalifu
ko'ach* (28)], as eagles grow new plumes; they shall run and

not grow weary, they shall march and not grow faint" (Isaiah 40:31).

Vilna Gaon

From Fins to Hands

[Lemech had a son.] He named him Noah, saying, "This one will bring us relief from our work and the anguish of our hands, from the soil that God has cursed" (Genesis 5:29).

Commenting on this verse, *Midrash Avkir*[4] makes the astonishing remark that before the days of Noah, man had fins instead of hands, which explains Lemech's statement that working the soil caused a great deal of anguish. In the days of Noah, a change occurred, as fins were replaced with hands, giving man the dexterity of fine and varied movements that form the basis for the handling of tools, weapons, and instruments. Surprisingly, *Midrash Avkir* observes that the human hand has the ability to make 58 movements, which is equivalent to the numeric value of the name נח *Noach* (*nun* = 50; *chet* = 8).

The *Midrash* is corroborated by the findings of modern science. Researchers have indentified 58 free movements in the hand, including flexion, extension, and abduction (ability to move the thumb forward of the fingers). The thumb is extremely important because of its unique action of opposition, by which it can be brought across the palm and to the tips of the slightly flexed fingers, enabling man to grab and handle tools.

It is interesting to note that the word *noach* means ease, to rest. The anatomical change from fins to hands that is associated with Noah made life indeed much easier for mankind.

With Raised Hands

The *Mishnah* (*Sotah* 38a) teaches that based on the verse, "And Aaron lifted his hands toward the people and blessed them" (Leviticus 9:22), the *kohanim* (priests) raise their hands when they bless the people.

According to the *Zohar*, the specific way in which the *kohanim* position their hands during the blessing is derived from the verse, "He is looking through the windows, peering through the lattices" (Song of Songs 2:9). This refers to God, who is standing behind the *kohanim* and looks at Israel through the spaces (lattices) between their fingers. The *kohanim* separate their fingers in such a way that there are five spaces between them. The congregation, on their part, avoid looking at the hands of the *kohanim,* for that would appear as though they were trying to look at the *Shechinah,* the Divine Presence.

The palms of the *kohanim* must be turned downward. The *Kedushat Levi*[5] explains the reason for this. When someone receives an object, he holds his hands with the palms facing upward. But when he gives away something, the giver's palm is downward. Since the *kohanim* are bestowing a blessing on the congregation, their palms are turned downward.

The Work of the Righteous

The *Gemara* expounds: The work of the righteous is greater than the creation of heaven and earth. God created heaven and earth with one hand, as it says, "My own hand has founded the earth, My right hand spread out the skies" (Isaiah 48:13), while in regard to the *Bet Hamikdash,* which is the work of the hands of the *tzaddikim,* it is stated, "The shrine of God Your hands have founded" (Exodus 15:17).

Ketubot 5a

The Hands of Esau

[When Jacob approached his father, Isaac, whose eyesight was fading, in order to receive his blessing,] Isaac touched him and said, "The voice is Jacob's voice, but the hands are the hands of Esau" (Genesis 27:22).

Maharal:[6] "The voice is Jacob's voice, but the hands are the hands of Esau." Jacob's hallmark is his voice, the sound that emerges from a person's interior. By contrast, Esau is distinguished by his hands, the limbs that deal with the outside world, the most exterior parts of the body. In the conflict between the voice and the hands, the interior and the exterior, spirit and physicality, the voice that emanates from the interior prevails over the external hands.

The Hand that Gives

Rabbi Meir of Premyshlan said: Through the *mitzvah* of *tzedakah* a person has an impact on the order in the highest spiritual worlds. In fact, when he gives charity he assembles the four letters of the Divine Name, *Yud-Hei-Vav-Hei*, thus unifying the name of God. How is this accomplished?

When you give *tzedakah*, the small coin you give represents the letter *yud*, the smallest letter in the *alef-bet*. Your hand that gives the coin has five fingers; it stands for the first letter *hei* of the Divine Name (*hei* = 5). Your outstretched arm resembles the elongated letter *vav* of the Name, and the poor man's hand that receives the coin corresponds to the second *hei* of the Name.

However, when it comes to giving *tzedakah*, make sure that you take the initiative, for if the poor man extends his hand before you are ready to give, the letters of God's name are reversed: the hand and the arm of the poor man (*hei* and *vav*) come before your hand holding the coin (*hei* and *yud*).

Divrei Meir

Serving God with Our Bodies

Rabbi Baruch of Medzhibozh[7] declared: During the Yamim Tovim of Tishrei, we serve God with our entire body. On Rosh Hashanah, the Day of Remembrance, we serve Him with our brain, since we remember with our brain; on Yom Kippur, with our heart, because fasting weakens the heart;

on Sukkot with our hands, since we hold the *lulav* in our hands; on Simchat Torah with our feet, since we dance with the Torah.

Sifran shel Tzaddikim

Nails

The *Zohar*[8] says that the *klippot* (literally, shells; the coarse, impure spirits of the world) attach themselves to the nails. Why is this so?

We know that the blood is the soul and life force that is centered in the heart. It thrusts life to all parts of the body. The nails are the parts of the body that are farthest removed from the heart. Therefore, they possess the least amount of life force and soul, to the point that they become separated from the body. That is the reason why the impure spirits can attach themselves to the nails.

THE FEET

Aphorisms in the Talmud

Hillel used to say: "To the place that I love, there my feet lead me" (*Sukkah* 53a). He means to say that no matter where I plan to go, I always wind up going to the *bet hamidrash*, the place I love most; instinctively my feet take me there.

Rabbi Yochanan said: A man's feet are responsible for him; they lead him to the place where he is wanted. [His feet will lead him to the place where he is destined to die (Rashi)].

Sukkah 53a

Rabbi Yochanan said: A man should always be eager to run to see the kings of Israel. And not only to see the kings of Israel but also the kings of the gentiles.

Berachot 9b

One who goes to the house of study but does not study has the reward for going; one who studies at home but does not attend the house of study has the reward for accomplishment.

Avot 5:17

A person should sell the beams of his house in order to buy a pair of shoes.

Shabbat 129a

Don't withhold shoes from your feet.

Pesachim 112a

It is unbecoming for a scholar to walk around in patched sandals.

Berachot 43b

Shmuel said: He who wants to taste death should put on his shoes and go to sleep. [Sleeping in your shoes is dangerous.]

Yoma 78b

The rabbis taught: If a person walks with a proud bearing even for four cubits, it is as if he pushed against the heels of the *Shechinah* [he acts arrogantly against God], since it is written, "The whole earth is full of His glory" (Isaiah 6:3).

Berachot 43b

In the way in which a person wants to go, in that way he is led (*Makkot* 10b). Heaven propels us in the direction we choose in life. If a person chooses the right path, heaven will help him to realize his aspirations. By the same token, if he chooses the road of evil, heaven will make it easy for him to achieve his corrupt goal.

Rabbi Chelbo said: When you leave the synagogue, you should not take large strides, but when you go *to* the synagogue, it is a *mitzvah* to run. . . . You should always run to listen to a lecture on *Halachah*, even on *Shabbat* [when it is improper to take large strides].

Berachot 6b

The Footsteps of Mashiach

How welcome on the mountain are the footsteps of the herald
Announcing peace, heralding good fortune,
Announcing victory,
Telling Zion, "Your God is King!"
Hark! Your watchmen raise their voices,
As one they shout for joy;
For every eye shall behold
The Lord's return to Zion.

Isaiah 52:7, 8

Agile in Old Age

How long is a person regarded as young and healthy? Rabbi Ila said: As long as he is able to stand on one foot and put on and take off his shoes.

They said about Rabbi Chaninah that when he was eighty years old, he was able to stand on one foot and put on and take off his shoes. Said Rabbi Chaninah: The warm baths and the oil my mother poured on me when I was young have stood me in good stead.

Chullin 24b

The Whole Torah While Standing on One Foot

A certain heathen once asked Hillel to teach him the entire Torah while he (the heathen) stood on one foot. Hillel answered him: What is hateful to you, do not do to your neighbor, that is the whole Torah; the rest is commentary. Go and study it!

(*Shabbat* 31a)

His Boot Would Not Fit

During the Roman siege of Jerusalem, Rabbi Yochanan ben Zakkai, the foremost sage of his time, was smuggled out of the city in order to negotiate with Vespasian, the Roman general. While Rabbi Yochanan and Vespasian were talking, a messenger arrived from Rome, reporting to Vespasian, "Caesar has died, and the leaders of the Roman senate have decided to appoint you as the new Caesar."

Vespasian had just finished putting on one boot, but when he tried to put on the other he could not.

"Why has my foot swollen, so that the shoe no longer fits?" Vespasian wondered.

"Don't worry," replied Rabbi Yochanan. "You have received good news, and that is why your foot is swollen, as Scripture states, 'Good news makes the bones fat' (Proverbs 15:30). Now, if you wonder what you can do so that the shoe will fit, let someone whom you dislike come and let him pass in front of you, as it is written, 'A despondent mood dries up the bones'" (Proverbs 17:22). Vespasian followed Rabbi Yochanan's advice, and the boot went on.

Gittin 56b

9

Milah—Circumcision

THE *MITZVAH* OF *MILAH*

This is My covenant between Me and between you and your offspring that you must keep: You must circumcise every male. You shall be circumcised through the flesh of your foreskin. This shall be the mark of the covenant between Me and you. Throughout all generations, every male shall be circumcised when he is eight days old. . . . The uncircumcised male whose foreskin has not been circumcised shall have his soul cut off from his people; he has broken My covenant (Genesis 17:10–14).

The *mitzvah* of *milah* (circumcision) is among the most important of all commandments, since all of Judaism depends on it. *Milah* is the mark of the covenant between God and the Jewish people, the sign that is indelibly sealed in our flesh. It is the sign indicating that we are God's servants who obey His commandments.

MILAH MEANS PERFECTION

[The following verse introduces the covenant of *milah*.] Abram was ninety-nine years old. God appeared to Abram and said to him, "I am Almighty God. Walk before Me, and be perfect" (Genesis 17:1).

THE MAGNIFICENCE OF *MILAH*

The *Gemara* (*Nedarim* 31 a, b) cites the following considerations to show the greatness of the *mitzvah* of *milah*:

Milah is a great *mitzvah*, for no one was as diligent as Abraham in fulfilling God's commandments, yet he was called perfect only because of the *mitzvah* of *milah*, as it says [in reference to *milah*], "Walk before Me, and be perfect" (Genesis 17:1).

Milah is a great *mitzvah* because it is equal in importance to all the other commandments combined. The *Zohar* finds an allusion to this in the numeric value of ברית *brit*, which equals 612 (*bet* = 2; *reish* = 200; *yud* = 10; *tav* = 400). We have a total of 613 *mitzvot*. Therefore the *mitzvah* of *brit*, *milah*, is equivalent to the other 612 *mitzvot*.

Milah is a great *mitzvah*, since if it were not for the covenant of *milah*, God would not have created the universe, as it is written, "Thus says God: If it were not for my *brit* (covenant) by day and night, I would not have instituted the laws of heaven and earth" (Jeremiah 33:25).

Milah is a great *mitzvah* because it overrides the severity of *Shabbat*. [Circumcision involves the drawing of blood, which is forbidden on *Shabbat*. Nevertheless, if the newborn child is eight days old on *Shabbat*, the *milah* must be performed.]

Rabbi Yishmael said, "Great is the *mitzvah* of *milah* since thirteen covenants were based on it" (*Nedarim* 31a, b).

The Rambam explains: In the section dealing with God's command to Abraham to circumcise himself (Genesis, chap. 17) the word *brit* (covenant) occurs thirteen times (Rambam, *Hilchot Milah* 3:9).

MILAH TAKES PRECEDENCE OVER *SHABBAT*

The *Gemara* (*Nedarim* 31a) teaches that if a newborn child is eight days old on *Shabbat*, the *milah* must take place on *Shabbat*, even though drawing blood is forbidden on *Shabbat*. The Ramban (Nachmanides) offers the following rationale why *milah* sets aside *Shabbat*: Since *milah* is a mark that is permanently fixed on a man's body, it is an uninterrupted, never-ending sign. *Shabbat*, on the other hand, is a cyclic sign because it ends on *Motza'ei Shabbat*, (at the departure of *Shabbat*). The continuous sign of *milah* supersedes the intermittent sign of *Shabbat*.[1]

THE PSALM FOR THE EIGHTH

The Talmud relates: King David once entered the bath and saw his naked reflection. He felt very bad and said, "Woe is to me. I am naked of all *mitzvot*." Then he recalled the *mitzvah* of *milah* that was on his body, and he felt better. When he emerged, he composed the "Psalm for the Eighth" (Psalm 12). [This is a psalm in which David thanks God for sanctifying him with a *mitzvah* that is fulfilled on the eighth day after birth.]

Menachot 43b

NAKED OF ALL *MITZVOT*

Ahavat Dodim, in a commentary to Song of Songs 3:1, offers the following homiletic interpretation of the above-mentioned passage: Whenever a person performs a *mitzvah*, his good intentions are tainted to a certain degree by some ulterior motive. Subconsciously, he may want to impress others with his piety or be admired for his generosity. David entered the bath in a figurative sense; he wanted to cleanse himself of all selfish interests that had invaded his thoughts when he was doing *mitzvot*. Upon examining himself, he discovered to his dismay that "he was naked of all *mitzvot*"— he could not find even one *mitzvah* he had done without an ulterior motive. But when he recalled the *mitzvah* of *milah* that was performed when he was eight days old, he felt better. Surely, as an eight-day-old infant he did not yet have any selfish thoughts. Here he had found the only *mitzvah* he had performed without an ulterior motive.[2]

THE REWARD FOR *MILAH*

The Shelah says: The reward for the *mitzvah* of *milah* is extraordinary. There are special angels who take this blood and store it in a special place. When God is angry at His people, he looks at this blood and has mercy on them.[3]

SAVED FROM PURGATORY

The *Midrash* says: God swore to Abraham that all his descendants who would be circumcised would never descend to *Gehinnom*. Abraham stands guard at the gate of *Gehinnom* so that none of his descendants bearing the mark of circumcision should enter this place of divine punishment. However, when a person follows his sexual desires and sins and dies without repenting, then specially appointed angels come and reattach his foreskin. He is then once again uncircumcised and can be thrust into *Gehinnom*. Abraham does not help him, since this person is uncircumcised.

Bereishit Rabbah 48:8

TWO REASONS FOR THE *MITZVAH* OF *MILAH*

First reason: It is an indelible sign that remains with a person in life and in death. It is sealed in our flesh, indicating that we are servants of God; we must obey His commandments and not violate them, for this is the reason we were created. Obviously, we do not come to the world merely to eat and drink but to keep the *mitzvot*.[4]

Second reason: Although God could have created man circumcised, He desired to create him with a foreskin that must be removed. Man is therefore created with a defect, and just as he can remove the defect on his body, so can he rectify the defects in his soul. Man has the free will to do good and not sin.

Sefer Hachinuch

THE EMPEROR'S PROPOSAL

The [Roman] emperor proposed to Rabbi Tanchum, "Come, let us all be one people."

"Very well," Rabbi Tanchum replied. "But we who are circumcised cannot possibly become like you [circumcision cannot be reversed]. So you become circumcised and be like us!"

"You have spoken well," replied the emperor. "Nevertheless, anyone who gets the better of the king in debate must be thrown to the wild beasts in the arena."

So they threw him to the lions, but he was not eaten.

Then a heretic remarked, "The reason that the beasts did not eat him is that they are not hungry." Thereupon they threw the heretic in, and he was eaten.

Sanhedrin 39a

ELIJAH PRESENT AT EVERY *BRIT*

At the *brit milah* ceremony, a chair is prepared in honor of the prophet Elijah, who attends every circumcision. One reason that Elijah must be present at every *brit* is because he spoke against the Jews and said, "The children of Israel have forsaken Your covenant" (1 Kings 19:10). As punishment for this accusation, he is obliged to attend every circumcision to see with his own eyes how the Jews keep this covenant with great enthusiasm.

Zohar 1:3, 1:93; *Pirkei deRabbi Eliezer* 29

ELIJAH'S PUNISHMENT

It happened that a nonobservant Jew invited the Gerer Rebbe (the Chidushei Harym[5]) to be the *sandek*[6] at the *brit* of his son, which was to take place on *Shabbat*. On the Rebbe's arrival, all the guests threw away their cigarettes. The Rebbe, who noticed the desecration of the *Shabbat*, said: The *Midrash* tells us that the prophet Elijah was punished for accusing Israel of forsaking God's covenant. He is forced to attend every *brit*. I have always wondered why being present at a *brit* should be considered a punishment. But now I see that it can be a severe penalty to attend some ceremonies, for example, a *brit* such as this.

Siach Sarfei Kodesh 4:147

MAN'S WORKS ARE MORE PLEASING THAN GOD'S

The *Midrash* relates that Tinneius Rufus[7] once asked Rabbi Akiva, "Which are more pleasing, God's works or man's works?"

"The works of man are more pleasing," replied Rabbi Akiva.

To prove his point, Rabbi Akiva then asked that some bread rolls and a few ears of grain be brought in.

Rabbi Akiva said, "The rolls were made by man; the grain was produced by God. Don't you agree that the rolls are more pleasing than the grain?"

Tinneius Rufus persisted. "If God wanted man to be circumcised," he asked, "why doesn't a baby emerge from his mother's womb circumcised?"

Replied Rabbi Akiva, "When a baby is born, the umbilical cord comes out with the infant. Now, if what you say is true, and a baby comes into the world in a state of per-

fection, why does the mother cut the umbilical cord? But let me tell you why an infant is not born circumcised. Because the Holy One, Blessed be He, gave commandments to the Jewish people in order to refine and purify them, as David says, 'The word of the Lord purifies'" (Psalm 18:31).
                                        Midrash Tanchuma, Tazria 7

Rabbi Akiva implied that Creation was left unfinished. God gave us the task of bringing Creation to completion. He gave us the Torah and the *mitzvot* as the means by which we can accomplish this task. *Milah*, more than any other *mitzvah*, expresses this idea: At birth, man is an unfinished product. Through the *mitzvah* of *milah* his body becomes perfect. He is inducted in the Torah nation and is given the means—the *mitzvot*—of attaining perfection for himself and the world.

❧

THE *SEFIRAH* OF *YESOD*

The sages of Kabbalah teach that the Infinite Light, the *Or Ein Sof*, which is of a purely spiritual nature, descends through a succession of Ten *Sefirot* (emanations) to the physical universe that is our world. The first three *Sefirot* are the fountainhead of spiritual wisdom from which flow the succeeding seven *Sefirot*. The ninth *Sefirah*, called *Yesod* (Foundation), blends the preceding emanations and conveys the divine flow of abundance to the tenth and lowest emanation, the *Sefirah* of *Malchut* (Kingship), which is our world, which is to say that the *Sefirah* of *Malchut* is the revelation of God's will in the physical world. Therefore, in the system of the *Sefirot*, *Yesod* (the *Sefirah* that gives to *Malchut*), represents the male and corresponds to the reproductive function in man.

Following this line of thinking, the kabbalists note that

Joseph, in his capacity as viceroy of Egypt, supplied the country with food during the seven years of famine. He told the people, "Here is seed for you" (Genesis 47:23). In kabbalistic writings, Joseph, as the "giver of seed," is the epitome of *Yesod*, the *Sefirah* that "gives."

Furthermore, Joseph controlled his sexual desire and mastered his reproductive organ when Potiphar's wife tried to seduce him—another reason why, in kabbalistic literature, Joseph personifies the *Sefirah* of *Yesod*.

The function of *Yesod* is to bring God's light into the *Sefirah* of *Malchut*, the material world. In our world, this task is carried out by the *tzaddik*, the righteous man who teaches the words of the Torah to the people and who brings blessing upon the world, as stated in the Talmud (*Chagigah* 12b): "What does the world rest on? On one pillar, which is the *tzaddik* [the righteous one], as it says, *Tzaddik yesod olam*, 'The foundation of the world is the *tzaddik*'" (Proverbs 10:25).

TZADDIK YESOD OLAM

Rabbi Yochanan said: As long as there is one *tzaddik*, the world will continue to exist, as it says, *Tzaddik yesod olam*, "The *tzaddik* is the foundation of the world" (Proverbs 10:25).

Yoma 38b

Abbaye said: In any generation, there are no fewer than thirty-six perfect *tzaddikim* in the world (*Sanhedrin* 97b). *Tikkunei Zohar* derives from a verse in Hosea that there are seventy-two perfect *tzaddikim* in the world at all times— thirty-six of them living in *Eretz Yisrael* and thirty-six scattered throughout the rest of the world. (In Hebrew the number thirty-six is *lamed-vav* [*lamed* = 30; *vav* = 6]. That is why in popular usage, a hidden *tzaddik* is called a *lamed-vavnik*, "one of the thirty-six.")

✦

A SMALL ORGAN

Rabbi Yochanan remarked, "Man has a small organ. When he satisfies it, it is hungry; but when he keeps it hungry, it is satisfied." [The more a person satisfies his sensual appetite, the greater his desire becomes.]

Sukkah 52b

✦

WHO SHALL GO UP TO HEAVEN?

This mandate that I am prescribing to you today is not too mysterious or remote from you. It is not in heaven, so that you should say, "Who shall go up to heaven and bring it to us that we can hear it and keep it?" (Deuteronomy 30:11).

This verse contains a fascinating allusion to *milah*. The initials of the words *mi yaaleh lanu hashamaymah*, "Who shall go up to heaven," are *mem, yud, lamed, hei*. Together they form the acronym *milah*. The last letters of these four words are *yud-hei-vav-hei*, the Tetragrammaton.

Homiletically, the combination of these letters conveys the idea that the *mitzvah* of *milah* removes the barrier that separates us from the heavenly spheres and enables us to reach the nearness of God.

✦

AMALEK, SYMBOL OF THE FORESKIN

In kabbalistic thought, the concept of Amalek takes on a transcendent meaning. Amalek is not only the nation that cravenly attacked the Israelites from the rear on their way out of Egypt but, under different guises, Amalek has reappeared continually in Jewish history as Israel's archenemy. As such it is the personification of evil, Satan, and the primeval serpent. Being Israel's physical and spiritual implacable adversary, Amalek must be totally annihilated, as it says, "Remember what Amalek did to you on your way out of Egypt. . . . You must obliterate the memory of Amalek" (Deuteronomy 25:17, 19).

In an insight drawn from Kabbalah, the Sefat Emet[8] describes Amalek as the foreskin that covers the *brit*, the divine seal that God placed on a Jew. The corona of the membrum is shaped like the letter *yud*, the first letter of God's name, which is concealed by the foreskin. It is revealed through *milah* and *peri'ah* (the uncovering of the corona),[9] so that *milah* serves as a constant reminder of the covenant between God and the Jewish people. The essence of a Jew is *zachor*, remembering. By contrast, the essence of Amalek is forgetting, which is the antithesis of remembering. Amalek wants a Jew to forget his identity and dissolve his bond with God and the Torah.

When a Jew remembers his history and his God, the source of his soul, Amalek cannot latch on to him, because by remembering, the foreskin (Amalek) is removed from the holy *brit*.[10]

UNCOVERING THE *ATARAH* (CORONA)

What is the deeper meaning of *brit milah?*
Rabbi Yitzchak Eizik Chaver: *Shefa*, the stream of God's

abundant bounty, reaches our world via the *Sefirah* of *Yesod* (Foundation), but here, this divine benevolence is hidden under a dense cover of physicality. What this means is that people do not recognize God as the Giver of life who sustains them and the world around them. Erroneously, they attribute life and the existence of the universe to an undefined force they call nature. At his *brit milah*, on the eighth day of his life, a Jew learns the truth.

The corona of the male organ resembles the letter *yud*, the first letter of God's name. More precisely, the corona represents *Yesod*, the *Sefirah* through which divine *shefa* flows to the world. It is hidden from view by the *orlah*, the foreskin, symbol of physicality and denial of God. At the *brit milah*, we remove the foreskin and reveal the *atarah*, corona. We thereby uncover the source of *shefa* (flow of divine abundance) and recognize God as the ruler of our destiny.

III

THE JEW
AND HIS FAMILY

A Jew can fulfill his destiny only in the framework of marriage, for God "who formed the earth and made it, did not create it a waste, but formed it for habitation" (Isaiah 45:18). And so, at the very outset of the story of Creation, God said, "It is not good for man to be alone. I will make a compatible helper for him" (Genesis 2:18). Accordingly, the sages consider an unmarried man as incomplete, as living without happiness, blessing, and peace (*Yevamot* 63a). They view the family as the cornerstone of the Jewish nation, indeed, a number of talmudic tractates are devoted exclusively to the subject of marriage and related topics.

The selections in Parts I and II deal with man as an individual, analyze him from head to toe, establishing correlations between his physical and his spiritual aspects. The entries in Part III take aim at marriage and the exalted role of the Jewish woman. In a wealth of pithy sayings and incisive observations, the rabbis of a bygone age offer sage counsel that is utterly relevant to modern-day couples and addresses many of the problems they face. An entire chapter is devoted to Torah attitudes regarding pregnancy, birth, and infertility. Assembled under the heading of "Preserving Life" are rabbinic insights about health, pain and suffering, physicians, and hygiene. A section about sleep and dreams divulges the fascinating talmudic approach to the interpretation of dreams. The closing chapter on visiting the sick appropriately ends this book on a note of *chesed*, selfless kindness. For God created the world in an act of consummate *chesed*; we, in turn, emulate Him by bestowing *chesed* (kindness) on all men and all classes.

10

Man and Wife

HUSBAND, WIFE, AND THE *SHECHINAH*

Rabbi Akiva expounded: When man and wife are worthy,
the *Shechinah* dwells among them; when they are unworthy, fire consumes them.

Sotah 17a

For a better understanding of Rabbi Akiva's statement,
we must consider the spelling of the Hebrew words for man
and wife, אִישׁ *ish*, "man," and אִשָּׁה *ishah*, "woman." *Ish* is
spelled: *alef, yud, shin; ishah: alef, shin, hei.* If we join the
yud of *ish* and the *hei* of *ishah* we obtain the Divine Name,
Yud-Hei, an indication that the *Shechinah* literally dwells
among them. But if the *yud* is removed from *ish* we are left
with *alef-shin*, or אֵשׁ *eish*, "fire." Similarly, if we take away
the *hei* from *ishah, alef-shin, eish*, "fire," remains.

FINDING THE RIGHT *SHIDDUCH* (MATCH)

In the days of the *Mishnah*, young men and women found
a suitable match in an unusual way. The *Gemara* describes
how it was done.

There were no greater festive days for the Jewish people
than the fifteenth of *Av* and Yom Kippur. On these two
auspicious days, the daughters of Jerusalem would all dress
up in white dresses, which they borrowed from each other
so as not to embarrass the girls who did not own a beautiful dress; then they would go out and dance in the vine-
yards. What did the young girls say? "Young man, lift up
your eyes and see whom you are going to choose as your
bride." The beautiful girls would say, "See whom you would
like to choose, for a bride has to be pretty." The girls who
lacked beauty but came from a good family would say,
"Don't look at beauty, look at the family" (*Ta'anit* 26b, 31a).

Eitz Yosef[1] comments that these declarations were re-
frains of a song they all sang. They were not directed at the
boys, since that would have been immodest.

THE *SHECHINAH* BLESSES THE MARRIAGE

The *Midrash* says: In the beginning, Adam was created from
the dust, and Eve was created from Adam. Since the time
of Adam and Eve, every human being is formed "with [God's]
image and likeness" (Genesis 1:26). A man cannot exist
without a wife, and a woman cannot exist without a husband. And both cannot live together without the *Shechinah*
(Divine Presence).

Bereishit Rabbah 8:8

SEARCHING FOR A LOST OBJECT

The *Gemara* says: The usual way is for a man to pursue a woman, rather than for a woman to pursue a man. Why is this so?

If someone lost something, who does the searching? Of course, it is the owner who goes looking for his lost possession.

Maharsha explains that the analogy refers to Adam, who lost one of his ribs and does not rest until he finds it. [Following Adam's example, it is the man who courts the woman.]

Kiddushin 2b

APHORISMS ABOUT MARRIAGE

They only match a woman to a man according to his deeds [He receives the wife he deserves; only if his actions are righteous will he have a virtuous wife.] (*Sotah* 2b).

It is as difficult to match a woman and a man as was the parting of the Red Sea (*Sotah* 2a).

When choosing a wife, take your time to probe her character to make sure that she is not quarrelsome. Don't marry a woman who is of a higher social status than you are, for you will not be acceptable to her (*Yevamot* 63a).

Forty days before the embryo is formed, a heavenly voice announces on high, "The daughter of so-and-so is to be the wife of so-and-so. . . ." A woman is destined to a man by God. Nevertheless, a man should be concerned lest a rival suitor anticipate him by means of prayer (*Mo'ed Katan* 18b).

A woman prefers a poor young man to a rich old man (*Yalkut Shimoni*, Ruth 606).

As much as a man may wish to get married, a woman's desire to be married is even greater (*Yevamot* 113a).

A Jew without a wife is an incomplete man (*Yevamot* 63a).

A Jew who has no wife lives without joy, without blessing, without goodness, and without peace (*Yevamot* 62b).

A man can easily be placated, but it is not easy to appease a woman (*Bereishit Rabbah* 17).

If your wife is short, bend down to listen to her, and follow her advice (*Bava Batra* 59a).

Before contemplating marriage with a girl, you should inquire into her brother's character traits, because most children turn out like their mother's brother (*Bava Batra* 110a).

Rabbi Ashi said: The reward of attending a wedding lies in the engrossing speeches you hear [that are addressed to the bride and groom] (*Berachot* 6b).

The *Mishnah* says: Do not engage in too much idle talk with women. They said this even about one's own wife; surely it applies to another's wife (*Avot* 1:5).

Rabbi Samson Raphael Hirsch comments: A man who truly respects his wife will have more to offer than just trivial talk and idle chatter. He will want to discuss the serious concerns of life. Moreover, this kind of jesting with other women can loosen the bounds of morality and lead to sin.

The death of a man is felt only by his wife; the death of a woman is felt only by her husband (*Sanhedrin* 22b).

THE *YETZER HARA* IS "VERY GOOD"

Rabbi Shmuel bar Nachman said: In the story of Creation it says, "God saw that it was good" (Genesis 1:12). This is an allusion to the *yetzer tov*, man's good inclination. In the same chapter it says in one passage, "Behold, it was very good" (Genesis 1:31). This is an allusion to the *yetzer hara*, man's evil inclination. Now you may exclaim: This is strange! How can the *yetzer hara* be characterized as "very good"? The answer is, that the *yetzer hara* is very good indeed. For without a *yetzer hara*, a man would not build a house, he would not get married, have children, and earn a living.

Bereishit Rabbah 9

A YOUNG WOMAN'S CHOICE

When the future wife of Rabbi Moshe of Ujhel was becoming of marriageable age, her father said to her, "Three prospective matches have been suggested for you. One young man is poor but a scholar; another is rich but not well versed in the Talmud; the third is very wealthy but quite ignorant of Jewish studies."

The girl replied, "What good is a man's wealth if he is ignorant or of limited knowledge! The first young man may be poor, but he must be brilliant if you, father, call him a scholar!"

And so she married Rabbi Moshe Teitelbaum,[2] who became famous as the author of *Yismach Moshe* and the founder of the chasidic dynasty of Ujhel-Sighet-Satmar.

A COMPATIBLE HELPER

The Talmud teaches: When Rabbi Yosi met the prophet Elijah, he asked him, "It is written, 'God said: I will make a compatible helper for him' (Genesis 2:18). Please tell me, in what way does woman help man?"

Elijah replied, "A man brings in wheat from the field,

but can he chew the raw seeds? The seeds need to be ground, the dough has to be kneaded and baked into bread. A man harvests flax, but can he wear the linen fibers without spinning, weaving, and sewing? These are the labors his wife performs for him; so you see, she lights up his eyes and puts him on his feet."

Yevamot 63a

On the surface, this *Gemara* teaches a husband to appreciate his wife and to be grateful for the things she does for him. On a deeper level, Rabbi Yosi's question implies an unspoken reproach. He insinuated that since woman (Eve) brought sin into the world and caused man to work "by the sweat of his brow," she made life more difficult for him rather than helping him. Elijah replied that even if the earth had not been cursed, and wheat and flax would have grown without arduous labor, man still could not have eaten raw kernels and worn flax. Hence, the woman who makes bread from wheat and clothes from flax, who, in other words, takes care of the home, is indeed a "compatible helper."

THE BLESSINGS OF MARRIED LIFE

The *Gemara* teaches: A man who has no wife knows no joy, no blessing, no goodness, no Torah, and no peace. . . . Furthermore, the sages of the *Gemara* say: He who loves his wife as much as he loves himself, and respects her more than he respects himself, about him Scripture says, "You will know that all is well in your tent" (Job 5:23).

Yevamot 62b

PRESCRIPTION FOR A HAPPY MARRIAGE

The Rambam (Maimonides) offers the following guidelines for a happy marriage:

The sages have ordained that a man should honor his wife more than himself, and love her as himself; if he has money, he should increase his generosity to her according to his means; he should not intimidate her, and his conversation with her should be gentle. He should lean neither to gloom nor to anger.

The sages have similarly ordained that a wife should honor her husband exceedingly and revere him; she should arrange her affairs according to his wishes, and she should regard him as if he were a prince or a king. She should behave according to his wishes and refrain from doing anything that is repugnant to him.

This is the way of the daughters and sons of Israel who are holy and pure in their union, and in these ways their life together will be happy and praiseworthy.

Rambam, *Hilchot Ishut* 15:19–20

A DEVOTED WIFE

The wife of one of Rabbi Levi Yitzchak of Berditchev's enemies met him one day in the street and poured a pail of water over his head. The Rebbe ran into the *bet midrash* and prayed, "O God, do not punish the 'good woman.' She must have done this on the order of her husband, and she should be praised as a devoted wife."

Sifran shel Tzaddikim

HONOR YOUR WIFE

Rabbi Chelbo said: Be careful to give your wife the honor that is due to her, because a man's home is blessed only on account of his wife, for it says, "And he treated Abram well because of her" (Genesis 12:16). With that in mind, Rava said to the townspeople of Mechuza:[3] Honor your wives, so that you will become rich.

Bava Metzia 59a

SOME LOSE, OTHERS GAIN

Some people lose by following their wife's advice. For example, Adam was hurt when he listened to his wife and ate from the Tree of Knowledge. Others, like Abraham, are rewarded for listening to their wives, as it says, "Abram heeded Sarai" (Genesis 17:2).

Devarim Rabbah 4

BE FRUITFUL AND MULTIPLY

A person who does not get married causes the *Shechinah* to depart from Israel, for it says, "I will be a God to you and to your offspring after you" (Genesis 47:17). Which means, if you have children, the *Shechinah* will dwell among you. But if there are no children, among whom should the *Shechinah* dwell? Among trees or rocks?

Yevamot 68b

WOMEN'S GREATER MERIT

The Talmud teaches: The promise women received from the Holy One, Blessed be He, is greater than that of the men, for it says, "You carefree women, attend to my words! You confident ladies, give ear to my speech!" (Isaiah 32:9). [The women are described as "carefree" and "confident," which is more than is said of men (Rashi).]

Rav said: Whereby do women earn merit? By making their children go to the synagogue, where they are taught Torah, and their husbands to the *bet hamidrash* to learn *Mishnah*, and waiting for their husbands until they return from the *bet hamidrash*. [Women are the mainstay of the Jewish family. The education of the children primarily rests on their shoulders, and they encourage their husbands, who are preoccupied with earning a livelihood, to study Torah.]

Berachot 17a

EVERYTHING DEPENDS ON THE WIFE

The *Midrash* relates the following anecdote to illustrate the paramount role of the wife in a marriage.

A devout man was married to a devout woman. After their divorce, he married a wicked woman, and she changed him into an evil person. She married a corrupt man and turned him into a *tzaddik* (righteous man).

Bereishit Rabbah 17

THE WORLD IS LIKE A WEDDING

The *Gemara* says, "This world is like a wedding feast" (*Eruvin* 54a). The Toledot Yaakov Yosef gave the following interpretation: "Just as the purpose of the wedding is to unite the groom with his bride, so it is the purpose of man in this world to unite himself with God."[4]

Rabbi Chanoch Henach of Alexander[5] explained this saying with a parable: A villager came on a visit to Warsaw. In the evening, he heard the music and singing of a wedding coming from the next house. This happened night after night.

The villager asked his host, "How is it possible that a single householder should have so many weddings?"

The host explained, "The house next door is a wedding hall; today one person holds a wedding there; tomorrow another."

"That is the meaning of the saying, 'The world is like a wedding feast,'" remarked the Rebbe. "There are always some people who enjoy themselves. But some days it is one person, and on other days it is someone else. No one is happy all the time."

Siach Sarfei Kodesh

PARTAKING OF A WEDDING FEAST

Rabbi Chelbo said: He who takes part in a wedding banquet and makes the bridegroom happy is considered as if he had rebuilt one of the ruins of Jerusalem (*Berachot* 6b).

The Sefat Emet asked: The *Gemara* is puzzling. Is it not preferable to erect a new edifice in the Holy City rather than rebuild one of its ruins? He answered: A Jewish home should be built on the solid foundation of our ancient tradition. When a bride and bridegroom pledge to maintain their home according to the Torah, the Jewish nation will endure.

MATCHES ARE MADE IN HEAVEN

The *Midrash* relates an illuminating tale: A [Roman] matron once asked Rabbi Yosi bar Chalafta, "Tell me, Rabbi. Since God finished creating the world, what is He doing all day?"

"He makes matches between men and women, pairing the daughter of so-and-so to so-and-so," Rabbi Yosi replied.

"Is that all?" the matron shot back. "I can do that too. I own a large staff of slaves and maidservants. I can pair them off in less than one hour!"

"It may seem easy to you," said Rabbi Yosi. "But to God it is as difficult as was parting the Red Sea."

She thereupon summoned one thousand slaves and one thousand maidservants and lined them up opposite each other. She then commanded, "You marry this one, and you marry that one!" and paired them off for one night. When they emerged the next morning, one had a bruised head, the other had an eye put out, and a third had broken legs. One shouted, "I don't want this slave!" Another yelled, "I don't want this maidservant!"

The matron immediately sent for Rabbi Yosi.

"Rabbi," she said. "I realize that your Torah is true. It is beautiful and admirable. Whatever you told me is absolutely correct" (*Vayikra Rabbah* 8).

[The point of this *Midrash* is that by making matches God decides what kind of people will populate the world. He thereby determines the flow of events and the course of history.]

MARRIAGE IS LIKE AN OCEAN VOYAGE

The *Midrash* says: There are many who leave on a voyage across the sea. Most of them return safely; only a few are shipwrecked and do not come back. Marriage is the same way. Most marriages succeed, and only a few fail.

Bamidbar Rabbah 9

THE ALTAR WEEPS

If a man divorces his first wife, even the altar sheds tears, as it says:

And this you do as well: You cover the altar of God with tears, weeping and moaning, so that He refuses to regard the oblation any more and to accept what you offer. But you ask, "Because of what?" Because God is a witness between you and your wife with whom you have broken faith, though she is your partner and covenanted spouse" (Malachi 2:13, 14).

Gittin 90b

DIVORCE

The Hebrew word for bill of divorce is גט *get*, hence the name of the talmudic tractate dealing with the laws of divorce is *Gittin*. The word *get* is not found in biblical Hebrew, and its etymology is obscure. The Vilna Gaon discovered that nowhere in the entire Torah are the two letters ג *gimel* and ט *tet* paired, neither within one word nor even as the last and first letters of adjoining words. Since these letters are always distant from each other, they form a fitting name for a document that separates husband and wife from one another.

Dvar Eliyahu

11

Pregnancy and Childbirth

THE SYSTEM OF PROCREATION

Malbim: In the Ten Commandments, the fifth commandment to honor your father and mother follows the fourth
commandment to remember the *Shabbat* and keep it holy.
The close connection between these two commandments
is evident also in the verse, "Every person must respect his
mother and father and keep my *Shabbat*" (Leviticus 19:3).

What is the factor that links these two commandments?

During the six days of Creation, God brought into being
a prototype of each species, including man. If God had not
stopped the process of creation but continued to fashion
living things, the system of procreation—of parents beget-
ting offspring—would not exist. God Himself would create
each individual. When God ceased creating on *Shabbat*, He
ensured the continuance of life on earth by instituting procreation, giving parents the power to beget children. Thus
we can say that parents are partners of God. They engen-
der the child's body, while God bestows the soul and
breathes life into the physical form.

The fact that one is born of a father and a mother is
the direct result of God's resting on *Shabbat*. And this is

the key to understanding the juxtaposition of "Honor your father and mother" and "Keep the *Shabbat*."

Malbim to Exodus 20:12

DURATION OF PREGNANCY

The Talmud teaches: Shmuel said, "A woman can give birth only on the two hundred and seventy-first day, the two hundred and seventy-second day, or the two hundred and seventy-third day of pregnancy." [Two hundred and seventy-one days are nine months of thirty days each, and on the first day of the tenth month she gives birth (Rashi).]

Mar Zutra said, "It is stated, "God gave [Ruth] conception [*herayon*], and the numeric value of הריון, *herayon* [pregnancy] is two hundred and seventy-one" (*hei* = 5; *reish* = 200; *yud* = 10; *vav* = 6; *nun* = 50).

Niddah 38a

THREE PARTNERS

The *Gemara* states: There are three partners in man: The Holy One, Blessed be He, the father, and the mother. The father supplies the white substance (sperm) from which are derived the child's bones, sinews, nails, his brain, and the white in his eyes. The mother supplies the red substance (the menstrual blood) from which are derived skin, flesh, blood, hair, and the black of the eyes. The Holy One, Blessed be He, gives the spirit and the soul, beauty of features, eyesight, the power of hearing, the ability to speak, to walk, understanding, and discernment. When the time arrives for the person to depart from this world, God takes His portion back and leaves the portions contributed by the father and the mother with them.

Niddah 31a

FOR THREE TRANSGRESSIONS

The *Mishnah* teaches: For three transgressions women die during childbirth: for being careless regarding the laws of *niddah* (menstruation), the tithe from the dough, and kindling the *Shabbat* light (*Shabbat* 2:6).

The *Gemara* (*Shabbat* 31b) explains that since these three *mitzvot* were specifically assigned to women, they are held accountable for ignoring them. Childbirth is a time of danger, when punishments are most likely.

FROM WHICH PART DOES THE EMBRYO DEVELOP?

The Talmud records the following discussion:

From which part is the embryo formed? The sages say: From the head. Abba Shaul says: It is formed from the navel, and its roots spread out in all directions from there. You may even say that Abba Shaul agrees with the sages, because Abba Shaul's statement only applies to the formation, that when an embryo is formed, it is formed from the center, but with respect to existence all agree that its source is in the nose, for it says, "All in whose nostrils was the merest breath of life" (Genesis 7:22).

Sotah 45b

AN ANGEL NAMED NIGHT

Rabbi Chaninah bar Papa expounded: The angel who is in charge of conception is named Night [meaning the night is set aside for conception], and he takes up a drop and places it before the Holy One, Blessed be He, saying, "Master of the Universe, what shall be the fate of this drop? Shall it produce a strong or a weak man, a wise man or a fool, a rich or a poor man?" However, the angel does not mention "a wicked man or a righteous one."

This is in accordance with the view of Rabbi Chaninah, who stated: Everything is in the hands of heaven except the fear of God. [A person's physical strength, intelligence, and material wealth are predetermined by God, but man is given the free will to make moral choices.]

Niddah 16b

THE MIRACLE OF PREGNANCY

Rabbi Elazar said: What does an embryo resemble when it is in its mother's womb? A nut floating in a bowl of water. If someone puts his finger on it, it would sink to one side or the other.

The Rabbis taught: During the first three months of pregnancy, the embryo occupies the lowest chamber, during the middle ones, it occupies the middle chamber, and during the last months it occupies the uppermost chamber; and when its time to emerge arrives, it turns over and then emerges, and this is the cause of the woman's pains at childbirth.

Rav Chinena bar Papa expounded: Consider the contrast between the power of God and that of mortal man. A man puts his things in a skin bottle (a vessel for holding liquids made of the skin of an animal) whose holes are tied

up and whose opening is turned upward, and yet it is doubt-
ful whether or not the things will be preserved. God, on the
other hand, fashions the embryo in a woman's internal
organ that is open and whose opening is turned downward,
and yet it is preserved.

Rabbi Elazar said: What is implied by the verse, "Who
alone does wondrous things; blessed is His glorious name
forever"? (Psalm 72:18). Even the person for whom the
miracle is performed is unaware of the miracle. [Only God
alone knows it.]

Niddah 31a

THERE IS NO ARTIST LIKE GOD

Rabbi Yochanan said: Look how the capacity of human
beings falls short of God's capacity. A human being is able
to draw a picture on the wall, but he cannot give it breath
and spirit, bowels and intestines. But God is not so; He
shapes one form in the midst of another and invests it
with breath and spirit, bowels and intestines. And this is
what Hannah[1] said, "There is no *tzur* (rock) like our God"
(1 Samuel 2:2). What means "there is no *tzur* like our God"?
There is no artist (*tzayar*) like our God.

Berachot 10a

WHEN DOES THE SOUL ENTER THE BODY?

The Talmud relates the following eye-opening discussion:
Antoninus[2] asked Rabbi Yehudah: When does God
place the soul in man—at the time of conception or when

the embryo is actually formed? Rabbi Yehudah answered: From the moment of formation [which occurs forty days after conception (Maharsha)]. Antoninus countered: Is it possible that a piece of meat should remain unsalted for more than three days without becoming spoiled? [By the same token, if the soul entered the body only at the time of formation, how could the impregnated semen remain alive in the mother's womb without becoming spoiled? (Rashi).] Rabbi Yehudah agreed and said: I learned something from Antoninus' words.

Sanhedrin 91b

WHEN DOES THE EVIL INCLINATION ENTER MAN?

Antoninus asked Rabbi Yehudah: When does the evil inclination begin to dominate a person: at the time of formation of the embryo or at birth? Rabbi Yehudah replied: At the time of formation. Antoninus demurred: If what you say is true, the child would rebel in the mother's womb, tear the womb, and go out. Therefore, the evil inclination must begin to hold sway only at birth. Rabbi Yehudah agreed and quoted a Scripture to support this view, "Sin is crouching at the door" (Genesis 4:7).

Sanhedrin 91b

THE EMBRYO IN THE MOTHER'S WOMB

Rabbi Simla'i lectured: What does an embryo resemble when it is in its mother's womb? It looks like folded writing tablets. Its hands rest on its two temples, its two elbows on its two thighs, and its two heels against its buttocks. Its head lies between its knees, its mouth is closed, its navel is open, and it eats what its mother eats and drinks, but it produces no excrement because otherwise it might kill its mother. As soon as it is born, the closed organ (the mouth) opens and the open one (the navel) closes; otherwise the fetus could not live even one single hour.

A light burns above the head of the fetus, and it looks and sees from one end of the world to the other [meaning, each person has unlimited potential]. And do not be surprised at this, because a person who sleeps here [in Babylon] might see a dream in Spain. And there is no time in which a person enjoys greater happiness than in those days [in the womb], for it says, "O that I were as in months gone by, in the days when God watched over me" (Job 29:2).

The fetus is also taught all the Torah from beginning to end. As soon as it is born, an angel approaches, slaps it on its mouth, and causes it to forget all the Torah completely.

Niddah 30b

DEVELOPMENT OF THE FETUS

Abba Shaul explained: In the beginning of its development, a fetus resembles a locust, and its two eyes are like two eyes of a fly, but they are far removed from one another. Its two nostrils are like two eyes of a fly but very near one another. The mouth of the fetus is stretched like a hair-thin thread; its male organ is the size of a lentil, and in the case of a female, the organ has the shape of a slit of barley grain, but it has no shaped hands or feet. The fetus is described in Job 10:10–12:

You poured me out like milk, congealed me like cheese;
    You clothed me with skin and flesh and wove me of bones
and sinews.
    You bestowed on me life and care; your providence
watched over my spirit.

Niddah 25a

THE WOMAN'S CURSE

To the woman He said, "I will greatly increase your pain
and your pregnancy. It will be with anguish that you will
give birth to children. Your passion will be to your husband,
and he will dominate you" (Genesis 3:16).

    Rabbi Chaim Volozhiner: "I will greatly increase your
pain and your pregnancy." The *Gemara* (*Eruvin* 100b) interprets "your pain" to refer to the pain of bringing up children, and "your pregnancy" to denote the discomfort of
pregnancy.

    The verse thus places the bringing up of children ahead
of pregnancy and childbirth. Why is the natural order of
things reversed?

    By mentioning the pain of raising children before the
discomforts of childbirth, the Torah hints at an additional
curse for women. The implication is that while a woman is
raising her small children with all the toil and distress this
entails, she will become pregnant again, which will greatly
compound her troubles.

Iturei Torah

LIKE A STOREHOUSE

Rav Chisda said: God built Eve after the model of a store-house. Just as a storehouse is narrow at the top and broad at the bottom in order to hold the produce safely, so is a woman narrower above and broader below in order to hold the fetus.

Berachot 61a

THREE KEYS

Rabbi Yochanan said: Three keys God keeps under His control and does not entrust to a messenger: the key of rain-fall, the key of childbirth, and the key of the revival of the dead. [The three keys encompass all of man's existence: his coming into the world; his livelihood, since rainfall is the factor that determines the economy; and his resurrection in the days of *Mashiach*.]

Ta'anit 2b

CHILDLESSNESS

The Talmud states: Why were our ancestors [Abraham and Sarah, Isaac and Rebeccah and Rachel] childless? Because the Holy One, Blessed be He, longs for the prayers of the righteous (*Yevamot* 64a).

Rabbi Yehoshua ben Levi said: A person who is child-less is considered as dead, for it says, "[Rachel said to Jacob:] Give me children, or else I am dead!" (Genesis 30:1) (*Nedarim* 64b).

THE BIRTH OF JOSEPH

[Rachel] became pregnant and gave birth to a son [Joseph]. "God has gathered away (*asaf*) my humiliation," she said (Genesis 30:23).

The *Midrash* explains the phrase "my humiliation": As long as a woman does not have a son, she has no one on whom she can blame her shortcomings. As soon as she has a son, she pins her blunders on him. From now on, [Rachel said,] if Jacob says to me, "Who broke this cup?" I can answer, "Your son did it." "Who ate these figs?" I'll say, "It was your son" (*Bereishit Rabbah* 73).

MICHAL'S BARRENNESS

We read in *Tanach* that when King David brought back the ark from the land of the Philistines, he "whirled with all his might before God." Michal, his wife, came out to greet him and criticized him for dancing publicly, which she considered unbecoming. The episode closes with the heartrending verse, "To her dying day Michal, the daughter of Saul, had no children" (2 Samuel 6–23).

Rabbi Yosef Yonah Tzvi Horowitz of Unsdorf comments that this punishment seems to be unduly harsh. Rabbi Horowitz suggests that the verse should be read in a different light. Michal's infertility should not be viewed as a punishment but rather as an explanation for her condemnation of David. David was jumping, skipping, and dancing like a father playfully cavorting with his little child. The passage is telling us that, sad to say, Michal was childless; she had never played the fool with a little baby. Therefore she could not understand how a grown man could lose his head and frolic and jump out of sheer happiness.

THE GRAVE AND THE WOMB

The *Gemara* states: It is written, "The grave and a barren womb are never satisfied" (Proverbs 30:15, 16). Why does the Scripture place the grave next to the womb? It comes to teach you that just as the womb takes in and gives forth again, so the grave takes in and gives forth again. And we can draw a logical inference from this: If the womb which takes in silently gives forth with loud noise (the crying of the newborn baby), doesn't it stand to reason that the grave, which takes in with loud noise (the wailing of the mourners), will give forth with loud noise (in the messianic era, when the dead will return to life.)[3]

Berachot 15b

HER IMPULSIVE OATH

Rabbi Shimon ben Yocha'i was asked by his students: Why did the Torah ordain that a woman after childbirth should bring a sacrifice? He replied: When giving birth, every woman swears impulsively that she will have no intercourse with her husband again. The Torah, therefore, ordained that she should bring a sacrifice, [because she regrets her oath].

Niddah 31b

THE PLACE OF THE BREASTS

The Talmud expounds the verse, "Bless the Lord, O my soul, and do not forget all His bounties" (Psalm 103:2). What did David mean when he said "all His bounties"? Rabbi Abbahu said: When David sucked from his mother's bosom and looked at her breasts, he broke into song, praising God for placing the breasts at the source of understanding [namely, the heart, which is the seat of understanding]. Rabbi Abbahu connects the word *gemulav* (His bounties) with *gamal* (weaned).

Berachot 10a

TORAH COMPARED TO BREASTS

The *Gemara* quotes the verse, "A loving doe, a graceful mountain goat. Let her breasts satisfy you at all times" (Proverbs 6:13). (This is an allegorical reference to the Torah.)

Rabbi Shmuel ben Nachmani expounded: Why are the words of the Torah compared to a breast? Just as a breast, no matter how often a child sucks it, he always finds milk in it, so is it with the words of Torah. As often as you study them, you always find delight in them.

Eruvin 54b

HANNAH'S PRAYER

Hannah, who was childless, fervently prayed to God. The Talmud records Hannah's prayer: "Master of the Universe, among all the things you have created in woman, you have not created one without a purpose: eyes to see, ears to hear, a nose to smell, a mouth to speak, hands to do work, legs to walk with, breasts to nurse. These breasts that You have placed on my heart, are they not meant to nurse? Give me a son, so that I may nurse with them" (*Berachot* 31b).

The sages are telling us that, just as every limb in the human body serves a purpose, so every one of the myriad God's creations is here for a specific purpose. Hannah's prayer teaches us that the human body is whole only if all the limbs or organs are functioning properly. If one limb is missing, the entire body is in disarray.

WHEN A CHILD IS BORN

Rabbi Ammi said: When a boy is born, peace comes into the world. He also said: When a boy is born, his bread (i.e., sustenance) comes with him (*Niddah* 31b).

If the firstborn child is a daughter, it is a good sign for the boys [since she helps her parents in raising her brothers] (*Bava Batra* 141a).

SEXTUPLETS

The Israelites [in Egypt] were fertile and prolific, and their population increased. They became so numerous that the land was filled with them (Exodus 1:7).

Rashi, quoting the *Midrash* (*Shemot Rabbah* 1:8), tells us that every woman gave birth to sextuplets.

The Gemara also tells of the births of sextuplets. Rabbi

Eliezer expounded the verse, "God blessed Oved-edom's house . . . because of the Ark of God" (2 Samuel 6:12). [After King David brought the Holy Ark out of Philistine captivity, he diverted it to the house of Oved-edom, where it remained for three months, whereupon God blessed him.]

What was the blessing with which God blessed Oved-edom? His wife and her eight daughters-in-law each gave birth to sextuplets.

Berachot 63b

THE LETTER *TET*

The numeric value of the letter ט *tet* is nine. In Kabbalah, the letter *tet* is viewed as an allusion to the nine months of pregnancy, and the shape of the *tet* is seen as a representation of the mother's womb in which new life is being nurtured. Thus, the number nine holds profound significance in the structure of all of existence. This is evident in the remarkable phenomenon that the sum of the digits of all multiples of nine add up to nine. For example, 5 x 9 = 45, and 4 + 5 = 9; 27 x 9 = 243, and 2 + 4 + 3 = 9; 368 x 9 = 3312, and 3 + 3 + 1 + 2 = 9. The same holds true for the reduced value of many fundamental concepts of the Torah. For example, the reduced value of אמת *emet*, truth, is also 9 (1 + 40 + 400 = 441, and 4 + 4 + 1 = 9); and ברית *brit* (covenant) adds up to 9 (2 + 200 + 10 + 400 = 612, and 6 + 1 + 2 = 9). So does אור, or light (1 + 6 + 200 = 207, and 2 + 7 = 9); as well as שבת, *Shabbat* (300 + 2 + 400 = 702, and 7 + 2 = 9).

12

Sleep

RABBINIC SAYINGS ABOUT SLEEP

Ten measures of sleep descended to the world; nine were taken by slaves, and only one by the rest of the world (*Kiddushin* 49b).

Sleep is one sixtieth part of death (*Berachot* 57b).

Putting your hand to your forehead will help you fall asleep (*Pesachim* 112a).

If someone swears not to sleep for three days, he is flogged [as a punishment for making a vain oath, because it is impossible to stay awake for three consecutive days], and he may sleep immediately (*Nedarim* 15a).

A daughter of Rav Chisda once asked her father: "Wouldn't you like to sleep a little?"

"There will soon come days that are long and short," he replied, "and we shall have time to sleep long" (*Eruvin* 65a).

He meant to say that the days in the grave are long in quantity but short in quality, because in the grave you cannot study Torah or do *mitzvot*.

Sleeping on *Shabbat* is a joy—*Sheinah BeShabbat Taanug*. (The initials of this Hebrew phrase, *shin, bet, tav*, form the word Shabbat) (*Yalkut Reuveni, Va'etchanan*).

247

Sleep and wine are a pleasure for the wicked and a pleasure for the world [While the wicked are sleeping and intoxicated they cannot cause any harm.] (*Sanhedrin* 71b).

In *Tanach*, old age is described as the time "when one rises up at the voice of the bird" (Ecclesiastes 12:4). An old man sleeps lightly; even the chirping of a bird wakes him up (*Shabbat* 152a).

Rabbi Acha said: A *mil*'s walk or a little sleep counteracts the effects of wine. Rabbi Nachman said: This applies only to one who has drunk no more than a *revi'it*; but if he has drunk more, the walk will only cause more fatigue, and the sleep more drunkenness! (*Sanhedrin* 22b).

Rav said: Adda the fisherman told me, "After eating fish, eat watercress (a plant used in salads) and drink milk, occupy your body (go for a walk), and don't occupy your bed" (*Mo'ed Katan* 11a).

Rabbi Chaninah ben Chachinai said: One who stays awake at night . . . endangers his life (*Avot* 3:5).

DON'T WASTE TIME

Rabbi Dosa ben Harkinas said: Late-morning sleep, midday wine, children's chatter, and sitting in the company of the ignorant drive a man from the world (*Avot* 3:14).

Rabbi Samson Raphael Hirsch comments: Sleeping away the morning hours and indulging in strong drink dulls the mind. The *Mishnah* frowns on each of these four idle pursuits as squandering of time—the most precious gift given to man.

DAVID'S HARP

The *Gemara* relates: A harp was hanging above David's bed. As soon as midnight arrived, a north wind came and blew on it, and it played by itself. He rose immediately and studied Torah until the break of dawn (*Berachot* 3b).

A WORKER'S SLEEP

A worker's sleep is sweet, whether he has little or much to eat; but the rich man's abundance doesn't let him sleep (Ecclesiastes 5:11). The reference is to the many possessions of the rich man. His worries about losing his wealth deprive him of his sleep (Rashi). According to an alternate explanation, it is the worker who cannot sleep because envy of the rich man's wealth keeps him awake.

HOW LONG SHOULD YOU SLEEP?

Rambam (Maimonides, a great Torah scholar and famous physician): A day and night are twenty-four hours. It is sufficient if you sleep one-third of that, i.e., eight hours. . . . You should not sleep facedown or faceup, only on your side. The first part of the night you should lie on your left side, the latter part of the night on your right side. Don't sleep immediately after eating; wait about three or four hours before going to sleep. And don't sleep in the daytime.

Hilchot Dei'ot 4:4, 5

THE CONSIDERATE WIVES
OF THE TORAH SCHOLARS

In vain do you rise early and stay up late, you who toil for the bread you eat; He provides as much to those who chase away their sleep (Psalm 127:2).

Rabbi Yitzchak explained: "Those who chase away their sleep" refers to the wives of the Torah scholars who chase the sleep from their eyes in this world [sitting up all night waiting for their husbands to return from the *yeshivah*] and achieve thereby the life of the world to come [as a reward for the consideration they show their studious husbands.]

Ketubot 62a

ASLEEP FOR SEVENTY YEARS

The Talmud relates that the saintly Choni Hame'aggeil (Choni the circle-drawer) once, while riding on his donkey through the countryside, noticed an elderly farmer planting a carob tree. He approached the old man.

"How long will it take until this tree bears fruit?" he asked.

"Seventy years," replied the farmer.

"Do you really expect to live that long, so that you will eat the fruit of your labor?" Choni retorted.

"Dear Rabbi," the farmer answered, "it is not necessary for me to enjoy the fruit of this tree. I enjoy the fruit of the tree my father planted; and so I hope that my son will enjoy the fruit of the tree I am planting."

Pleased with the answer, Choni sat down in the grass and ate a slice of bread. He suddenly got tired and fell asleep. Around him a rock formation rose up from the ground that shielded him from view, and so he slept for seventy years. When at last he awoke, he saw a man picking fruit from the carob tree, eating it with obvious delight. Choni walked over to the man.

"Are you the farmer who planted this tree?" he asked.

"No, my grandfather planted this tree seventy years ago."

Realizing that he had been sleeping all that time, Choni went home and inquired if his son was still alive.

"He died long ago," was the answer. "But Choni's grandson lives in this town."

"Look at me, folks," Choni said. "I am the old Choni Hame'aggeil himself." But no one believed him, since everyone knew that old Choni had died long ago.

Then he went to the *bet midrash* (house of study) and expounded the Talmud to the local sages.

"This man analyzes the *Gemara* the same way the late Choni used to do. We still remember his discourses," the scholars said to one another.

"Look at me! I am Choni Hame'aggeil, can't you see?" Choni exclaimed.

The scholars did not believe him and did not accord him the proper respect. Since people did not recognize him and simply ignored him, he became deeply distressed and prayed to God to take back his soul. Soon after that he died. Rava said that Choni's story illustrates the popular adage: "Death rather than solitude" [Alternate translations: "Give me companionship or give me death," or "Loneliness is worse than death," or "Better dead than desolate/friendless."] (*Ta'anit* 23a).

SLEEPING AND GROWING OLD

The Hebrew word *yashan* means both *sleeping* and *growing old*. The story of Choni Hame'aggeil is a perfect illustration of both meanings coinciding. By sleeping for seventy years, Choni found himself old and behind the times.

If a person remains awake, he stays young and stays at-
tuned with the changing generations. Vibrantly alive, he is
capable of presenting the eternal Torah values to the new
generation in the contemporay idiom, using up-to-date
educational methods.

✤

PHARAOH'S SLEEP

"[Pharaoh dreamed that] the ugly, lean cows ate up the
seven handsome, fat cows. Pharaoh then woke up. He fell
asleep again and had a second dream" (Genesis 41:4, 5).

Rabbi Aharon of Karlin: Pharaoh then woke up. He fell
asleep again. Jacob also woke up from a dream in which
he dreamed about the ladder whose top reached upward
to heaven. When Jacob's dream ended, we read, "Jacob
awoke from his sleep, and he said . . . " (Genesis 28:16).
When a Jew arises, the first thing he does is "he says." He
recites the *berachot* of the morning service, the *Shema*, the
Shemoneh Esrei, he studies Torah. . . . Compare this with
Pharaoh: "He wakes up," turns over on his other side, "and
goes back to sleep."

✤

THE BEDTIME *SHEMA*

The *Gemara* says: On going to bed you should say the first
section of the *Shema* and the *berachah Hamapil*: "Who casts
the bonds of sleep upon my eyes and slumber on my eyelids" (*Berachot* 60b). Rabbi Yitzchak said: If you recite the
bedtime *Shema*, it is as though you held a two-edged sword

in your hand [to protect you against the evils of the night (Rashi). (*Berachot* 5a).

THE REBBE SLEPT SOUNDLY

Rabbi Mordechai of Lechovitz[1] used to say: "If there is a single coin left in my house at night, I cannot fall asleep. But if I don't have a penny to my name I sleep soundly, knowing that as soon as I wake up, I must immediately look to God for help."

Or Yesharim

SERVING GOD IN YOUR SLEEP

The Chozeh of Lublin[2] said: You can serve the Creator even while you are asleep. If you are attached to God's Torah, the purpose of your sleep is to gain strength to serve God. Thus you are fulfilling the Torah twenty-four hours each day.

Zot Zikaron

DECENCY COMES FIRST

[After he had a vision in a dream of the ladder that reached into heaven,] Jacob arose from his sleep and said, "God is truly in this place, but I did not know it" (Genesis 28:16).

Rabbi Nosson Tzvi Finkel:[3] Rashi comments: By saying, "But I did not know it," Jacob implied that, had he known it, he would not have slept in this holy place. In other words, Jacob reproached himself for showing disrespect by sleeping at the sacred site, even though it was during this sleep that he rose to the peak of prophetic vision.

There is an important ethical lesson in this: Above all, we must adhere to the rules of common decency and respect, even if by violating these rules we could attain the loftiest spiritual heights. Ethical conduct takes precedence to Torah.[4]

Or Hatzafun

13

Dreams

INSTRUMENTS OF PROVIDENCE

Dreams and the interpretation of dreams play a major role in the Torah and the Talmud. One might say that dreams and their interpretation were instruments God used to bring the Jewish people into being. Jacob's dream of the ladder that connected earth and heaven held the message of God's guidance of all events in the world. Joseph's dreams kindled the envy of his brothers to such an extent that they sold him into slavery. Joseph's interpretation of the dreams of Pharaoh's butler and baker, and subsequently, that of Pharaoh's own dreams led to his ascendancy to viceroy of Egypt. This resulted in the migration to Egypt of Jacob and his sons, which eventually brought in its wake the centuries of Egyptian bondage culminating in the Exodus, the Giving of the Torah, and the birth of the Jewish nation at Sinai.[1] The ultimate fulfillment of Jewish history, too, is associated with dreaming, for the final redemption is described as, "When God will return the captivity of Zion, we will be like dreamers" (Psalm 126:1).

The sages of the Talmud and *Midrash* offer profound psychological insights into the significance of dreams and the interpretation of dream symbols.

APHORISMS ABOUT DREAMS

A dream is one sixtieth part of prophecy (*Berachot* 57b).

There are three things for which you should pray: a good king, a good year, and a good dream (*Berachot* 55a).

Rav Chisda said: A dream that is not interpreted is like a letter that is not read [It is neither good nor bad, since all dreams follow the suggestion of the interpreter (Rashi).] (*Berachot* 55a).

Rabbi Yochanan said: Three kinds of dreams are fulfilled: an early-morning dream, a dream that a friend has about you, and a dream that is interpreted in the middle of a dream. Some add also, a dream that is repeated (*Berachot* 55b).

Rabbi Yonatan said: A man is shown in a dream only that which is suggested by his own thoughts. This is proved by the fact that a person never dreams of a date palm of gold or an elephant going through the eye of a needle, [because he never thinks of such things] (*Berachot* 55b).

There cannot be a dream without some nonsense (*Berachot* 55b).

If a man goes seven days without a dream he is called evil (*Berachot* 55b).

Rav Huna said: A good man is not shown a good dream, and a bad man is not shown a bad dream [A good man is shown a bad dream, and a bad man is shown a good dream. The purpose is to turn the good man to repentance, and to give the bad man his reward in this world (Rashi).] (*Berachot* 55b).

Rabbi Chanan said: Even if a person is told in a dream that he will die the following day, he should not stop praying (*Berachot* 10b).

Rabbi Elazar said: All dreams follow the mouth. [The fulfillment of the dream depends on the suggestion of the interpreter], because it says, ["The butler said to Pharaoh], 'Things turned out just as [Joseph] said they would'" (Genesis 41:12) (*Berachot* 55b).

Rabbi Meir said: Dreams have no effect one way or the other (*Gittin* 52a).

A RIVER, A BIRD, AND A POT

Rav Chanan said: There are three kinds of dreams that signify peace, namely, a dream about a river, a bird, and a pot (*Berachot* 56b).

A pot symbolizes abundant food, and when there is plenty of food in the house there is peace. An alternate interpretation sees a pot as the peacemaker, because a pot separates the fire underneath it from the food inside it.

The Ketav Sofer[2] suggests that the three dream symbols presage three kinds of peace: the pot brimming with nourishing food hints at domestic peace; the meandering river that serenely traverses a country signifies tranquility in the territory of that country; the bird that wings its way unencumbered across international boundaries, mountains, and seas stands for global peace and harmony.

DREAMING OF A PUMPKIN

The *Gemara* states: Pumpkins are shown in a dream only to a person who fears heaven with all his might (*Berachot* 56b).

Rashi explains that although pumpkins are large in

size, they do not grow high above the ground. Thus they are symbolic of the God-fearing man who, despite his many merits, remains lowly and humble.

DREAMING OF A VINE

If you dream of a vine laden with fruit, your wife will not have a miscarriage, because it says, "Your wife shall be like a fruitful vine" (Psalm 128:3). [Unlike all other foods and beverages, wine improves with age, hence the analogy to the growing fetus is very apt.]

If you dream of a choice vine, you can look forward to seeing *Mashiach*, because it says, "[*Mashiach*] loads down his donkey with a single grapevine, his young donkey with a single vine branch" (Genesis 49:11). [Like wine, Israel's unwavering belief in the coming of *Mashiach* becomes stronger as the years go by.]

Berachot 57a

MISCELLANEOUS OTHER DREAMS

If you see wheat in a dream, you will see peace, as it says, "He makes your borders peace and satisfies you with choice wheat" (Psalm 147:14).

If you see a goat in a dream, you will have a blessed year, as it says, "The goats' milk will be enough for your food" (Proverbs 27:27).

If you see a goose in a dream, you may hope for wisdom, since it says, "Wisdom cries aloud in the street" (Proverbs 1:20).

If you see a snake in a dream, it means that your livelihood is assured [because a snake eats dust, which is always available in abundance.] (*Berachot* 57a).

JACOB'S OTHER DREAM

[Before leaving Laban, Jacob told Rachel and Leah about a dream he had, saying,] "During the breeding season, I lifted my eyes and saw in a dream that the bucks mounting the sheep were ringed, spotted, and flecked" (Genesis 31:10).

In the portion of Vayeitzei, Jacob has two dreams that stand in sharp contrast to one another. When leaving *Eretz Yisrael* he had a dream of a ladder uniting heaven and earth, with angels ascending and descending and God standing at its head. This was the dream of a man steeped in spirituality.

But after twenty years of living close to the corrupt Laban, Jacob has the dream described in the present verse in which he sees visions of goats that are ringed, spotted, and flecked. Obviously, his mind is now occupied with acquiring wealth and material possessions. And so the angel of God appears to Jacob in a dream and tells him, "I see all that Laban has done to you" (Genesis 31:12). The angel is telling Jacob that some of Laban's attitudes have rubbed off on him and affected his outlook on life. It is time for him to leave. The angel continues, "Now set out and leave this land. Return to the land where you were born" (Genesis 31:13).

Rabbi Shlomoh Riskin

THREE KINDS OF DREAMS

Rabbeinu Bachya,[3] commenting on Pharaoh's dreams in Genesis 41:1, speaks about the origins of dreams. He says: Some dreams are attributable to the food one has eaten, others are induced by thoughts, and then there are dreams that are rooted in the soul. The dreams that are produced by food stem from internal chemical processes that affect the brain. Such dreams have no meaning or value. A dream induced by thought is a reflection of the ideas that occupy a person's mind during the day. The mental images he focuses on during his waking hours reappear in his dreams.

A dream that is rooted in the soul is inspired by one's imagination. When a person sleeps, his conscious mind is dormant. It is then that the dreamer's imagination gains the upper hand to the point that he believes that the fantasies he sees are reality. A dream of this kind, one that is not prompted by prior reflection or planning, arises both in the righteous and the wicked. . . . God planted these dreams in Pharaoh's mind and caused him to be upset by them. Then He made the Egyptian magicians offer foolish interpretations of these dreams,[4] all in order to raise Joseph to the high office of viceroy.

THE GREEDY INTERPRETER OF DREAMS

The Talmud relates: Bar Hedya was an interpreter of dreams. If you paid him, he gave a favorable interpretation, but if you did not pay, he gave an unfavorable interpretation.

Abbaye and Rava each had a dream. Abbaye gave him a *zuz*, but Rava did not give him anything. They told him: In our dream we had to read the verse, "Your ox will be slaughtered before your eyes" (Deuteronomy 28:31). To Rava he said: Your business will fail, and you will be so upset that you will have no appetite to eat. To Abbaye he said: Your business will prosper, and you will not be able to eat from sheer joy. . . . They said to him: In our dream we had to read the verse, "All the nations of the world will realize that God's name is associated with you" (Deuteronomy 28:10). To Abbaye he said: Your name will become famous as head of the *yeshivah*, and you will be greatly feared. To Rava he said: The king's treasury will be broken into; you will be arrested as a thief, and everyone will draw an inference from you [saying: if Rava is suspect, then surely we are]. The next day, the king's treaury was broken into, and they came and arrested Rava. . . . Finally, Rava gave him a fee. Then he said to him: I dreamed that I saw a wall fall down. He replied: You will become extremely wealthy. . . . He said to him: [In my dream] I saw my own villa collapse, and everyone came and took a brick. He said to him: Your teachings will be spread throughout the world. . . . [The story ends with the greedy Bar Hedya's gruesome execution by the Romans.] "They tied together two cedars with a rope, and tied one of Bar Hedya's legs to one cedar and the other to the other. Then they released the rope so that each tree rebounded to its place. He was decapitated and his body was split in two."

Berachot 56a

PRAYER REGARDING DREAMS

The *Gemara* states: If one had a dream and does not remember what he saw, [meaning, he is not sure whether the dream portended good or evil] let him stand before the *kohanim* at the time when they spread their hands in blessing, and let him say, "Master of the world! I am Yours and my dreams are Yours. I have dreamed a dream, and I do not know what it indicates. . . . May it be acceptable before You, God, that all my dreams be good ones. If they are good dreams, strengthen them, fortify them, like the dreams of Joseph, and if they require healing, heal them."[5]

Berachot 55b

THE INTERPRETATION OF VARIOUS DREAM SYMBOLS

Following is a sampling of dreams and their interpretations drawn from the large selection that is found in the Talmud in *Berachot* 56b–57b.

If you see a myrtle in your dream, you will have good luck with your property (like a myrtle, which has many leaves).

If you see eggs, your petition remains pending; if they are broken, your petition will be granted. The same with nuts and cucumbers and all vessels of glass and breakable things like these.

If one dreams that he goes up on a roof, he will attain a high position; if he dreams that he goes down, he will be degraded. . . . If you see an elephant in a dream, a miracle will happen to you. All kinds of fruit are good signs in a dream, except unripe dates. All kinds of birds are a good sign in a dream, except the owl, the horned owl, and the bat. . . . If one dreams that he is tearing his garment, his evil decree (against him from heaven) will be torn up.

If one sees a rooster in his dream, he may expect a male child.

If one sees David in a dream, he may hope for piety; if Solomon, he may hope for wisdom; if Ahab,[6] let him fear for punishment.

If one dreams that he has been arrested by the police, protection will be offered him [he is placed in custody and watched, a sign that he will be protected from harm (Rashi)].

If one dreams that he walks into a marsh, he will become head of a *yeshivah*. [Big and small reeds grow in a marsh, an indication that advanced students and beginners will gather to hear his lectures (Rashi).]

Berachot 56b–57b

14

Preserving Life and Maintaining Health

SAVING A LIFE HAS HIGHEST PRIORITY

The Talmud states: There is nothing that comes before saving a life except idolatry, incest, and bloodshed (*Ketubot* 19a).

The Torah regards the saving of human life as supreme. Every law must yield to the preservation of life. If a person is told: Violate this or that law, otherwise you will be killed, he should violate the law and not be killed. The exceptions are the three cardinal sins: idolatry, incest, and murder. One should rather lose one's life than commit these transgressions.

✦

VIOLATE *SHABBAT* TO SAVE A LIFE

Although the observance of *Shabbat* is of overriding importance, *Halachah* requires you to violate *Shabbat* in order to save a life. The *Gemara* gives this rationale: "The Torah

265

tells you to violate one *Shabbat* to save a man's life, for you enable him thereby to observe many *Shabbat* days [during the rest of his life]."

Shabbat 15b

YOU SHALL LIVE BY THEM

Keep My decrees and laws, which if a person keeps them, he shall live by them; I am God (Leviticus 18:5).

The Talmud teaches that the phrase "he shall live by them" implies that God's commandments should be a means of life and not of destruction. Therefore, you must transgress any commandment of the Torah to save a life, except for committing idolatry, adultery, or murder.

Yoma 85b

A MORAL DILEMMA

In a famous passage, the Talmud poses the following agonizing moral dilemma: Suppose two people are traveling on a journey [far from civilization], and one has a pitcher of water. If both drink, they will both die, but if only one drinks, he can reach civilization. The Son of Patura taught: It is better that both should drink and die, rather than that one should watch his companion die. Until Rabbi Akiva came and taught: [It is written:] "He shall live with you" (Leviticus 25:35), [this means] that your life takes precedence over your companion's life.

Maharsha explains that the phrase "with you" implies that your life takes precedence, but that the other fellow too has a right to live after your survival is assured. However, Rabbi Akiva will agree, that if the pitcher belonged to both of them, both should drink and die (Maharsha).

Bava Metzia 62a

A PREEMPTIVE STRIKE IS PERMITTED

If someone comes to kill you, be quick and kill him first (*Berachot* 58a).

The *Gemara* derives this from the verse, "If a burglar is caught in the act of breaking in, and is struck and killed, it is not considered an act of murder" (Exodus 22:1). It is assumed that the burglar would not hesitate to take a life, since he knows that the owner does not stand idly by when his possessions are taken. Therefore, killing him is not considered murder (Rashi).

AN APPALLING PREDICAMENT

The Talmud tells of a man who posed the following distressing question to Rava: "The county governor ordered me to kill so-and-so, and if I refuse, I will be killed. Master, what am I to do?"

"Give your life, but do not kill another man," replied Rava. "After all, how do you know that your blood is redder than the other fellow's blood? Maybe his blood is redder than yours." [Who can say that your blood is more pleasing to God than your fellowman's blood? Therefore, the rule that you should violate any commandment to save your life does not apply in this case (Rashi).]

Sanhedrin 74a

APHORISMS ABOUT HEALTH

The stones on which we sat when we were young are waging war against us in our old age [The poor health habits of our youth are the cause of the aches and pains of our old age.] (*Yerushalmi Beitzah* 1:7).

Eat a third and drink a third and leave a third for when you are angry, and then you will have had your fill [Leave one third of your stomach empty, otherwise when you get angry you will burst (Rashi).] (*Gittin* 70a).

Three things weaken a man's strength, namely, anxiety, traveling, and sin (*Gittin* 70a).

The Talmud says: The Torah weakens a man's strength [through constant study] (*Sanhedrin* 26b).
Commented the Amshinover Rebbe: Do you know what kind of strength is weakened by Torah study? The "strength" of an arrogant man who says, "My own strength and the might of my own hand have won this wealth for me" (Deuteronomy 8:17). When he studies Torah, he realizes that it is God who gives him power to become prosperous. Arrogance is the "strength" that is weakened by Torah study.

Shmuel [who was a physician] said: All illness is caused by the wind (by dust and germs that are carried by the air) (*Bava Metzia* 107b).

Most sick people recover (*Gittin* 28a).

A sick person's own prayers are more effective than the prayers others utter on his behalf (*Bereishit Rabbah* 53).

If someone prays on behalf of his friend while he himself is in need of the same thing, he will be answered first, as it is written: God restored Job's fortunes when he prayed for his friends (Job 42:10) (*Bava Kamma* 92a).

The *Zohar* says: All cures are in God's hand. However, some cures are sent through a messenger, and although these cures are effective, the disease sometimes recurs. But the illnesses that God Himself heals never recur. God's cures are flawless (*Zohar, Vayikra* 303b).

Resh Lakish said: The Holy One, Blessed be He, does not smite Israel unless He has created a remedy for them beforehand. Maharsha explains that since God has promised never to destroy the Jewish people, He creates a remedy before He smites them, for He will definitely use the remedy (*Megillah* 13b).

Rabbi Alexandri said: The miracle that happens when the sick recover is greater than that of Chananiah, Mishael, and Azariah (the three companions of Daniel, who miraculously emerged from a fiery furnace unharmed where they had been thrown for refusing to bow to Nebuchadnezzar's golden idol). The miracle of Chananiah, Mishael, and Azariah concerned a fire kindled by man that all can extinguish, whereas that of a sick person is related to a heavenly fire (the temperature rises), and who can extinguish that? (*Nedarim* 41a).

The Ba'al Shem Tov said: You may be free from sin, but if your body is not strong, your soul will be too weak to serve God properly. Maintain your health and preserve your strength.

Keter Shem Tov[1]

The life of the mother takes precedence over the life of the fetus (*Ohalot*, end of chapter 7). [If the mother's life is threatened, the fetus is regarded as a *rodeif*, a killer in hot pursuit of his victim. *Halachah* rules that the killer must be destroyed to save the life of his intended victim (*Sanhedrin* 72b). Analogously, if the mother's life is at risk, an abortion must be performed to save the life of the mother.]²

SOUND ADVICE

Beware of three things: Do not sit too long, for long sitting aggravates one's abdominal troubles; do not stand too long, because long standing is harmful to the heart; and do not walk too much, because excessive walking is harmful to the eyes. Rather spend one-third of your time sitting, one-third standing, and one-third walking. Standing is better than sitting when you have nothing to lean against.

Ketubot 111a

COLD AND HEAT

Everything is "by the hand of heaven," except cold and heat. (All diseases are ordained from above, and there is nothing you can do to protect yourself. But you can avoid catching a cold or being overcome by heat [by dressing properly and staying indoors or in the cool shade].)

Ketubot 30a

DON'T TAKE AN OVERDOSE

Rabbi Simchah Bunam of Pshis'cha said: We are taught that words of wisdom are "healing for one's body" (Proverbs

4:22). That's why Avtalyon said, "Scholars, be cautious with your words" (*Avot* 1:11). Since words are like medicine, they must be carefully measured, and precaution must be taken against an overdose.

Simchat Yisrael[3]

THE HEALING POWERS OF HERBS

Rabbi Yitzchak Luria, the great kabbalist known as the Holy Ari, revealed the concept of *shevirat hakeilim*. He taught that during Creation there occurred a cosmic cataclysm. In that primordial disaster, the vessels that conveyed the Divine Light to the material world were unable to contain the abundant flow of spirituality. They broke, spilling sparks of holiness, *nitzotzot hakedoshim*. These holy sparks became embedded in all elements of the physical world. It is the sacred mission of the Jewish people to redeem these fallen sparks. By performing *mitzvot* and living a Torah-centered life, a Jew transforms even the most mundane acts, like eating and drinking, into a service of God. He thereby releases the captive sparks.

Rabbi Baruch of Medzhibozh[4] made the following insightful comment:

At the time of Creation, many holy sparks were trapped inside shells of physicality and became lodged in the four forms of existence: mineral, vegetative, animal, and man. How can the holy sparks inside an animal be released? When a Jew eats meat and uses the energy he gains from this meat to serve God, then the sparks that are trapped inside the animal that produced the meat are elevated. Similarly, the sparks in plants attain their destiny when a Jew eats fruits and vegetables and recites the appropriate *berachah* over them. The sparks in the minerals that nourished the plants are freed indirectly when a Jew who obeys God's will consumes fruits and vegetables. But how will the sparks that are trapped inside poisonous and noxious weeds ever be released? No Jew will use them for a *mitzvah*. God in His wisdom arranged it that poisonous herbs also should have a *tikkun* (restoration) by endowing them with marvelous therapeutic powers. The fallen sparks in these herbs are released when a Jew who is ill is cured through medicine derived from such plants and can resume a life of Torah study and performance of mitzvot.

Butzina Denehora, p. 50

AGENTS OF RESCUE

After having killed an Egyptian, Moses was forced to flee from Pharaoh. He ended up in the land of Midian, where he was sitting near the well. When Jethro's daughters came to water their father's sheep they were chased away by other shepherds, but Moses came to their aid and watered their sheep. The daughters told their father, "An Egyptian rescued us from some shepherds" (Exodus 2:19).

The *Midrash* comments: This incident is reminiscent of the case of a man who was bitten by a poisonous lizard and who ran to the river to wash out his wound. When he got there, he saw a child drowning in the waves. He pulled out the child, saving his life. Said the child, "If it had not been for you, I would be dead right now." "Don't thank me," replied the man. "It isn't I who saved you but the lizard who bit me and caused me to run to the river. The lizard is the one who saved you."

When Jethro's daughters thanked Moses for saving them from the shepherds, Moses replied, "The Egyptian whom I killed, he is the one who saved you." Therefore, the girls reported to their father, "An Egyptian rescued us." ("An

Egyptian" does not refer to Moses but to the Egyptian whom Moses had killed.)

The *Midrash* comes to teach us that God's ways are mysterious. He uses many messengers to achieve His rescue, and what may appear as a disaster often is a blessing in disguise.

Shemot Rabbah 1

GUARD YOUR HEALTH

Watch yourselves very carefully (Deuteronomy 4:15).

The Chafetz Chaim[5] said: This verse teaches that a Jew must take care of his health just as a coachman takes care of his horse. The coachman watches that it does not go hungry, because the horse is his livelihood.

Accordingly, a Jew is forbidden to damage his health [by smoking] or inflicting physical pain on himself, for a healthy body means a healthy soul.

The story is told that the Chafetz Chaim once admonished a prominent *rosh yeshivah* (dean) who denied himself even the smallest portion of meat at his daily meal, leaving it for his students. He gently chided him, "Among the many concerns of a *rosh yeshivah*, there is one matter that should be uppermost in his mind: he should see to it that his students have a *rosh yeshivah* who is in good health."

Chafetz Chaim al Hatorah

15

Cleanliness
and Hygiene

CLEANLINESS LEADS TO HOLINESS

Rabbi Pinchas ben Yair says: Cleanliness leads to abstinence, abstinence leads to purity, purity leads to saintliness, saintliness leads to humility, humility leads to fear
of sin, fear of sin leads to holiness, holiness leads to the
Holy Spirit, and the Holy Spirit leads to the Revival of the
Dead.

Avodah Zarah 20b

CLEANLINESS IS A *MITZVAH*

The *Midrash* says: When Hillel the Elder took leave of his
disciples, they asked him, "Rabbi, where are you going?"
He replied, "I am going to perform a *mitzvah*."
"What *mitzvah*?" they inquired.
"I am going to bathe in the bathhouse," he replied.
"Is that considered a *mitzvah*?" they asked.

"Indeed it is," he answered. "Look, the fellow who is in charge of the statues of the emperor in the theaters and circuses cleans and shines them every day. I am created in the image of God, as it says, 'For God made man with His own image' (Genesis 9:6). Surely I should be meticulous about my cleanliness."

Vayikra Rabbah 34

THE BATHHOUSE OF APHRODITE

The Talmud relates that the heathen Proclus asked Rabban Gamliel, "Why are you bathing in the pool of Aphrodite (the Greek goddess of love)? After all, it says in your Torah, 'Let nothing that has been doomed stick to your hand'" (Deuteronomy 13:18).

Rabban Gamliel replied, "I did not enter [Aphrodite's] territory. She is the one that intruded on my territory." [The pool was here long before the Greeks came, and it was open to everyone. Aphrodite does not have the power to deprive the public of their ancient rights (Rashi).]

Avodah Zarah 44b

NEITHER THE PAIN NOR ITS REWARD

We read in the Talmud: Rabbi Chiya fell ill and Rabbi Yochanan came to visit him. He said to him, "Do you welcome your sufferings?" [He implied that if he lovingly accepts the pain, his reward in the world to come will be very great.]

Rabbi Chiya replied: "I want neither the pain nor its reward."

Rabbi Yochanan then held his hand and cured him by the touch of his hand.

On another occasion, Rabbi Yochanan fell ill and Rabbi Chaninah went to visit him. He asked him, "Do you welcome your sufferings?" Rabbi Yochanan replied, "I want neither the pain nor its reward." Rabbi Chaninah then cured him by the touch of his hand.

The *Gemara* asks: If Rabbi Yochanan could cure Rabbi Chiya, why couldn't he cure himself? The rabbis replied: "A prisoner cannot free himself from jail." [And a patient cannot cure himself.]

Berachot 5b

❖

THREE PRECIOUS GIFTS

Rabbi Shimon bar Yocha'i said: The Holy One, Blessed be He, gave Israel three precious gifts, and all of them were given only through suffering. They are: The Torah, the Land of Israel, and the world to come.

Berachot 5a

❖

THE ORDEAL OF RABBI CHANINAH BEN TRADYON

We find in the Talmud the moving story, told in stark simplicity, of the martyr's death of a great sage:

The Romans found Rabbi Chaninah ben Tradyon sitting and teaching Torah to large assemblies [in defiance of the Roman prohibition]. They brought him to the place of execution, wrapped him in a Torah scroll, surrounded him with bundles of branches, and set them on fire. They brought unwoven wool soaked in water and placed it over his heart so that he should not die too quickly.

His daughter said: Father, that I should see you like this! He answered her: If I had been burned alone it would have worried me, but since I am burned with the *Sefer Torah*—He who will seek redress for the *Sefer Torah* will seek redress for me.

His disciples said to him: Rabbi, what do you see? He answered: The parchment is burning, but the letters fly in the air. The executioner said to him: Rabbi, if I increase the flames and remove the wool from over your heart, will you bring me to the life of the World to Come? He answered: Yes. The executioner said: Swear it to me. He swore it. Immediately, he increased the flames and removed the wool from over his heart. His soul departed in purity. The executioner also leaped into the fire. At that moment, a heavenly voice was heard to say: Rabbi Chaninah and the executioner are destined for the life of the World to Come.

When Rabbi Yehudah Hanassi heard this, he wept, saying: Some acquire their world in one hour, while others have to fight for it during seventy long years (*Avodah Zarah* 18a).

THE *BA'AL TESHUVAH* AND THE *TZADDIK*

Commenting on the above-mentioned *Gemara*, Rabbi Eliyahu E. Dessler,[1] the famous teacher of *Mussar*, says: Why did Rabbi Yehudah Hanassi cry when he heard that this lifelong evildoer had succeeded in gaining *Olam Haba* in one brief moment? And how are we to understand the opinion that states: "The place where *ba'alei teshuvah* stand [in the World to Come] is not accessible even to the greatest *tzaddikim*?" (*Berachot* 34b). In what sense can a *ba'al teshuvah* be greater than a *tzaddik*?

The answer is this. The purpose of Creation is to reveal the glory of God. This can occur in two ways. It can be brought about by *tzaddikim* who reveal God's majesty by their actions. It can also come about by our seeing the way God conducts His world. When the veil is lifted and the misconceptions are finally removed, all the depth of God's wisdom will stand revealed. The precision of His justice and truth, the immensity of His unending mercy, will all become manifest. This tremendous revelation can also in part be credited to man, for it occurs as a result of his actions. The Rabbis said: "Open for Me an opening like the point of a needle, and I will open for you gates like the gates of the Sanctuary."[2] This means that to every effort a person makes in His service, God responds with heavenly aid in this tremendous proportion—the ratio of a mighty gateway to a needle point.

The sinner has been occupied all his life in obscuring the glory of God. When he decides he wants to return to a better way of life, his effort, slight and ineffective though it may be, gives rise to heavenly aid to an unimaginable extent. He reveals the infinite mercy of God to a degree never achieved by a *tzaddik*. He reveals the mercy of *teshuvah*. He finds himself taken by the hand and raised to the heights in one great leap. His "needlepoint" of effort is a puny one indeed. But the very minuteness of his personal contribution ensures that the revelation of God's love and mercy is all the more wondrous. It is a revelation that in the nature of things can never be achieved by a *tzaddik*. It is in this sense that we may understand how "complete *tzaddikim* are unable to stand in the place occupied by *ba'alei teshuvah*." And this is why Rabbi Yehudah wept. He realized that he could never have a share in that great illumination of God's glory uniquely brought about by the *ba'al teshuvah*.

THE PHYSICIAN'S RIGHT TO HEAL

It is written: [If two men fight and one hits the other with a stone or with his fist] . . . the one who struck him must provide for the victim's complete cure (Exodus 21:19). The Talmud says: From this we learn that permission has been given to the physician to heal. [Without this explicit permission, a physician's practice of healing might be considered the unwarranted removal of a divinely mandated sickness.]

Berachot 60a

MEDDLING IN GOD'S AFFAIRS?

While walking through the streets of Jerusalem, Rabbi Yishmael, Rabbi Akiva, and a third man came upon a sick man.

"Please, Rabbis," said the sick man. "Tell me what medicine I should take to get better."

"Take such-and-such herbs," they replied, "until you feel better."

"Who made this man sick?" said the third man. "The Holy One, Blessed be He. And you, Rabbis, intrude on God's affairs. When He smote, do you have a right to heal?"

The Rabbis replied, "What kind of work do you do?"

"I am a farmer," answered the third man. "Look, here is my scythe."

"Well, tell us, who created the earth?" asked the Rabbis. "The Holy One, Blessed be He, right? Well, aren't you intruding on God's affairs?"

"If I did not plow, fertilize, and cultivate the field, nothing would grow," countered the third man.

"Well, the body is just like the field," retorted the Rabbis. "The fertilizer is the medicine and the physician is the farmer."

The point the rabbis were making is that just as a farmer must cultivate the earth, so does a physician have a moral obligation to heal the sick.[3]

APHORISMS ABOUT PHYSICIANS

A physician who heals for nothing is worth nothing. A physician who is far away has a blind eye [he is not concerned about the fate of the patient (Rashi)] (*Bava Kamma* 85a).

A door that is not opened to give charity to the poor will be opened to admit a physician (*Midrash Rabbah* 9).

The best doctor will end up in *Gehinnom* ["The best doctor" is a reference to an arrogant physician who thinks he is better than any other and who does not believe that he is God's messenger in bringing healing to the sick.] (*Kiddushin* 82a).

A Torah scholar should not live in a city that has no physician (*Sanhedrin* 17b).

ABRAHAM'S HEALING STONE

A precious stone was hanging from Abraham's neck. Any sick person who looked at it was healed immediately (*Bava Batra* 16b).

Rabbi Yitzchak Eizik Chaver, in his commentary *Or Torah*,[4] offers the following metaphorical explanation of the mystifying stone on Abraham's neck:

Abraham spread the knowledge of the unity of God and Divine Providence among his heathen contemporaries. With the words and voice that emanated from his throat he converted them to monotheism. By revealing the Light of God that is concealed in Creation, he healed them of their spiritual affliction. Thus it may be said that every sick person was cured by heeding Abraham's message, which is to say, they were restored to health by means of the voice and the words that proceeded from Abraham's neck and throat.

+

THE GREATEST SPECIALIST

It happened that a *chasid* came to Rabbi Mordechai of Neshchiz[5] complaining of a serious ailment, asking the Rebbe for advice.

"Go and see the great specialist in Hanipol," counseled the Rebbe.

Arriving in Hanipol, the *chasid* was ridiculed by the villagers. "Hanipol is a small village. There is no great specialist here. We don't even have a horse doctor."

"Well, what do you do if someone gets sick?" the *chasid* asked.

"We can do nothing except pray to God," was the reply.

Returning to the Rebbe of Neshchiz, the *chasid* voiced his disappointment. "They don't even have an ordinary doctor in Hanipol."

"Did you ask them what they do when they become ill?" the Rebbe asked.

"They told me that since they have no alternative, they place their trust in God," the *chasid* replied.

"Fool that you are!" the Rebbe exclaimed. "God is the great specialist I sent you to see, for it is written, 'I am God who heals you'" (Exodus 15:26).[6]

+

REMEDIES FOR A STOMACH AILMENT

Rebbe (Rabbi Yehudah Hanassi) once suffered from abdominal pain. They searched and found a non-Jew who owned three hundred barrels of seventy-year-old apple wine. He drank from it and was cured.

Avodah Zarah 40b

WHOLESOME DATES

Dates are healthful in the morning, at noon, and in the evening. They are not good in the afternoon [after a rest (Rashi)], and they do away with three things: evil thoughts (worry), stress of the bowels, and abdominal troubles.

Ketubot 10b

THE CURE FOR ALL DISEASES

You will then serve God your Lord, and He will bless your bread and your water. I will banish sickness from among you (Exodus 23:25).

Rabbeinu Bachya wonders what is the connection between God's blessing the bread and water and His banishing sickness. He notes that disease is caused by internal and external factors. Eating the wrong kinds of food and drinking contaminated water or harmful beverages are internal causes of illness. Infections, exposure to extreme cold or heat, and germs are some of the external causes of disease. In the present verse, God pledges that if you live according to the Torah, He will bless the food you ingest so that it will rectify any internal imbalance and heal any internally caused disease. Likewise, God promises to banish sickness, meaning illness that is generated by external factors, so that you will not need to turn to a physician for help.

SAYINGS ABOUT CLEANLINESS AND HYGIENE

Better than all the eye ointments in the world is a drop of cold water on the eye in the morning and bathing hands and feet in the evening (*Shabbat* 108b).

He who washes his face and does not dry it well will develop a scab (*Avodah Zarah* 28b).

You should bathe your face, hands, and feet every day in honor of your Creator [because man is created in the image of God (Rashi)] (*Shabbat* 50b).

A Torah scholar may not live in a town that has no bathhouse (*Sanhedrin* 17b).

"The delights of the sons of men" (Ecclesiastes 2:8) are ornamental pools and baths (*Gittin* 68a).

HANDWASHING IN THE MORNING

When you get up in the morning, you are like a newborn creature. Therefore you should prepare yourself for worship by washing your hands out of a vessel, just as the priests used to wash their hands out of a washbasin before performing their service in the *Bet Hamikdash*. There is another reason given by the kabbalists (*Zohar*, quoted in *Bet Yosef*), for this morning handwashing. When a person is asleep, his soul departs from his body, and an unclean spirit descends on him. When he gets up from sleeping, the unclean spirit leaves his entire body except for his fingers and does not depart until one spills water on them three times alternately.

Shabbat 109a; *Kitzur Shulchan Aruch* 3:1

WASHING THE HANDS BEFORE MEALS

Before eating bread you must wash your hands. The water used for washing hands must be poured out of a vessel. Before drying the hands we say the *berachah*, "Blessed are You, God, our Lord, King of the Universe, who has sanctified us with His commandments and has commanded us regarding washing the hands."

Kitzur Shulchan Aruch 40:1, 3, 5

MISTAKEN IDENTITY

In connection with washing the hands before meals, the *Midrash* relates the following revealing story:

During the persecution of the Jews under Hadrian, a Jewish innkeeper, in order to hide his Jewish identity, sold also pork. If someone did not wash his hands before he ate, the innkeeper assumed he was a non-Jew and served him pork. If someone washed his hands first, the innkeeper recognized him as a Jew and served him *kosher* meat. Once a Jew entered the inn and sat down to eat without first washing his hands. The innkeeper, assuming that he was a non-Jew, served him pork. When the Jew examined the bill and found out what he had eaten, his hair stood on end and he became very frightened. "I am a Jew, and you served me pork!" he exclaimed. "It's your own fault," replied the innkeeper. "You should have washed your hands before the meal."

Bamidbar Rabbah 20:21

16

Old Age

FOREVER YOUTHFUL

The Talmud relates: Until Abraham there was no old age [old age did not show on a person's face or body]. Whoever wanted to speak to Abraham would speak to Isaac, and whoever wanted to speak to Isaac spoke to Abraham [because they looked exactly alike]. Thereupon Abraham prayed, and old age came into being, as it says, "Abraham was old, well advanced in years" (Genesis 24:1).

Bava Metzia 87a]

HE ASKED FOR OLD AGE

The *Midrash* says: Abraham requested the marks of old age. He said: Master of the Universe, [under present conditions] when a man and his son enter a city, people don't know to whom they should show respect [because father and son look alike]. If You crown a person with old age, people will know whom to honor.

The Holy One, Blessed be He, replied: Well spoken! You asked for a worthwhile thing. And I will start with you. And so, from the first page of the Torah until the story of Abraham, there is no reference to old age. Only when Abraham appeared on the scene, old age is mentioned for the first time, for it says, "Abraham was old, well advanced in years" (Genesis 24:1).

Bereishit Rabbah 65

SCHOLARS AND IGNORAMUSES IN OLD AGE

Torah scholars, the older they get, the more wisdom they acquire. Ignoramuses, on the other hand, the older they get, the more foolish they become (*Shabbat* 52a).

TORAH STUDY AT A YOUNG AND AT AN OLD AGE

Elisha ben Abuya said: One who studies Torah as a child, to what can he be likened? To ink written on fresh paper. And one who studies Torah as an old man, to what can he be likened? To ink written on smudged paper (*Avot* 4:25).

[Whatever you write on fresh paper is clear and does not fade. Therefore, you should study Torah while you are young and your mind is fresh and receptive.]

Rabban Shimon ben Gamliel said: He that studies Torah as a child is like a young man who marries a young girl; for she is suited to him, and he is suited to her. She is drawn to him and he is drawn to her. He that studies Torah in his old age is like an old man who marries a young girl. She may be suited to him, but he is unsuited to her. She may be drawn to him, but he withdraws from her (*Avot deRabbi Natan* 24).

Rabbi Shimon ben Elazar said: He that studies Torah as a child is like a physician who, when a wound is brought before him, has a scalpel to cut it and drugs to heal it. He that studies Torah in his old age is like a physician who, when a wound is brought before him, has a scalpel to cut it but has no drugs to heal it. [The Torah is compared to healing drugs.][1]

Elisha ben Abuyah said: When a person studies Torah as a child, the words of the Torah are absorbed by his blood and come out of his mouth distinctly. But if he studies Torah in his old age, the words of the Torah are not absorbed by his blood and do not come out of his mouth distinctly. And so the saying goes: If you did not desire them in your youth, how will you acquire them in your old age? (*Avot deRabbi Natan* 24).

SCRIPTURES AND APHORISMS ABOUT OLD AGE

"You shall rise before the aged and give respect to the old" (Leviticus 19:32).

Rabbi Yochanan used to rise before an elderly gentile. He said: "Just think how many reverses and setbacks this man has experienced during his lifetime [and how many miracles he has witnessed (Rashi)]" (*Kiddushin* 33a).

The crown of the aged is grandchildren, and the splendor of children is their fathers (Proverbs 17:6).

Many an old camel is loaded with the hides of younger ones [many an old man outlives the young] (*Sanhedrin* 52a).

"In the winter, the lazy man does not plow; at harvest-time he seeks, and finds nothing" (Proverbs 20:4). This refers to a person who did not study Torah in his younger years, and in his old age he finds that it is beyond his grasp (*Devarim Rabbah* 8).

The glory of youths is their strength; the majesty of old men is their grey hair (Proverbs 20:29).

Youth is like a wreath of roses; old age is like a wreath of thorns (*Shabbat* 152a).

Four things hasten the onset of old age: fear, anger over one's children, a cantankerous wife, and war (*Midrash Tanchuma, Chayei Sarah* 1).

Two are better than three [The two legs of youth are better than the three legs of old age, because an old man needs a cane.] (*Shabbat* 151b).

The plain carobs we ate when we were young tasted better than the delicate peaches we ate in our old age (Jerusalem Talmud, *Pe'ah* 7:4).

Why is Israel compared to a bird? Just as a bird cannot fly without wings, so is Israel helpless without the advice of their elders (*Yalkut Torah* 520).

People say, "An old man in the house is a burden in the house, an old woman in the house is a treasure in the house!" [A woman is never too old to be useful in the house.] (*Arachin* 18b).

Old age and hoary age befit the righteous and befit the world, as it says, "Ripe old age is a crown of splendor, it can be found in the path of righteousness" (Proverbs 16:31) (*Avot* 6:8).

WHEN OLD MEN DEMOLISH

Rabbi Shimon ben Elazar said: If old men advise you to demolish, and young men advise you to build, then demolish and do not build, because the demolishing of old men is really building (it is beneficial), and the building of youths is really demolishing (it is harmful) (*Megillah* 31b).

THE SUPERIORITY OF EARLIER SAGES

The preeminence of earlier over later sages is one of the fundamental principles of *Halachah*. Therefore, later scholars will never challenge rulings of earlier authorities. This concept is clearly reflected in the following selections.

The *Gemara* says: The heart of the ancients was open to understanding like the width of the entrance hall of the *Bet Hamikdash*; of the later sages, like the width of the Sanctuary, but our heart is like the eye of a narrow needle (*Eruvin* 53a).

A similar saying reads: If the ancients were like angels, we are like humans. If the ancients were human, we are like donkeys (*Tosafot, Chullin* 5b, s.v. *tzaddikim*).

EITHER WAY I LOSE

The Talmud relates: When Rabbi Ammi and Rabbi Assi were sitting before Rabbi Yitzchak, one of them said to him, "Will you please tell us some legal points?" The other said, "Will you please give us some homiletical instruction?" When he began a homiletical discourse he was prevented by the one,

and when he started a legal discourse he was prevented by
the other. So he said to them: "I will tell you a parable: This
is like a man who had two wives, one young and one old.
The young one used to pluck out his white hair, whereas
the old one used to pluck out his black hair. Thus he finally
became bald on both sides" (*Bava Kamma* 60b).

✤

A BIRD NAMED *CHOL*

The *Midrash* says: After eating from the fruit of the Tree of
Knowledge, Eve offered some of it to her husband and to
all the animals and birds. All of them partook of the fruit
[and, as a result, became mortal] except for one bird, named
chol [phoenix]. Job is referring to this bird when he says, "I
thought I would be as long-lived as the *chol* [phoenix]" (Job
29:18). This bird lives for one thousand years, after which
it is consumed by fire and rises from the ashes to return to
life once again.

Bereishit Rabbah 19

✤

THE DAYS OF OUR YEARS

The *Mishnah* teaches: A sixty-year-old attains seniority; a
seventy-year-old attains ripe old age; an eighty-year-old
shows strength; a ninety-year-old becomes stooped over; a
hundred-year-old is as if he were dead, passed away and
ceased from the world.

Avot 5:25

✤

THE INFIRMITIES OF OLD AGE

Solomon depicts the infirmities of old age in poetic imagery. He describes the autumn of life, the years in which the powers of the organs of the body begin to wane, as the time "when the light, the moon, and the stars grow dark" (i.e., the forehead, the nose, the soul, and the cheeks lose their vibrancy), "and the clouds return after the rain" (i.e., the eyesight is weakened by weeping) (*Shabbat* 151b); "the day when the guards of the house will tremble" (the hands and the arms which protect the body from harm now are feeble) (Ibn Ezra); "and the powerful men will stoop" (i.e., the legs that support the body [Rashi]); "and the grinders are idle because they are few" (i.e., the teeth) (*Shabbat* 152a); "and the gazers through the windows are dimmed" (i.e., the eyes) (*Shabbat* 152a) (Ecclesiastes 12:2, 3).

TO WHAT DID THEY ATTRIBUTE THEIR LONGEVITY?

The *Gemara* relates: The disciples asked Rabbi Zakkai, "In the merit of which good practice did you attain your longevity?" He replied, "In all my life I never called my colleague by his nickname, and I never neglected to recite *Kiddush* on *Shabbat*."

The disciples asked Rabbi Eleazar ben Shamua, "In the merit of which good practice did you attain longevity?" He replied, "In all my days, I never used the synagogue as a shortcut."

When the disciples asked Rabbi Pereida the same question, he answered, "In all my days, no person ever preceded me to the house of study."

Rabbi Nechunya ben Hakanah, replying to the same question, said, "In all my days, I never gloated over the shame of my fellow, I forgave those who tormented me, and I was liberal with my money."

Rabbi Yehoshua ben Korcha answered the question about his longevity by saying, "I never gazed at the face of a wicked person."

Megillah 27b, 28a

YOUTHFUL AT 120 YEARS OF AGE

"Moses was 120 years old when he died, but his eyes had not dimmed and his natural powers had not left him" (Deuteronomy 34:7).

ABRAHAM'S MEDALLION

The *Midrash* says: Abraham had a medallion. On one side the image of an old man and an old woman was engraved. The other side displayed the image of a boy and a girl. [The *Midrash* makes the point that Abraham's teachings about the unity of God and the obligation of "keeping God's way, doing charity and justice" will endure because the children are following in their parents' footsteps.]

Bereishit Rabbah 39:16

WHAT IS AN OLD MAN?

In Jewish tradition, the elderly are treated with utmost respect, as old age is synonymous with maturity and wisdom. This reverent attitude is expressed by the talmudic sages, who say that the Hebrew word for old man, *zakein*, is an abbreviation of the phrase *zeh shekanah chochmah*, "one who acquired wisdom."

Kiddushin 32b

RESPECT FOR THE AGED

Rabbi Abba Hakohen said: Whenever I used to see a gathering of people in the street, I would detour so as not to inconvenience them by making them rise before me. When I told this to Rabbi Yosi bar Zavda, he told me: Quite the contrary; you should pass in front of them and afford them the opportunity to get up when they see you. You thereby instill the fear of God in them, for it says, "Stand up before a white head. You shall thus fear your God" (Leviticus 19:32).

Midrash Rabbah 15

17

Visiting the Sick

BIKKUR CHOLIM

Visiting the sick (*bikkur cholim*) is a *mitzvah* of paramount importance. At a time of illness, *bikkur cholim* relieves the patient's forced isolation and brings him or her the comfort of companionship which in itself is a powerful aid to recovery. It is one of the precepts enumerated in the Talmud, "the fruit of which man eats in this world, while the principal remains for him in the world to come" (*Shabbat* 127a).

The *Gemara* infers the *mitzvah* of *bikkur cholim* from the verse, "Follow God your Lord" (Deuteronomy 13:5), which is interpreted to mean that we are to follow God's example. "The Holy One, Blessed be He, visited the sick, so should you also visit the sick" (God visited Abraham on the third day after his circumcision,[1] when one is particularly weak, to inquire after his health.) (*Sotah* 14a).

✤

LOVE YOUR NEIGHBOR

The Rambam (Maimonides) states: Visiting the sick is a positive *mitzvah*. It is an act of kindness you do with your entire body, a good deed for which there is no prescribed measure of how much is involved. When you visit the sick you are fulfilling the commandment to "love your neighbor as you love yourself" (Leviticus 19:18) (*Mishneh Torah*, Laws of Mourning 14:1).

JETHRO'S ADVICE

[Jethro counseled Moses,] "Clarify the decrees and laws for the people. Show them the path they must take, and the things they must do" (Exodus 18:20). According to Rabbi Eliezer Hamoda'i, the phrase "the things they must do" implies charitable deeds, specifically, visiting the sick and burying the dead (*Mechilta, Yitro, 2*).

PROVIDING FOR A BRIDE

The *Gemara*[2] lists among the acts of kindness whose fruits a person enjoys in this world but whose principal remains intact for him in the world to come: visiting the sick, providing for a bride, and attending a funeral.

Rabbi Chanoch Henach of Alexander[3] was asked: Why is the *mitzvah* of providing for a bride interposed between the sick and the dead?

He replied: The *Gemara* wants to teach us that if, God forbid, a member of the family is sick, we should give charity toward the wedding expenses of a poor bride. The merit of this *mitzvah* will protect us from having to attend the funeral of the sick person (*Siach Sarfei Kodesh* 1:559).

MI SHEBEIRACH, PRAYER FOR A SICK PERSON

The following prayer for the recovery of a sick person is said in the synagogue at the time of the reading of the Torah: He who blessed our forefathers Abraham, Isaac, and Jacob, Moses and Aaron, David and Solomon—may He bless and heal the sick person (patient's Hebrew name) son/daughter of (patient's mother's name) because (name of supplicant) will contribute to charity on his/her behalf. In reward for this, may the Holy One, Blessed be He, be filled with compassion for him/her to restore his/her health, to heal him/her, to strengthen him/her and to revivify him/her. And may He send him/her speedily a complete recovery from heaven for his two hundred forty-eight organs and three hundred sixty-five blood vessels, among the other sick people of Israel, a recovery of the body and a recovery of the spirit, swiftly and soon. Now let us respond: Amen.

When one prays in the presence of a patient, the prayer should be short and should be said quietly. It may be said in any language, since the *Shechinah* is present at the head of the patient (*Yoreh Dei'ah* 335:5). An appropriate short prayer is:

May the Almighty have mercy upon you among the other sick people of Israel, or

May the Almighty speedily send you a complete recovery together with the other sick people of His nation Israel.

The customary *berachah* wishing the sick person a *refuah shelemah*, a complete recovery, may of course be said directly and audibly to the patient.

The *Gemara* says: When you visit a sick person, you

should pray for him and include the name of the patient
"among the other sick people of Israel," saying, "May the
Almighty have mercy over you and over the other sick people
of Israel." On *Shabbat* we add, "Though the *Shabbat* pro-
hibits us from crying out, may a recovery come speedily with
great mercy, and have a peaceful *Shabbat*" (*Shabbat* 12a).

✤

PSALMS OF HEALING

The reading of psalms is balm for the soul that enhances
the healing process. The person reading these psalms identifies with the psalmist in his pain and longing. He feels
uplifted and is inspired with renewed hope and faith.

The Rabbis suggest the reading of any of the following
thirty-six psalms whose contents are particularly suited to
the spiritual needs of a sick person and his concerned rela-
tives and friends: Psalms 2, 6, 9, 13, 16, 17, 18, 22, 23,
25, 30, 31, 32, 33, 37, 38, 39, 41, 49, 55, 56, 69, 86, 88,
89, 90, 91, 102, 103, 104, 107, 116, 118, 128, 142, and
143.

✤

RULES FOR VISITORS

A visitor should not sit on the patient's bed. He should speak
comforting words and make sure not to frighten the patient
or cause him to worry. He should obey the doctors' and
nurses' instructions. The visitor should ask the patient
whether he needs financial aid to regain his health. He
should help him, pray for him, and leave (*Kolbo* 112).

If a patient is sleeping, he should certainly not be disturbed. The visitor should leave a note informing him of his visit, and this itself will bring gladness to the patient (*Rosh al Hatorah, Vayeira*).

Do not stay too long. At no time should the visit become tiresome or burdensome to the patient (*Yoreh De'ah* 335:2).

You should dress in an appropriate manner when performing the *mitzvah* of *bikkur cholim*, in deference to the *Shechinah*, which rests at the head of the patient (*Yalkut Me'am Lo'ez, Vayeira*).

No one should assume the role of a medical expert, offering unsolicited layman's advice as to what should be done to cure the patient. The differing opinions of various people can easily cause more harm than benefit (*Gesher Hachayim*, p. 28, para. 3).

✤

BRINGING CHEER AND CONFIDENCE

Rabbi Shimon Schwab related: A lady once bought a new raincoat as a present for a sick woman. Usually one brings flowers, a nightgown, or similar present. When the sick woman inquired about the unusual gift, the visitor responded in surprise, "What do you mean? The weather is bad outside; soon you'll need the raincoat!" The patient's face lit up, and it was obvious that she was greatly encouraged and heartened by these words and the very thoughtful gesture.[4]

✤

A SINCERE PRAYER

The Yehudi Hakadosh,[5] the Holy Jew, once was seriously ill. The people of his town, Pshis'cha, proclaimed a day of fasting, repentance, prayer, and charity for the Rebbe's speedy recovery. A villager happened to arrive in town and went to the tavern for a drink of brandy.

"Today is a public fast because our Rebbe is sick," the townspeople cried out. "You cannot have a drink."

The villager immediately went to the synagogue and prayed, "*Ribbono shel Olam*, Sovereign of the Universe, please cure the Holy Rebbe so that I can have my drink."

Soon after that, the Rebbe began to feel better and said, "The prayer of the villager was more acceptable in heaven than any others. He prayed with the greatest sincerity for my prompt recovery" (*Siach Sarfei Kodesh* 2:263).

TALMUDIC TEACHINGS
ABOUT VISITING THE SICK

The *Gemara* teaches: There is no prescribed measure for visiting the sick. What does this mean? Rabbi Joseph explained: Its reward is unlimited. Abaye explained: Even a prominent person must visit a simple one. Rava said: If necessary, you should visit a patient even a hundred times a day (*Nedarim* 40a).

Rav Dimi said: He who visits a sick person causes him to live, whereas he who does not, causes him to die. How does he cause his death? Put it this way: He who does not visit the sick prays neither that he may live nor die [and through the lack of his prayers which might have been accepted he is said to cause his death] (*Nedarim* 40a).

Rav said: He who visits the sick will be delivered from the punishments of *Gehinnom*, as it says, "God will deliver him in the day of evil" (Psalm 41:2) Now, if one does visit, what is his reward in this world? God will preserve him from the evil urge and save him from sufferings, and he will be a source of pride to all, as it says, "God will preserve him and keep him alive" (Psalm 41:3) (*Nedarim* 40a).

As long as there is life, there is hope (Jerusalem Talmud, *Berachot* 9:1).

Rabbi Shisha said: One should not visit the sick during the first three hours or the last three hours of the day, because the visitor may be deceived by the patient's appearance and neglect to pray for him. In the morning, the patient looks better (consequently, a visitor may think that he is on the road to recovery and consider prayer unnecessary). In the evening, the patient seems worse (and the visitor may feel that prayer is hopeless) (*Nedarim* 40a).

Rabin said: From where do we know that the Almighty supports the sick? From the verse, "God will support him on his sickbed" (Psalm 41:4). Rabin also said: From where do we know that the Divine Presence rests above a patient's bed? From the verse, "God rests on his sickbed."[6] Therefore, he who visits the sick should not sit on the bed . . . because the Divine Presence rests above a patient's bed (*Nedarim* 40a).

Rabbi Alexandri said: When a sick man recovers from his illness all his sins are forgiven, as it says, "He forgives all your sins, heals all your diseases" (Psalm 103:3). Rav Hamenuna said: He then returns to the days of his youth, for it says, "His flesh shall be fresher than a child's; he shall return to his younger days" (Job 33:25) (*Nedarim* 41a).

Rabbi Abba said: He who visits a sick person takes away one-sixtieth of his sickness. They said to him: If so, let sixty

people visit him, and he will be cured. He replied: The sixtieth is to be understood as follows: Each visitor takes away
one-sixtieth of the illness that remains after an earlier visitor to this patient had taken away one-sixtieth of the illness [Thus, the patient would not be completely cured by
sixty visitors.] (*Nedarim* 39b).

Rabbi Akiva once went to visit a sick disciple. [Finding
the sickroom neglected] he gave orders to have the floor
swept and sprinkled. As a result, the disciple said, "Rabbi,
you have revived me!" Thereupon Rabbi Akiva went out and
taught, "He who does not visit the sick is like a shedder of
blood." (*Nedarim* 40a).

You should not visit patients suffering with bowel
trouble because of embarrassment, and you should not visit
people suffering with eye disease or from headaches because
speech is harmful to them (*Nedarim* 41a).

It is appropriate to visit non-Jews who are sick and to
pray for their welfare and recovery (*Sefer Bikkur Cholim* 3:2).

ONE ILLUSTRIOUS PATIENT VISITING ANOTHER

Rabbi Moshe Feinstein[7] was a patient at the New York
University Medical Center. When he learned that Senator
Jacob Javits had been admitted to the center, he immediately closed the volume he was studying, and over the vehe-
ment protests of his nurse, climbed down from his bed into
his wheelchair.

"What are you doing, Rabbi? Where are you going?" the
nurse asked in great dismay.

"Senator Javits is in the hospital," replied Reb Moshe.
"A Jew such as he who has done so much for the Jewish

people—I must pay him a *bikkur cholim* call." He then proceeded to wheel himself out of the room.

GEMILUT CHASADIM (ACTS OF KINDNESS)

The main theme of this book is that since man was created in God's image, his mission in life is to emulate the attributes of God. God created the world in a supreme act of *chesed*, pouring out an abundant stream of love and kindness on man. It is fitting, therefore, that we conclude this book with a chapter on visiting the sick, which is *gemilut chasadim*, a human act of unselfish kindness that is a reflection of God's kindness.

In a succinct statement, the *Gemara* sums up the paramount importance of *gemilut chasadim*:

The Torah begins with an act of *gemilut chasadim* [kindness] and ends with an act of *gemilut chasadim*. It begins with an act of kindness, for it says, "God made leather garments for Adam and his wife, and He clothed them" (Genesis 3:21); and it ends with an act of kindness, for it says, "He (God) buried [Moses] in the valley" (Deuteronomy 34:6).

Sotah 14a

In the final analysis, kindness is one of the pillars of the Jewish faith, as the prophet states,

He has told you, O man, what is good,
And what God requires of you:
Only to do justice
And to love kindness
And to walk humbly with your God.

Micah 6:8

Notes

INTRODUCTION

1. Rabbi Chaim Volozhiner, *Nefesh Hachayim* 1:17 (end of chapter) (Vilna, 1824; most·recent edition, B'nei B'rak, 1989).

CHAPTER 1

1. One of the minor tractates of the Talmud and an amplification of the famous mishnaic tractate of *Avot*.

2. The cheeks shine like stars. In *Shabbat* 121b, *lesatot* (cheeks) is translated as stars (*Binyan Yehoshua* by Rabbi Yehoshua Falk).

3. Author of *Binyan Yehoshua*, commentary to *Avot deRabbi Natan* (Duerenfurth, 1788).

4. The total number of body parts—248 limbs and 365 sinews or blood vessels—equals 613, the same number as the amount of commandments in the Torah. The sages say that each of the 613 parts of the body is associated with a corresponding *mitzvah*.

5. In the days of Noah, "the world was corrupt before God, and the land was filled with lawlessness" (Genesis 7:11).

6. The universe was thrown into chaos when Adam transgressed.

7. Rabbi Yehudah Loew of Prague (1525–1609). See my *Great Torah Commentators* (Northvale, NJ: Jason Aronson Inc., 1990), pp. 227–229.

8. Rabbi Yehudah Loew, *Tiferet Yisrael* (Prague, 1593), chap. 13.

9. *Avot deRabbi Natan*, chap. 16.

10. 1135–1204, Rabbi Moshe ben Maimon, popularly known as Rambam, after the initials of his name. He is revered as an illustrious halachic authority, codifier, philosopher, and physician. His commentary on the *Mishnah* and his great code *Mishneh Torah* are works of genius.

11. *Moreh Nevuchim*, one of the greatest philosophical works of all time, written by the Rambam in Arabic in 1185. Translated into Hebrew by ibn Tibbon. First published in Rome before 1480; Venice, 1551.

12. Earth, air, fire, and water.

13. The fifth or celestial essence, ether, above the four elements of earth, air, fire, and water.

14. He lived in Spain in the eleventh century.

15. First printed in Naples in 1490. Written in Arabic, it was translated into Hebrew by Rabbi Yehudah ibn Tibbon in 1611. Translated into English by Moshe Chaim Hyamson (New York, 1924). See *The Great Torah Commentators*, pp. 197–199.

16. The human body originates from semen, which comes from the food that man has consumed. Food is a product of the vegetative state, which, in turn, derives its nourishment from the mineral state. Thus, man passes all the stages that lead from mineral to his becoming a living, rational, speaking human being.

17. As opposed to an angel who lives but is immortal.

18. 1089–c. 1164. See *The Great Torah Commentators*, pp. 6–8.

19. In *Tanach* (the Bible) and the Talmud, the heart is considered the seat of the soul.

20. This passage refers to the story where Joseph had instructed the overseer to place his silver chalice on top of Benjamin's pack. After the brothers left the city, the overseer, on Joseph's orders, chased them and accused them of stealing Joseph's chalice. The brothers denied it. The overseer then inspected their packs, *beginning with the oldest and ending with the youngest*. The chalice was found in Benjamin's pack.

The Hebrew *gadol* can be rendered both "large" and "oldest," and *katan* translates both as "small" and "youngest."

21. c. 1080–c. 1145. See *The Great Torah Commentators*, pp. 200–202.

22. Fano, 1506.

23. Rabbi Bachya ben Asher, 1263–1340, a *dayan* (rabbinical judge) in Saragossa, Spain, is the author of a celebrated commentary on the Torah, *Midrash Rabbeinu Bachya* (Naples, 1492). See *The Great Torah Commentators*, pp. 14–16.

24. 1740–1810, popularly known as the Berditchever, author of *Kedushat Levi* (Slavita, 1798). See my *Great Chasidic Masters* (Northvale, NJ: Jason Aronson Inc., 1992), pp. 51–54.

25. *Niflaot Beit Levi*, comp. A. J. Kleinman (Pietrkov, 1911).

26. Rabbi Meir Leib ben Yechiel Michael Weiser (1809–1879). Popularly known as Malbim, the initials of his name, he is the author of a monumental commentary on the Torah and *Tanach* (Warsaw, 1860–1876). See *The Great Torah Commentators*, pp. 36–38.

27. Compare *Targum Yonatan* and Ramban.

CHAPTER 2

1. *Sanhedrin* 37a.

2. *Midrash Rabbah, Naso*, 14:2; *Etz Chaim*, beginning of chapter *Abiyah. Etz Chaim* is a compilation of the kabbalistic teachings of Rabbi Yitzchak Luria, the *Ari Hakadosh*. It was written by his disciple, Rabbi Chaim Vital (1543–1620) and first published in Koretz, 1782. See *The Great Torah Commentators*, pp. 225–226.

3. Degel Machaneh Efraim, *Bereishit*, Rabbi Moshe Chaim of Sadilkov (Koretz, 1810). See *The Great Chasidic Masters*, pp. 77–80.

4. From the prayer said after the Counting of the *Omer*.

5. *Mesillat Yesharim* (Amsterdam, 1740), by Rabbi Moshe Chaim Luzzatto (1707–1747), foremost ethicist, kabbalist, and poet. See *The Great Torah Commentators*, pp. 133–135.

6. 1823–1900. See the *Great Torah Commentators*, pp. 176–178.

7. *Resisei Laylah* (Lublin, 1901).

8. Terach, Achaz, and Amon were idol worshipers.

9. 1892–1953. *Rosh yeshivah*, eminent *Mussar* teacher and educator. See *The Great Torah Commentators*, pp. 150–152.

10. Rabbi Eliyahu E. Dessler, *Michtav MeEliyahu*, vol. 1 (B'nei B'rak, 1955), p. 32.

11. Ibid., 1:38–39.

12. 1704–1772. Influential leader of the chasidic movement and successor of the Ba'al Shem Tov. See *The Great Chasidic Masters*, pp. 8–11.

13. Rabbi Yisrael Berger, *Eser Orot* (Warsaw, 1913).

14. Died in 1827. See *The Great Chasidic Masters*, pp. 115–117.

15. Cracow, 1842.

16. Rabbi Klonymos Kalman Epstein, *Ma'or Vashemesh*, commentary on Genesis 17:1.

17. Rabbi Dov Ber, the Maggid of Mezritch, *Maggid Devarav LeYaakov* (Koretz, 1781).

18. *Megillah* 31a.

19. *Pirkei deRabbi Eliezer* 3, a midrashic work attributed to the Tanna Rabbi Eliezer ben Hyrkanos.

20. *Midrash Rabbah* 12:4, *Shemot Rabbah* 2:9.

21. Ramban on Genesis 2:17; *Nefesh Hachayim*, 1:2.

22. The first Gerer Rebbe (1799–1866). His work, *Chidushei Harym*, was first published in Warsaw, 1870. See *The Great Chasidic Masters*, pp. 150–153.

23. Rambam (Maimonides), *Mishneh Torah*, *Hilchot Teshuvah* 5:1. First printed in Rome, 1475. See *The Great Torah Commentators*, pp. 99–103.

24. Galen, a Greek physician of the second century, developed a theory that human personality was determined by four basic body fluids or humors: blood, phlegm, black bile, and yellow bile. Their dominance of one over another within a person produced these temperaments: sanguine (warm, pleasant), phlegmatic (slow-moving, apathetic), melancholic (depressed, sad), and choleric (hot-tempered).

25. *Shemonah Perakim* (*The Eight Chapters*), chap. 8. *Shemonah Perakim* constitutes the Rambam's introduction to his commentary on the *Mishnah*, tractate *Avot*. It discusses the nature of the soul, its afflictions and their cures, man's purpose in the world, prophecy, and the problem of free will versus divine omniscience.

26. 1808–1888. Rabbi S. R. Hirsch was a historic leader of Orthodox Jewry. His monumental Torah commentary was first

published in Frankfurt am Main, 1867–1878. See *The Great Torah Commentators*, pp. 33–35.

27. As in *adameh le'Elyon*, "I will match the Most High" (Isaiah 14:14).

28. A commentary on *Maalot Hatorah*, which was written by Rabbi Avraham, the brother of the Vilna Gaon (Koenigsberg, 1851).

29. *Rosh Yeshivah* of the Mirrer Yeshivah (1901–1979). See *The Great Torah Commentators*, pp. 153–156.

CHAPTER 3

1. Maimonides in his commentary on the *Mishnah* (*Sanhedrin* 10:1).

2. 1522–1570. See *The Great Torah Commentators*, pp. 222–223.

3. Salonica, 1584.

4. Also described by Rabbi Chaim Vital in *Etz Chaim*, beginning of chapter *Abiyah*.

5. See *The Great Torah Commentators*, p. 223.

6. C. 1790–c. 1784. The foremost disciple of the Ba'al Shem Tov, popularly known as the Toldos. See *The Great Chasidic Masters*, pp. 12–16.

7. Rabbi Moshe Romi, *Shaarei Gan Eden* (Venice, 1589); also Rabbi Moshe Chaim Luzzatto, *Maamar Hachochmah*, discourse on the Ten *Sefirot* (Amsterdam, 1783).

8. Attributed to the Patriarch Abraham, with commentaries by Raavad, Ramban, Rabbi Moshe Botarel, Rabbeinu Saadiah Gaon, and Rabbi Eliezer of Worms. First published in Mantua, 1562.

9. *Likutei Amarim* (*Tanya*), chap. 3, by Rabbi Shneur Zalman of Liadi, the Baal Hatanya (1745–1813). First published in Slavita, 1796. See *The Great Chasidic Masters*, pp. 73–76.

10. *Zohar* to Korach.

11. Rabbi Chaim Vital, *Etz Chaim*, *Shaar Hatikun*, chap. 3.

12. Rashi on Deuteronomy 13:5 and *Sotah* 14a.

13. Rashi on Genesis 18:1.

14. *Pirkei D'Rabbi Eliezer*, chap. 31. A midrashic work attributed to the *Tanna* Rabbi Eliezer ben Hyrkanos (Constantinople, 1514).

15. In *Shemonah Perakim* (the introduction to his commentary on *Avot*) and in *Mishneh Torah, Hilchot Dei'ot* 1:4.

16. Discourse on Purim. Also *Zohar, parashat Acharei* 57b and *Tzofnat Panei'ach* 118a.

17. Rambam, *Hakdamah lePeirush Hamishnayot*.

18. Rabbi Dov Ber, *Or Torah on Vayeitzei* (Koretz, 1804). See *The Great Chasidic Masters*, pp. 8–11.

19. C. 1710–c. 1784. Profound thinker and author of *Toledot Yaakov Yosef*, prime expounder of the Ba'al Shem Tov's thoughts. See *The Great Chasidic Masters*, pp. 12–16.

20. *Toledot Yaakov Yosef, Lech Lecha* (Koretz, 1780).

21. *Zohar Chai, Yitro* 40b.

22. *Zohar* 1:16b.

23. Introduction to *Tikkunei Zohar*.

24. *Zohar, Emor* 103b.

25. Composed by the kabbalist Rabbi Shlomoh Halevi Alkabetz (1505–1584), a brother-in-law of Rabbi Moshe Cordovero, the Remak.

26. *Zohar* 3:180b and *Pardes Rimonim, Sha'ar Ha'otiot* 3, by Rabbi Moshe Cordovero (1522–1570); see *The Great Torah Commentators*, pp. 222–223.

27. *Berachot* 57b.

28. Rabbi Chaim Finkel quoting the Maharal's commentary on the first *mishnah* of *Shabbat*.

CHAPTER 4

1. Rabbi Yitzchak Luria Ashkenazi (1534–1572), foremost kabbalist.

2. Rabbi Shmuel Rosenberg of Unsdorf, *Be'er Shmuel, Vayikra* 1:2 (Kleinvardein, 1938).

3. 1522–1570, in *Pardes Rimonim* 1:6.

4. *Sanhedrin* 90a.

5. *Shabbat* 61a, *Avot de Rabbi Natan* 31:3.

6. *Berachot* 61b.

7. God said, "My face, however, will not be seen" (Exodus 33:23).

8. Rabbi Moshe ben Maimon (Maimonides), in his work *Shemonah Perakim*, Eight Chapters on Ethics. See *The Great Torah Commentators*, pp. 99–103.

9. Rabbi Yisrael Friedman of Rizhin (1797–1850), known as the Rizhiner. See *The Great Chasidic Masters*, pp. 143–146.

10. The period of seven sabbatical cycles (forty-nine years) is followed by the fiftieth year, which is the *Yovel* or jubilee year (Leviticus 25:8–23).

11. *Sefer Yetzirah* 1:7.

12. Rabbi Yisrael Friedman, *Nachalat Yisrael*, Genesis 2:1 (New York: Ruzhiner Chassidic Publication Centre, 1951).

13. *Sefer Yetzirah* 1:7.

14. Jerusalem Talmud, *Nedarim* 3:2.

15. *Sefer Yetzirah* 5:1.

16. 1883–1954. See my *Contemporary Sages* (Northvale, NJ: Jason Aronson Inc., 1994) pp. 95–99.

17. Talmud, *Eruvin* 54a.

18. 1767–1827. See *The Great Chasidic Masters*, pp. 106–110.

19. *Ta'anit* 2a.

20. Tel Aviv, 1929.

21. *Gittin* 56b.

22. Rabbi Shmuel Eliezer Eidels (1555–1631). See *The Great Torah Commentators*, pp. 67–68.

23. 1901–1979. See *The Great Torah Commentators*, pp. 153–156.

24. Quoted by Rashi and Redak.

25. Rabbi Shmuel Shmelke Horowitz of Nikolsburg (c. 1726–1778); see *The Great Chasidic Masters*, pp. 29–33.

26. *Sifran shel Tzaddikim*, an anthology by R. Eliezer Dov (Warsaw, 1914).

27. From the prayer *Hineni Mechavein* that is said before putting on the tefillin. The basic laws of *tefillin* are discussed in chapter 10 of *Kitzur Shulchan Aruch*, Abridged Code of Jewish Law, available in English translation by Hyman E. Goldin (New York: Hebrew Publishing Co., 1961). Also available in linear translation (New York: Metsudah Publications, 1988).

28. Rabbi Pinchas Shapiro of Koretz (1728–1790), author of *Imrei Pinchas* (B'nei B'rak, 1988).

29. *Midrash Pinchas* (Warsaw, 1876).

30. Rabbi Meir Leib Weiser (1809–1979). See *The Great Torah Commentators*, pp. 36–38.

31. Rabbi Shmuel Eliezer Eidels (1555–1631). See *The Great Torah Commentators*, pp. 67–68.

32. *Berachot* 28a; *Shabbat* 16b.

33. *Midrash Tanchuma, Pinchas* 10, *Midrash Rabbah, Pinchas* 21:2.

34. Rabbi Shmuel Tzvi Danziger of Alexander (a city in Poland). *Tiferet Shmuel*, first printed in Lodz, 1920.

35. *Hameorot Hagedolim* (Jerusalem, 1969).

36. Rabbi Shimon Schwab, *Mayan Bet Hashoevah* (Brooklyn, NY: Mesorah Publications, 1994).

37. The creation of Eve is recorded only in Genesis 2:21–24.

38. Rabbi Yehudah Loew of Prague (1525–1609), great talmudist, kabbalist, and philosopher. See *The Great Torah Commentators*, pp. 227–229.

39. Maharal in *Gevurot Hashem*, chap. 28 (Prague, 1589).

40. *Irin Kaddishin,* by Rabbi Yisrael Friedman of Rizhin (1797–1850) (Warsaw, 1880). See *The Great Chasidic Masters*, pp. 143–146.

41. Died in 1826.

42. In the *Sephardi* version of the *Shemoneh Esrei.*

43. *Imrei Kodesh* (Lemberg, 1871).

44. Rabbi Moshe ben Nachman (Nachmanides) (1195–1270). See *The Great Torah Commentators*, pp. 11–13.

45. Rabbi Moshe Chaim Luzzatto, author of the seminal *Mesillat Yesharim* (1707–1747). See *The Great Torah Commentators*, pp. 133–135, 230.

46. *Yoma* 75a.

47. For a comprehensive discussion of the evils of *leshon hara* (gossip and slander), see the volumes *Chafetz Chaim* and *Shemirat Halashon*, by Rabbi Yisrael Meir HaKohen.

48. Great contemporary kabbalist. Author of *Hasulam*, commentary on the *Zohar*. Died on Yom Kippur, 1954.

49. R. Aharon Sorasky, *Marbitzei Torah* (B'nei B'rak, 1989).

50. *Ben Hamelech Vehanazir*, adages and allegories in Arabic, trans. Rabbi Avraham Halevi bar Chasdai (Constantinople, 1518).

51. Rabbi Samson Raphael Hirsch. See *The Great Torah Commentators*, pp. 33–35.

52. *Sefer Yetzirah* 1:1.

53. Vilna Gaon's commentary on *Sefer Yetzirah.*

54. The *Idra Rabba* in *Mishpatim.*

55. Nine times in Genesis, chapter 1, and once in Genesis 2:18.

56. *Parashat Shelach*, 5642.

57. See Deuteronomy 32:10, Psalm 17:8, Proverbs 7:2.

58. Rabbi David Kimchi (1160–1235), *Sefer Hashorashim*, a dictionary of the Bible, first published in Naples, 1590. See *The Great Torah Commentators*, pp. 9–10.

59. Rabbi Menachem Mendel Paneth of Fristik, *Divrei Menachem* (Lemberg, 1863).

60. Rabbi Yeshayah Horowitz (1565–1630). See *The Great Torah Commentators*, pp. 69–70.

61. Rabbi Meir Leib Weiser (1809–1879). See *The Great Torah Commentators*, pp. 36–38.

62. C. 1080–c. 1145. See *The Great Torah Commentators*, pp. 200–202.

63. *Kuzari*, chapter on Revelation of Godliness.

64. 1767–1827. See *The Great Chasidic Masters*, pp. 106–110, and *Contemporary Sages*, pp. 161–166.

65. Rabbi Simchah Bunam, *Kol Simchah* (Breslau, 1859).

66. Maimonides, *Moreh Nevuchim, Guide for the Perplexed* I:44.

67. Jerusalem Talmud, *Berachot* 1:5.

68. Rabbi Shem of Zoloshitz (1870–1943), *Ohalei Shem*. See *Contemporary Sages*, pp. 80–84.

69. The *mitzvah* to wear *tzitzit* is carried out by wearing the *tallit katan* (*arba kanfot*) and the *tallit*. The *tallit katan* is an undergarment that is worn all day, consisting of a rectangular piece of cloth with an opening in the middle to let it pass over the head. To its four corners the *tzitzit* are fastened. The *tallit* is worn during worship by day. For a detailed discussion of the laws of *tzitzit*, see *Kitzur Shulchan Aruch*, chapter 9.

70. Rabbi Samson Raphael Hirsch, "Tzitzit," chap. 39 in *Chorev*.

71. A gentile bought as a slave (Rashi).

72. A logical inference, from minor to major.

73. *Sanhedrin* 91a, *Megillah* 6a, *Menachot* 44a.

74. Also *Sotah* 17a, *Yerushalmi Berachot* 1:2, *Tanchuma, Shelach* 15, *Zohar* 3:301a.

75. Rabbi Meir Schiff (1608–1644), author of *Chidushei Halachot*, a commentary on many tractates of the Talmud (Homburg von der Hoehe, 1736/1737).

76. Rabbi Menachem Mendel of Kossov, *Ahavat Shalom* (Chernovitz, 1885).

77. Rabbi Shlomoh of Lutzk, *Dibrot Shlomoh, parashat Bo*.

Rabbi Shlomo (d. 1813) was one of the outstanding disciples of the Maggid of Mezritch; officiated in Skohl and Konitz.

78. Rabbi Chanoch of Alexander, *Chashavah Letovah*. Rabbi Chanoch (1798–1870), was a prominent disciple of R. Simchah Bunam of Pshis'cha, R. Menachem Mendel of Kotzk, and the Chidushei Harym of Ger.

79. Rabbi Naftali Tzvi Yehudah Berlin (1817–1893). See *The Great Torah Commentators*, pp. 42–43.

80. *Ketubot* 5b.

81. The fiftieth year of the *Yovel* cycle. See Leviticus 25:40; *Kiddushin* 21b; Rashi.

82. Rabbi Bachya ben Asher (1263–1340), Rabbeinu Bachya on Exodus 21:6. See *The Great Torah Commentators*, pp. 14–16.

83. Rabbi Shmelke of Nikolsburg (c. 1726–1778), *Imrei Shmuel* (Jerusalem, 1968). See *The Great Chasidic Masters*, pp. 19–33.

84. The "Holy Jew," Rabbi Yaakov Yitzchak of Pshis'cha (1766–1813).

85. *Berachot* 32b.

86. Rabbi Baruch of Medzhibosh, *Siach Sarfei Kodesh* (Lodz, 1928).

87. Also in *Pesikta Zutreti*, *Bereishit* 2:23; *Pirkei deRabbi Eliezer* 12.

88. Rabbi Shlomoh Hakohen Rabinowitz (1803–1866). See *The Great Chasidic Masters*, pp. 157–160.

89. The *berachot* of *Velamalshinim* and *Et Tzemach David* were added later.

90. By Don Yitzchak Abarbanel (Tarnopol, 1812).

91. Rabbi Yisrael Lipkin, founder of the *Mussar* movement (1809–1883). See *The Great Torah Commentators*, pp. 138–140.

92. Rabbi Elazar Dov, *Sifran shel Tzaddikim* (Warsaw, 1914).

93. *Sarei Hamei'a* (Jerusalem: Mossad HaRav Kook, 1951).

94. Rabbi Nachman of Bratzlav (1772–1811), *Likutei Moharan*, Psalm 139:5. See *The Great Chasidic Masters*, pp. 118–121.

95. Upon smelling fragrances the blessing, *Borei minei vesamim*, "Who creates species of fragrance," should be said.

96. Rabbi Yitzchak Kalish of Vorki (1779–1848), *Yalkut Sippurim*. See *The Great Chasidic Masters*, pp. 122–124.

97. The practice of *nezirut* disappeared after the destruction of the *Bet Hamikdash*. In recent times, however, there has been one notable exception, the *nazir* Rabbi David Cohen. In 1915,

while a student of philosophy at the University of Basel, Switzerland, he had an encounter with the illustrious Rabbi Avraham Yitzchak Kook, chief rabbi of Jaffa, who in 1920 became chief rabbi of *Eretz Yisrael* (he died in 1935). It was a mystical meeting that proved to be a turning point in young David Cohen's life. With his nazirite long black wavy hair flowing from beneath his black derby hat, he was a striking figure in the staid community of Basel. For the rest of his life, he followed Rabbi Kook and edited *Orot Hakodesh*, Rabbi Kook's magnum opus. The *nazir* Rabbi David Cohen died on 28 *Av*, 1972.

98. Rabbi Abraham Seba (1440–1508), *Tzeror Hamor*. First published in Venice, 1522. The author was driven from Spain in the 1492 expulsion and settled in Morocco and Algeria.

99. *Kol Hatorah* (*The Call of Torah*) (Brooklyn, NY: Mesorah Publications, 1993).

100. A nazirite vow of unspecified duration remains in force for thirty days (*Nazir* 5b).

101. In the *Mishnah* in *Berachot* 12b. This segment has been incorporated in the *Haggadah* of Passover.

CHAPTER 5

1. Rabbi Meir Shapiro was the founder and *rosh yeshivah* of Yeshivat Chachmei Lublin. He launched the worldwide Daf Yomi program (folio-a-day program of studying the Talmud). He died on October 23, 1933.

2. Rabbi Charles Wengrov and Mr. Martin H. Stern, "Introducing Dof Hayomi to Klal Yisroel," *The Jewish Observer*, November 1993, p. 26.

3. According to Bartinura, this refers to the penis and the testicles.

4. *Bechorot* 45a.

5. Dr. Yehudah Leib Kazenelson, *Hatalmud Vechochmat Harefuah*, p. 258, as quoted in *Mishnayot Mevuarot*, 12 vols., a new and easy-to-understand commentary on the *Mishnah* by Rabbi Pinchas Kehati (Jerusalem: Heichal Shlomoh, 1977). Commonly called simply *Kehati*.

6. Rabbi Meir Leib ben Yechiel Michel Malbim (Weiser) (1809–1879). See *The Great Torah Commentators*, pp. 36–38.

7. Rabbeinu Nissim (c. 1290–c. 1375). See *The Great Torah Commentators*, pp. 96–98.

8. Rabbi Avraham Borenstein (1839–1910), the Sochatchover Rebbe, author of *Avnei Nezer*. He is quoted in *Shem Mishmuel*, written by his son, Rabbi Shmuel Borenstein (Jerusalem, 1949).

9. 1780–1850.

10. *Shabbat* 127a.

11. *Yoma* 28b.

12. Bartfeld, 1909.

13. Rambam, *Sefer Hamitzvot*, Positive Commandment 1.

14. By Rabbi Avraham, brother of the Vilna Gaon, first published in Koenigsberg, 1851.

15. Rabbi Samson Raphael Hirsch, *Chapters of the Fathers* (Jerusalem and New York, 1967).

16. The *Ulam* and the *Heichal* were two chambers of the Sanctuary in the *Bet Hamikdash*.

17. 1890–1986. Eminent *rosh yeshivah* of Yeshivah Torah Vodaath, universally loved and admired as outstanding Torah leader. See *The Great Torah Commentators*, pp. 47–49.

18. Rabbi Nathan Nata Shapira (1585–1633), *Megaleh Amukot*. A great scholar of Kabbalah, he wrote *Megaleh Amukot* (Lemberg, 1795) and many talmudic works.

CHAPTER 6

1. Rabbi Yehudah of Stutchin (1892–1982), *Minchat Yehudah* (Brooklyn, NY, 1983). See *Contemporary Sages*, pp. 128–131.

2. The peace of mind that results from eating bread in the morning enables the litigant to plead his case convincingly (Rashi).

3. When a person is not contented he is easily angered (Rashi).

4. Rabbi Simchah Zissel Ziv of Kelm, in *Hameorot Hagedolim*, compiled by Rabbi Chaim Efraim Zeitchik (Jerusalem, 1969).

5. Rabbi Shmuel ben Meir (c. 1085–c. 1174), grandson of Rashi, author of monumental Torah commentary.

6. Rabbi Mendel of Rymanov (c. 1735–1815), *Be'erot Hamayim* (Lemberg, 1868). See *The Great Chasidic Masters*, pp. 81–84.

7. Rabbi Yitzchak Luria Ashkenazi (1534–1572), *Likutei Torah Arizal*. See *The Great Torah Commentators*, p. 224.

8. Rabbi Yisrael Meir Hakohen Kagan (1839–1933). See *The Great Torah Commentators*, pp. 118–121.

9. Rabbi Menachem Mendel Morgenstern of Kotzk (1787–1859).

10. Rabbi Menachem Mendel Morgenstern, *Emet Ve'emunah* (Jerusalem, 1940).

CHAPTER 7

1. Twelve thoracic and six lumbar vertebrae.

2. Rabbi Baruch of Mezhibozh (1757–1811) (a grandson of the Ba'al Shem Tov) *Butzina deNehora* (Lemberg, 1880).

3. Rabbi Yehudah Aryeh Leib Alter of Ger (1847–1905). See *The Great Chasidic Masters*, pp. 187–190.

4. *Yalkut Shimoni*.

5. Rabbi Yaakov Yosef of Polnoye, *Tzofnat Pane'ach*, first published in Koretz, 1782. Rabbi Yaakov Yosef was known as Toledot Yaakov Yosef (c. 1710–c. 1784). See *The Great Chasidic Masters*, pp. 12–16.

CHAPTER 8

1. Rabbi Chaim Schmulevitz (1901–1979), *Sichot Mussar* 5731/1971:5. Rabbi Schmulevitz was *rosh yeshivah* of the Mirrer Yeshiva in Jerusalem. See *The Great Torah Commentators*, pp. 153–155.

2. Each of the four fingers has three bones, and the thumb has two, for a total of fourteen.

3. In the story of Creation it says ten times, "God said," nine times in Genesis 1 and once in Genesis 2:18.

4. Annotated by Rabbi Salomon Buber (Vienna, 1885).

5. Rabbi Levi Yitzchak of Berditchev (1740–1810). See *The Great Chasidic Masters*, pp. 51–54.

6. Rabbi Yehudah Loew of Prague (1525–1609). See *The Great Torah Commentators*, pp. 227–229.

7. 1757–1811. He was a grandson of the Ba'al Shem Tov.

8. *Shemot*, p. 208.

CHAPTER 9

1. Rabbi Moshe ben Nachman (Nachmanides) (1195–1270), *Emunah Uvitachon* (Koretz, 1788). See *The Great Torah Commentators*, pp. 11–13.

2. (Lemberg 1793). Rabbi Binyamin of Zaloshitz, *Ahavat Dodim*.

3. Rabbi Yeshayah Horowitz (1565–1630), *Shenei Luchot Habberit*. See *The Great Torah Commentators*, pp. 21–24.

4. Rabbi Mordechai Yafeh (c. 1535–1612), *Levush* (Lublin, 1590).

5. Rabbi Yitzchak Meir Alter of Ger (1799–1866). See *The Great Chasidic Masters*, pp. 150–153.

6. The person who holds the infant during the ceremony, which is considered a great honor.

7. The Roman governor during the Bar Kochba revolt in 126 C.E. He is known in the Talmud as Turnus Rufus.

8. Rabbi Yehudah Aryeh Leib Alter, the Gerer Rebbe (1847–1905). See *The Great Chasidic Masters*, pp. 187–190.

9. The procedure of circumcision consists of three essential elements: (1) *milah* (also called *chituch*), the removal of the foreskin; (2) *periah*, the uncovering of the corona by tearing the inner membrane; (3) *metzitzah*, the sucking of the wound. The *mohel* takes a sip of wine, then sucks the wound and spits the wine out. In some places the mohel sucks through a glass tube into which a piece of cotton has been inserted (*Yoreh De'ah* 264:3). For the most comprehensive and authoritative discussion of all the laws and customs pertaining to *milah*, see Rabbi Moshe Bunim Pirutinsky, *Sefer Habberit* (Brooklyn, NY, 1973).

10. Rabbi Yehudah Aryeh Leib Alter, the Sefat Emet, *Thoughts on Parashat Zachor* (Pietrkov, 1904).

CHAPTER 10

1. Karlsruhe, 1763.

2. 1759–1841. See *The Great Chasidic Masters*, pp. 89–91.

3. A large city in Babylonia, situated on the Tigris River. Rava had his *yeshivah* there.

4. Rabbi Yaakov Yosef of Polnoye (c. 1710–c. 1784), *Toledot Yaakov Yosef.* See *The Great Chasidic Masters*, pp. 12–16.

5. 1798–1870.

CHAPTER 11

1. Hannah had been childless for many years. When her prayers were answered and she gave birth to Samuel, she thanked God with a hymn of exquisite beauty.

2. This is Emperor Marcus Aurelius Antoninus (121–180 c.e.), famous for his book *The Meditations* on Stoic philosophy. The emperor met Rabbi Yehudah about 165/166 c.e. and formed a close friendship with the great sage, based on the respect Marcus Aurelius felt for the lofty ideals of the Torah. The friendship had a lasting effect on the whole of Jewish history. The good relationship between the two leaders is mentioned many times in the Talmud, for example in *Avodah Zarah* 10 a, b, *Bereishit Rabbah* 67:6 and 75:5, and other sources.

3. The belief in the revival of the dead is one of the Thirteen Principles of Faith formulated by the Rambam (Maimonides) in his commentary to the *Mishnah* (*Sanhedrin*, chap. 10).

CHAPTER 12

1. 1742–1810.

2. 1745–1815. See *The Great Chasidic Masters*, pp. 65–68.

3. 1849–1927, leading exponent of the *Mussar* movement, popularly known as the Alter of Slobodka.

4. Rabbi Nosson Tzvi Finkel, *Or Hatzafun* (Kovno, 1928).

CHAPTER 13

1. "Today you have become a nation" (Deuteronomy 27:9).

2. Rabbi Avraham Shmuel Binyamin Sofer (Schreiber) (1815–1871). See *The Great Torah Commentators*, pp. 39–41.

3. 1263–1340. See *The Great Torah Commentators*, pp. 14–16.

4. They interpreted the seven lean cows eating the seven handsome cows to mean: Seven daughters you will beget and seven daughters you will bury (Rashi quoting *Bereishit Rabbah* 89).

5. This prayer is inserted in *Birkat Kohanim* (the priestly blessing). Before concluding with *veyishmerecha*, the *kohanim* sing a lengthy chant during which the congregation recites this prayer. It is repeated during the chant, which ends with *vichuneka*.

6. An idolatrous, evil king. See 1 Kings 16:30–33.

CHAPTER 14

1. Zolkova, 1794.
2. *Sanhedrin* 73a.
3. Pietrkov, 1910.
4. 1757–1811, a grandson of the Ba'al Shem Tov. A compilation of his Torah thoughts was published under the title *Butzina Denehora* (*Luminous Lamp*) (Lemberg, 1880).
5. Rabbi Yisrael Meir Hakohen Kagan (1839–1933), foremost Torah leader of his generation. See *The Great Torah Commentators*, pp. 118–121.

CHAPTER 15

1. Michtav MeEliyahu, p. 27. See *The Great Torah Commentators*, pp. 150–152.
2. *Shir Hashirim Rabbah* 5:2.
3. Rabbi Shmuel Aripol, *Aggadat Shmuel*, chap. 4 (Venice, 1576).
4. A commentary on *Maalot Hatorah* by Rabbi Avraham, the brother of the Vilna Gaon (Koenigsberg, 1851).
5. 1742–1800. See *The Great Chasidic Masters*, pp. 61–64.
6. *Sifran shel Tzaddikim* (Warsaw, 1914).

CHAPTER 16

1. See *Sifre*, Deuteronomy 85.

CHAPTER 17

1. Rashi to Genesis 18:1, *Sotah* 14a, *Bava Metzia* 86b.
2. *Shabbat* 127a.
3. 1798–1870.
4. Quoted in Rabbi Aaron Levine, *Bikkur Cholim* (Toronto, 1987).
5. Rabbi Yaakov Yitzchak of Pshis'cha (1766–1813).
6. This is a different rendering of the same verse.
7. 1895–1986, *rosh yeshivah* and preeminent Torah leader of our generation. See my *Responsa Anthology*, pp. 168–171.

Glossary

Aggadah   Nonlegal portion of the Talmud.
Aron Hakodesh   Holy Ark containing Torah scrolls.
Ba'al teshuvah   Returnee to Torah observance.
Bechirah   Freedom to choose between good and evil.
Berachah   Blessing.
Bet Din   Rabbinical court.
Bet Hamikdash   Holy Temple in Jerusalem.
Bet midrash   House of study.
Bikur cholim   Visiting the sick.
Bitachon   Trust, faith.
Brit Milah   Circumcision.
Chachamim   Sages.
Chasid   Adherent of Chasidism.
Chasidism   The movement of spiritual reawakening within
   Judaism.
Chatan   Bridegroom.
Chatunah   Wedding.
Chazal   Sages.
Chumash   Five Books of Moses.
Chupah   Wedding canopy.
Daven   Pray.
Din Torah   Torah judgment rendered by a rabbinical court.
Emunah   Faith.
Eretz Yisrael   Land of Israel.

Erev Shabbat   The eve of *Shabbat*, Friday.
Gemara   Talmudic tractate.
Gemilut chasadim   Kindness, benevolence, loan without interest.
Get   Religious divorce.
Hakadosh Baruch Hu   The Holy One, Blessed be He.
Halachah   Torah and rabbinic law.
Hashem   God.
Kallah   Bride.
Kavanah   Concentration.
Kedushah   Holiness.
Kehillah   Community, congregation.
Klippah (*klippot*)   Shell(s), the coarse, impure spirits of the world.
Kohen (*kohanim*)   Priest(s), descendant of Aaron.
Leshon Hara   Gossip, slander, talebearing.
Ma'ariv   Evening prayer.
Mashiach   The Messiah, a descendant of King David, who will redeem the Jewish people, rebuild the Temple, and usher in the messianic era.
Mazal   Fortune, good luck.
Menorah   Candelabra.
Mezuzah   Scroll affixed to the doorpost.
Midrash   Homiletic interpretation of the Scriptures.
Mikveh   Ritual bath.
Milah   Circumcision.
Minchah   Afternoon prayer.
Minyan   Quorum for prayer of ten adult men.
Mishnah   Oral Torah.
Mitzvah   Commandment, good deed.
Motza'ei Shabbat   Departure of *Shabbat*.
Mussar   Movement of ethical revival through introspection.
Navi   Prophet.
Neshamah   Soul.
Niggun   Wordless melody.
Nitzotzot hakodesh   Sparks of holiness, a kabbalistic concept.
Ohel Moed   Communion tent.
Olam Haba   World to Come.
Olam Hazeh   This world.
Olam katan   Miniature world.
Or En Sof   Infinite Light.

Orlah   Foreskin.
Parashah   Weekly Torah portion.
Pikuach nefesh   Saving a life.
Poseik   Authority on *Halachah*.
Rebbe   Chasidic rabbi.
Rosh yeshivah   Dean of a *yeshivah*.
Sefer Torah   Torah scroll.
Sefirah(ot)   Divine emanation(s), attributes.
Se'udah   A festive meal.
Se'udah Shelishit   Third meal on *Shabbat*.
Shacharit   Morning prayer.
Shavuot   Festival of Weeks, Pentecost.
Shechinah   Divine Presence.
Shefa   Flow of divine abundance.
Shema Yisrael   Hear, O Israel.
Shemoneh Esrei   Eighteen blessings of daily prayer, *Amidah*.
Shidduch   Match.
Shiur(im)   Lecture(s).
Shmuess   Ethical discourse.
Shochet   Ritual slaughterer.
Sofer   Scribe.
Sukkot   The festival of Tabernacles.
Tanach   Bible.
Tefillin   Phylacteries.
Teshuvah   Repentance.
Torah   The complete body of Jewish teaching.
Tzaddik   Righteous person, chasidic rebbe.
Tzedakah   Charity.
Tzelem Elokim   The image of God.
Tzimtzum   Divine restriction.
Tzitzit   Fringes, tassels; see Numbers 15:38.
Yahrzeit   Anniversary of death.
Yamim Nora'im   Days of Awe, Rash Hashanah and Yom Kippur.
Yeshivah   Talmudical college.
Yetzer hara   Evil inclination, carnal nature, selfish instinct.
Yetzer hatov   Good inclination.
Yom Kippur   Day of Atonement.
Zechut   Merit.
Zocheh   Worthy.

Bibliography

Sources are listed alphabetically by author or title, according to how they are known. Some works were published posthumously.

Ahavat Shalom. R. Menachem Mendel of Kossov. Chernovitz, 1885.

Bachya, Rabbeinu. *Commentary on the Torah.* Naples, 1492.

Ba'al Shem Tov. see *Sefer Ba'al Shem Tov.*

Bet Aharon. R. Aharon of Karlin-Stolin. Brody, 1875.

Bikur Cholim. R. Aaron Levine. Toronto, 1987.

Binyan Yehoshua. R. Yehoshua Falk. Duerenfurth, 1788.

Butzina Dinehora. R. Baruch of Mizhbizh. Lemberg, 1880.

Chafetz Chaim. Torah commentary. R. Yisrael Meir Hakohen Kagan. New York, 1943.

Chashavah Letovah. R. Chanoch of Alexander. Pietrkov, 1929.

Chidushei Halachot. R. Meir Schiff. Homburg von der Hoehe, 1736.

Chochmah Umussar. Rabbi Simchah Zissel of Kelm. New York, 1957.

Chorev. R. Samson Raphael Hirsch. Frankfurt am Main, 1926.

Chovot Halevavot. R. Bachya ibn Pakuda. Naples, 1490.

Degel Machaneh Efraim. R. Moshe Chaim Efraim of Sadilkov. Koretz, 1811.

Divrei Meir. R. Meir of Premyshlan. Bartfeld, 1909.

Divrei Menachem. R. Menachem Mendel of Fristik. Lemberg, 1863.

329

Dover Shalom. Thoughts of R. Shalom Rokeach, the Belzer Rebbe. Przemysl, 1910.

Dvar Eliyahu. R. Eliyah, the Vilna Gaon. Warsaw, 1854.

Emet Ve'emunah. R. Menachem Mendel Morgenstern of Kotzk. Jerusalem, 1940.

Entziklopedia Talmudit. R. Slomoh Yosef Zevin. Jerusalem, 1947.

Finkel, Avraham Yaakov. *Contemporary Sages.* Northvale, NJ: Jason Aronson Inc., 1994.

————. *The Essence of the Holy Days.* Northvale, NJ: Jason Aronson Inc., 1993.

————. *The Great Chasidic Masters.* Northvale, NJ: Jason Aronson Inc., 1992.

————. *The Great Torah Commentators.* Northvale, NJ: Jason Aronson Inc., 1990.

————. *The Responsa Anthology.* Northvale, NJ: Jason Aronson Inc., 1990.

Gesher Hachaim. R. Yechiel Michel Tikotzinsky. Jerusalem, 1947.

Gevurot Hashem. R. Yehudah Loew of Prague, the Maharal. Cracow, 1582.

Hirsch, Rabbi Samson Raphael. *Commentary on the Pentateuch.* Frankfurt am Main, 1867.

Imrei Kadosh. R. Uri of Strelisk. Lemberg, 1871.

Imrei Shefer. R. Naftali Tzvi Horowitz. Lemberg, 1884.

Imrei Shmuel. R. Shmuel Shmelke of Nikolsburg. Jerusalem, 1968.

Irin Kadishin. R. Yisrael Friedman of Rizhin. Warsaw, 1880.

Kedushat Levi. R. Levi Yitzchak of Berditchev. Slavita, 1798.

Kenesset Yechezkel. R. Yechezkel Rabinowitz of Radomsk. Bendin, 1913.

Kitzur Shulchan Aruch. R. Shlomoh Ganzfried. Ungvar, 1864.

Kol Hatorah. R. Elie Munk. Brooklyn, NY, 1993.

Kol Simchah. R. Simchah Bunam of Pshis'cha. Breslau, 1859.

Kuzari. R. Yehudah Halevi. Fano, 1506.

Levush. R. Mordechai Yafeh. Lublin, 1590.

Likutei Amarim. Tanya. R. Shneur Zalman of Liadi. Slavita, 1796.

Likutei Moharan. R. Nachman of Bratzlav. Ostroh, 1806.

Maalot Hatorah. R. Avraham, the brother of the Vilna Gaon. Koenigsberg, 1851.

Malbim, R. Meir Leib ben Yechiel Michael Weiser. *Commentary on the Torah.* Warsaw, 1860.

Maggid Devarav LeYaakov. R. Dov Ber of Mezritch. Koretz, 1781.

Maimonides. See R. Moshe ben Maimon.

Michtav MeEliyahu. R. Eliyahu E. Dessler. B'nei B'rak, 1955.

Maor Vashemesh. R. Klonymos Kalman Epstein of Cracow. Cracow, 1842.

Marbitzei Torah. R. Aharon Sorasky. B'nei B'rak, 1989.

Mashmia Shalom. R. Shimon Shalom Kalish of Amshinov. Jerusalem, 1969.

Mayan Beit Hashoevah. R. Shimon Schwab. Brooklyn, NY, 1994.

Meorot Hagedolim. A Zeilengold. Bilgoray, 1911.

Mesillat Yesharim. R. Moshe Chaim Luzzatto. Amsterdam, 1740.

Midor Dor. Mordechai Lipson. Tel Aviv, 1929.

Midrash Avkir. Annotated by R. Salomon Buber. Vienna, 1885.

Midrash Pinchas. R. Pinchas Shapiro. Warsaw, 1876.

Midrash Rabbah on the Torah. Constantinople, 1512.

Midrash Shocher Tov. Midrash on Tehillim (Psalms). Constantinople, 1512.

Midrash Tanchuma. R. Tanchuma bar Abba. Constantinople, 1520.

Minchat Yehudah. R. Yehudah of Stitchin. Brooklyn, NY, 1983.

Mishneh Torah. Rabbi Moshe ben Maimon, the Rambam. Mantua, 1566.

R. Moshe ben Maimon, the Rambam. *Moreh Nevuchim (Guide for the Perplexed).* Naples, 1492.

——. *The Eight Chapters.* Trans. Avraham Yaakov Finkel. Scranton, PA: Yeshivath Beth Moshe, 1994.

——. *Maimonides' Introduction to the Mishnah.* Trans. Avraham Yaakov Finkel. Scranton, PA: Yeshivath Beth Moshe, 1993.

——. "Letter to Yemen." In *Selected Letters to Maimonides.* Trans. Avraham Yaakov Finkel. Scranton, PA: Yeshivath Beth Moshe, 1994.

Ohalei Shem. R. Shem Klingberg of Zaloshitz. Jerusalem, 1961.

Or Hameir. Compiled by R. Reuven Margolis. Lemberg, 1926.

Or Yisrael. R. Yitzchak Blazer. Vilna, 1900.

Pardes Rimonim. R. Moshe Cordovero. Salonica, 1584.

Pesikta Rabbati. A midrashic work. Prague, 1653.

Pesikta Ze'irta. A midrashic work. Venice, 1546.

Pirkei deRabbi Eliezer. Attributed to the Tanna R. Eliezer ben Hyrkanos. Constantinople, 1514.

Pri Tzaddik. R. Tzadok Hakohen of Lublin. Lublin, 1901.

Sefat Emet. R. Aryeh Yehudah Leib Alter, the Gerer Rebbe. Pietrkov, 1905.

Sefer Ba'al Shem Tov. Brooklyn, NY, 1950.

Sefer Yetzirah. Attributed to Avraham Avinu. Mantua, 1562.

Shefa Chaim. R. Yekutiel Yehudah Halberstam of Klausenburg. Union City, NJ, 1983.

Shelah. R. Yeshayah Horowitz of Prague. Amsterdam, 1648.

Shem MiShmuel. R. Shmuel Borenstein of Sochatchov. Warsaw, 1929.

Shemen Hatov. R. Shmuel Shmelke Horowitz of Nikolsburg. Pietrkov, 1905.

Shulchan Aruch. R. Yosef Karo. Venice, 1564.

Sichot Mussar. R. Chaim Shmulevitz. Jerusalem, 1980.

Siach Sarfei Kodesh. Y. K. K. Rakatz. Lodz, 1928.

Sifran shel Tzaddikim. R. Elazar Dov. Warsaw, 1914.

Simchat Yisrael. R. Simchah Bunam of Pshis'cha. Pietrkov, 1911.

Tiferet Shmuel. R. Shmuel Tzvi Danziger of Alexander. Lodz, 1920.

Tiferet Shlomoh. R. Shlomoh Rabinowitz of Radomsk. Warsaw, 1887.

Tiferet Yisrael. R. Yehudah Loew of Prague. Prague, 1593.

Torat Moshe. R. Moshe Sofer. Pressburg, 1895.

Tzofnat Pane'ach. R. Yaakov Yosef of Polnoye. Koretz, 1782.

Tzror Hamor. R. Avraham Seba. Venice, 1522.

Zohar. Tanna Rabbi Shimon bar Yochai. Mantua, 1558.

Zot Zikaron. R. Yaakov Yitzchak Horowitz, the Chozeh of Lublin. Lemberg, 1851.

Passages Cited

TALMUDIC SOURCES

The talmudic tractates are arranged in alphabetical order and, except where otherwise indicated, are of Talmud *Bavli* (the Babylonian Talmud).

26a	219
35b	90
36b	56
38a	198
45b	235
46b	180

Sukkah

42b	120
52b	214
53a	201

Taanit

2a	161
2b	241
5b	167
8b	177
21b	175
23a	251
24a	101
26b	220
29a	104
31a	196

Yevamot

62b	222, 224
63a	175, 217, 221, 222, 224
64a	128, 241
68b	226
96b	125
97a	125
113a	221

Yoma

18b	169
29a	75
38b	213
74b	119
78b	202
85b	266

MIDRASHIC SOURCES

Bereishit Rabbah

1	171
8	220
9	223
12	143
14	182
17	222, 227
18	187
19	292
39	294
48	209
53	268
61	178
65	288
67	82, 87, 115
70	168
73	242
77	185
98	89
100	148

Shemot Rabbah

1	85, 183, 245, 273
5	171
24	167
27	116

Vayikra Rabbah

7	154
13	169
16	91
18	179
31	98
32	116
33	91
34	276

Bamidbar Rabbah

| 9 | 230 |

Subject Index